THE
DISCIPLINE OF
TEAMWORK

THE
DISCIPLINE OF
TEAMWORK

PARTICIPATION AND CONCERTIVE CONTROL

JAMES R. BARKER

SAGE Publications
International Educational and Professional Publisher
Thousand Oaks   London   New Delhi

For information:

SAGE Publications, Inc.
2455 Teller Road
Thousand Oaks, California 91320
E-mail: order@sagepub.com

SAGE Publications Ltd.
6 Bonhill Street
London EC2A 4PU
United Kingdom

SAGE Publications India Pvt. Ltd.
M-32 Market
Greater Kailash I
New Delhi 110 048 India

Printed in the United States of America

Library of Congress Cataloging-in-Publication Data

Barker, James R. (James Robert), 1957–
    The discipline of teamwork: Participation and concertive control / by
James R. Barker.
        p.   cm.
    Includes bibliographical references and index.
    ISBN 0-7619-0369-0 (cloth: alk. paper)
    ISBN 0-7619-0370-4 (pbk.: alk. paper)
        1. Teams in the workplace.   I. Title.
    HD66 .B364   1999
    658.4'02—dc21   99-6166

This book is printed on acid-free paper.

99   00   01   02   03   04   05   7   6   5   4   3   2   1

Acquiring Editor:	Harry Briggs
Editorial Assistant:	MaryAnn Vail
Production Editor:	Denise Santoyo
Editorial Assistant:	Nevair Kabakian
Typesetter:	Lynn Miyata
Indexer:	Juniee Oneida
Cover Designer:	Kristi White

For Linda, Sara, and Felicity

Contents

Preface

This book is about the social consequences of working in the participative, team-based organization that has marked the 1990s. During this time, organizations worldwide have been converting and restructuring into new forms in which their employees take on more of the responsibilities traditionally given to a supervisor. Workers in these "participative" organizations are highly involved in such matters as making day-to-day decisions, scheduling their work, solving their own problems, and supervising their own activity. The self-managing team-based organization is the most popular form that participative restructuring takes these days. The large-scale change to team-based organizations has brought with it significant repercussions for the way that we think about work in organizations and for the actual way that we do work in organizations, which is what I explore in this book.

The present book is not about teamwork, per se. We have been bombarded for some time now with books that extol the virtues of teamwork in general and of self-managing teams in particular. These books, mostly written by management consultants, commonly focus on helping business leaders engineer a successful change to a team environment and develop, cultivate, and manage teams. This book is not about how teams "work" in this sense. Rather, it is about how teams, as a part of the larger trend toward more participative but disciplinary organizational structures, "work" as a social phenomenon.

What the above statement means is that I have set out here to answer a lot of "how" questions:

- How do we create the social environment of "teams"?
- How do social consequences (e.g., the repercussions mentioned above) arise from our participation in team-based environments?
- How do these consequences shape and affect us as human beings?
- How should we live and work together in team-based environments in light of these consequences?

The rationale for such a focus is simple. Like it or not, we are living in an age of worker participation. Each day we find ourselves working in more team-based, or similar, environments. Certainly, we need to know how to make teams productive and efficient. But we also need to know the implications that such work holds for us as human beings, as people who spend much of our lives working together in organizations. We need to know how participation in teams affects us on a social level, both positively and negatively. We must be aware of these consequences before we can make informed decisions about the ultimate worth and usefulness of teams and other participation programs. Thus, my purpose in the pages that follow is to illuminate some of the "social" consequences of working in teams and to provoke you, the reader, to consider the potential effects of these consequences.

My analytical story about the social character of teamwork is set at "ISE Communications," a manufacturing company successfully using self-managing teams. It is a story created from the lived experiences of ISE's team workers, through their actions and actual words during work and from their reflections on their work as team members. The consequences of teamwork emerge from a real story of real people working on real teams. The people at ISE invited me to observe their work and to hear their voices in confidence, which is a confidence that I will protect in the following story. The company name and the name of all the workers at ISE are pseudonyms.

In addition to protecting their confidence, I have another important reason for wanting to preserve these people's anonymity. That lack of personal identity helps us to translate their experience into our own. In a sense, the team workers at ISE are members of an "everyteam." The social consequences of teamwork that they experienced are our consequences, too. Their experience can help us decide whether we like this era of greater worker participation, and their experience will help us decide what about teamwork we want to maintain and what we want to change.

Acknowledgments

I would never have finished this book without Kurt Heppard's selfless help and encouragement. After four years, three job changes, four moves, two kids, and all the rest life has to offer, the book was languishing on my back burner. During the past year, however, Kurt helped me get restarted, inspired me to develop the unfinished sections, and motivated me to finish. I will always appreciate his confidence and treasure his friendship.

Linda Macdonald and Graham Sewell both contributed immeasurably to the last few months of work on the book. Graham graciously took time to read the manuscript and gave me both excellent suggestions and strong encouragement to finish. Linda has been an invaluable editor, reading the manuscript with a keen sense for how the audience would respond while catching untold numbers of vagaries, densities, and grammatical errors. Kurt, Linda, and Graham's hard work have dramatically improved this book's quality. Thank you all.

Over the years, a number of others have generously assisted me with the various aspects of book writing. Here at the Air Force Academy, especially, I have had the luxury of extremely supportive colleagues who have graciously sustained me over the last 2 years. Steve Green provided strong encouragement and the logistical support I have needed. Julie Chesley and Christy Strbiak read manuscript drafts and offered very helpful comments. Sandi Long did close detail editing for me. Kevin Davis helped me arrange my teaching schedule, and Earl McKinney taught one of my classes to give me more time for the book. Rita Campbell and Chuck Yoos read earlier manuscripts for me, as did Liz Gilbert.

To all of my present colleagues, I am deeply grateful for your support and encouragement.

Hugh Willmott debated my more provocative assertions with me, and the arguments arc much improved as a result. Dave Whetten and Mary Jo Hatch helped me formulate some of my key arguments. Blake Ashforth, Michael Beyerlein, Anson Seers, Keith Murnighan, Chris Neck, and Charles Booth have all given much encouragement along the way. And I have a special thank you reserved for the ever-patient Marquita Flemming and Harry Briggs of Sage who stuck with me during all the trials and tribulations of book authorship.

At the University of New Mexico, Todd Wydra, Caleb Rabinowitz, and David Diamant all helped me analyze the ethnographic data, as did Rob Grice and Bill Pawlshyn at Marquette University. Karen Foss and Brad Hall read some of the earliest versions of my ideas and helped me formulate the core themes I have developed. I also received a grant from the College of Communication at Marquette University that funded a substantial part of the data analysis.

I am indebted to the Reverend Christine Robinson, who is one of our society's most insightful but lesser-known social critics. Her words guided my thinking as I formulated the last half of Chapter 7.

Back to the beginning, I am forever grateful to Bob Sutton, Linda Johanson, and the *ASQ* family for all their assistance over the years. Also, my original doctoral committee members, George Cheney, Phil Tompkins, Patti Adler, Brenda Allen, and Michael Pacanowsky, have continuously given warmly of their counsel and friendship over the years.

And there is Linda Macdonald, loving wife and partner as well as invaluable editor, and our children, Sara and Felicity, who all make life wonderful each day. Their love gives me the sense of purpose to write about the consequences of our organizational world and how we ought to make that world a better place.

Two final notes: First, I can never express enough thanks and appreciation to the team members at "ISE" who shared so much of their work intimacies with me. Obviously, without their and "Jack Tackett's" cooperation, willingness to let me into their lives, and support, I would have no book.

Last, at some point I have to write the following, and this is a good place: The opinions I have expressed in the following pages are my own and do not necessarily reflect the opinions or policy of the U.S. Air Force Academy, the Air Force, or the Department of Defense.

1

Setting the Stage

Overview

> The mind-set of a larger corporation makes you lazy. If you are
> getting by, you are OK. But, in a new company, and a small company,
> you can't just get by. You have to look forward and say, "What will it
> take to survive?" You can't look inwardly all the time. You can't look
> back and say, "Well, we survived this way," and keep maintaining the
> status quo. I took a hard look at my company, and I didn't see a
> pretty picture in the future. I told everyone that we weren't going to
> survive if we simply considered what we're doing now successful.
> We had to do something drastic.
>
> *Jack Tackett, ISE's vice president of manufacturing*

A DREAM OF RADICAL CHANGE

In the late 1970s, a group of developers turned their hopes and
dreams to a tract of land on the east side of a growing Rocky Mountain city.
They looked at this wide, scruffy grassland and envisioned a large, busy
industrial park. And the building began. Soon, though, the early 1980s oil bust
dashed their dreams. The eager developers built only three buildings, the largest
of which now stands vacant. For the most part, their imagined park remains a
huge open field criss-crossed with scantily used roads. Lonely stop signs
punctuate these roads and serve little function other than as amusement for the
inquisitive prairie dogs scampering in the vacant lots. Instead of regulating the
flow of hoped-for workers, the signs are only irritating reminders of what might
have been.

Yet, one part of the developers' dreams came true. The smallest of the three
buildings houses a modest, but fiercely competitive, manufacturing company.

With a workforce of about 150 people, "ISE Communications" manufactures voice and data transmission equipment, primarily electronic circuit boards, for the telecommunications industry. Originally, ISE was a division of a large communications corporation, which sold the company to the ISE management team in the early 1980s. The large firm still remains ISE's primary customer. Like many other small companies, ISE struggles daily to survive in a highly competitive, innovative, and technically complex business environment.

On the surface, ISE is quite similar to any other manufacturing company. The company has the traditional manufacturing, engineering, sales and marketing, human resources, and executive staffs. Its 90 manufacturing workers[1] are mostly hourly employees, whereas the support staffs are mostly salaried employees. As expected of a manufacturing company in a large metropolitan area, ISE's production employees represent a cross-section of the local working-class community. Among manufacturing workers, the ratio of females to males fluctuates, but it tends to stay around two-thirds female to one-third male. Latinos/Latinas, Chicanos/Chicanas, African Americans, and Asian Americans make up ISE's main ethnic cogroups, and they compose about 60% of the workforce at any given time.

The exact composition of ISE's manufacturing employees varies as workers come and go and as the work volume rises and falls. ISE maintains a temporary workforce that constitutes about 10% to 15% of its manufacturing employees, although this percentage has been as high as nearly 50% during peak production demands. ISE coordinates with two employment agencies to provide the temporary workers with in-house training. In fact, only one job in manufacturing assembly, an electronic technician, requires training not provided by ISE.

Manufacturing circuit boards involves requesting board parts (resistors, potentiometers, transistors, etc.) from the supply room, assembling these parts onto a circuit board, and soldering the parts to the boards. After the soldering process, the workers must test the boards for electronic problems, troubleshoot any problems they find, and make necessary repairs. Repair quickly becomes a time-consuming and labor-intensive process.

After a board passes the final tests, the workers must package it and process the necessary shipping paperwork. Building and testing boards requires repetitive tasks that easily become monotonous. Unfortunately, the errors that arise from monotony mean costly and lengthy retesting delays or repairs. All the work of building and testing circuit boards requires close attention to detail and tightly coordinated effort.

In many ways, ISE is a lot like other manufacturing companies: People come to work, they work, get paid, and go home. But ISE has a difference about it that helps the company to remain a survivor in that lonely industrial park. The difference is a function of the manufacturing structure, management system, and communicative practices by which the actual work gets done. To be a survivor, ISE has significantly changed the performance and management of its day-to-day production work.

This difference, the significant change on which the company's survival rested, came from "Jack Tackett," ISE's manufacturing vice president. During the mid-1980s, Jack had been strongly influenced by such popular books as *In Search of Excellence* (Peters & Waterman, 1982) and *Quality Is Free* (Crosby, 1979) and manufacturing philosophies like "JIT."[2] Jack foresaw a turbulent future for the telecommunications industry. As seen in his statement opening this chapter, Jack knew that ISE would have to do something "radical" to survive. In fact, Jack began saying that ISE had to perform "radical surgery" on itself, and his surgical prescription was "self-managing teams."

Over the last decade, self-managing teams have become a widely popular mechanism for changing the direct work structure of an organization into a form that is more participative—that is, into a structural form in which employees make many of the decisions that managers once made and supervise their own work behavior. Generally, contemporary self-managing teams are peer groups (about 10 to 15 people) totally responsible for manufacturing major components or for completing service functions. These groups make all the decisions, do all the coordination, and perform all the work required to build the items or perform the tasks under their responsibility. Self-managing teams have no first-line supervisors; the team does its own supervising. The team hires and disciplines its own members and coordinates directly with other departments for needed supplies or information and with other manufacturing teams to solve production problems and overcome obstacles.

Self-managing teams fit best in organizations characterized by interdependent tasks, complex processes, time sensitivity, and the need for rapid change and adaptation. As depicted in popular managerial literature, a self-managing system creates an environment that controls worker activity in ways quite different from the bureaucratic (hierarchical, rules-based) forms of control found in traditional organizational structures, which brings us back to Jack's performing "radical surgery" on his manufacturing department.

After 2 years of planning, Jack changed his manufacturing structure to teams in August 1988, amid a time of desperation for ISE. The company was losing money and struggling to meet new market demands. Jack knew in his heart that the change to teams, his radical surgery, would help save the company. It did. After struggling through 1988, 1989, and most of 1990, the company finally began to turn a profit. Aside from its change to teams, ISE's senior managers made several fortuitous marketing and engineering decisions that reestablished the company's customer base. Changing to teams also made Jack's manufacturing department leaner and more productive. Jack credited the new design with cutting his factory cost by 25% from 1988 to 1992. The dream of radical change had come true.

THE IMPULSE TOWARD TEAMS AND PARTICIPATIVE ORGANIZATIONS

These days, we find ourselves in the midst of a remarkable period of change in the ways that organizations and the people within them work together. Value-based organizing philosophies, such as total quality management, have swept our culture with the force of a powerful social movement. Everywhere we look, people are talking about restructuring, reengineering, outsourcing, teaming, and whatever else may be the buzzword of the moment. This fast-moving, ever-changing current is sweeping before it both our knowledge of and ways of knowing about how organizations and their members ought to work. Traditional ways of organizing are breaking down, and new methods are emerging to take their place.[3]

Self-Managing Teams

Currently, the most popular planned organizing innovation is the transformation of a traditional, hierarchically based organization to a flat confederation of self-managing teams, such as ISE's manufacturing teams. Many renowned corporations, including General Motors, Motorola, and General Mills, have initiated this kind of change over the last few years. Today, we find all types of organizations, for-profit, not-for-profit, governmental, educational, health care, and everything in between, experimenting with self-management.

Although self-managing teams have gained much of their popularity in recent years, they are not a new phenomenon. Research and writing on the subject originally dates from Trist's study of self-regulating English coal miners in the 1950s (Trist, 1981; Trist, Higgin, Murray, & Pollock, 1963) and includes the Scandinavian experience with semiautonomous teams (Bolweg, 1976; Katz & Kahn, 1978) and early U.S. team experiences, most notably the Gaines Dog Food plant in Kansas (Ketchum, 1984; Walton, 1982). The contemporary version of the self-managing concept draws on both the past experiences with teams in Europe and the United States and the more recent influence of Japanese-inspired quality circles in Western organizations (Sewell & Wilkinson, 1992; Sundstrom, De Meuse, & Futrell, 1990).

Typical of this participative strategy, self-managing workers assume for themselves much of the former tasks of the old supervisor. Instead of being told what to do by a superior, self-managing workers must gather and synthesize information, act on it, and take collective responsibility for those actions. Self-managing workers are generally organized into teams of 10 to 15 people who take on the responsibilities of their former supervisors. Top management often provides a value-based corporate vision that team members use to infer parameters and premises (norms and rules) that guide their day-to-day actions. Guided by their company's vision, self-managing team members direct their own work and coordinate with other areas of the company.

Usually, a self-managing team is responsible for completing a specific, well-defined job function, whether in production or service industries. The team's members are cross-trained to perform any task the work requires and also have the authority and responsibility to make the essential decisions necessary to complete the function. Self-managing teams may build major appliances, process insurance claims, assemble component parts for computers, or handle food service for a large hospital. Along with performing their work functions, members of a self-managing team set their own work schedules, order the materials they need, and do the necessary coordination with other groups. Besides freeing itself from some of the shackles of bureaucracy and saving the cost of low-level managers, the self-managing company also gains increased employee motivation, productivity, and commitment. The employees, in turn, become committed to the organization and its success (Barker & Tompkins, 1994).

Proponents of self-managing teams have described them as a dramatic revision of an organization's traditional managerial and authority structure (e.g., Orsburn, Moran, Musselwhite, & Zenger, 1990; Wellins, Byham, & Wilson, 1991). They assert that traditional management structures entail inflexible hierarchical and bureaucratic constraints that stifle creativity and innovation. These rigid organizations are top-heavy with managers and unresponsive to changing, dynamic markets, ultimately reducing their competitive viability. From the proponents' viewpoint, U.S. organizations must radically change their managerial structure by converting to worker-run teams and eliminating unneeded supervisors and other bureaucratic staff (traditional management structures). Proponents argue that self-managing teams make companies more productive and competitive by letting workers manage themselves in small, responsive, highly committed, and highly productive groups. Thus, the self-management perspective proposes a "radical change," to use Jack's words, from hierarchical supervision to hands-off, collaborative worker management.

The Participative Trend

On a broader level, the self-managing team phenomenon reflects a general evolutionary force in our society that presently is moving us away from the traditionally observed bureaucratic organization toward more participative forms of controlling work activity. Participation, here, refers to an organization's members playing a larger role in the day-to-day operations of the firm, such as a team of workers managing themselves and making business decisions in lieu of a former first-line supervisor. Today's organizations have found that they can survive better, be more productive, and find better solutions to the myriad of problems facing them if workers are more involved in both the day-to-day decision making and the self-supervision of their own work. Self-managing teams, as exemplified by ISE's experience, represent the most visible and popular form of a highly participative organization.

Four abstract but powerful social forces drive the current evolution toward participation. As these forces have coalesced and gained intensity over the last few years, they have dramatically shaped our ways of thinking about work in our organizations. The present interest in participation stems, for the most part, from our experience in responding to these abstract but pervasive social forces.[4] The first social force that shapes how workers organize and work is the rampant growth of technology. Whenever a new technology (either a hard or soft technology) is introduced, it changes the organization. New technology changes the organization's pattern and flow of information. New technology changes the way workers do work and the social structure of that work. Consequently, they have to adapt to the new technology in a variety of complex and systemic ways. One of the key pressures that companies such as ISE were experiencing during this time was the pressure to adopt the Just-in-Time production techniques mentioned above, a soft technological innovation. As we shall learn later, ISE could not adopt the JIT inventory control system without changing both the fundamental way that its workers assembled their circuit boards and the social structure of the plant.

A second powerful social force is the increasingly global and competitive economic marketplace. Today, few work organizations can escape the need to have strategic plans for local, regional, national, and global competitive contingencies (e.g., Drucker, 1992). Even today's not-for-profit and governmental organizations face pressures to "go global" as a result of sweeping advances in telecommunications and Internet technologies. Technology and global economics together dramatically increase the speed at which work happens in today's organizations. The logic behind most attempts at *empowerment,* as the term is popularly used, is to push decision-making power down to lower and lower levels in the organization so that its people can be more productive, effective, and efficient. At the time Jack was becoming a convert to self-management, ISE was facing stiff competition from within the United States and was forecasting growing competition from foreign companies. Jack believed in the popular rhetoric of empowerment, teamwork, and change. He had to find a way for his manufacturing personnel to work better, faster, and smarter. ISE's existence depended on it because its competitive market demanded it.

The increasing education level of the workforce is a third powerful social force that pushes us toward participative forms of organizing. Expanding technological innovations require workers with advanced skills and training. The demands of the global marketplace require smart workers who can make decisions about their work and understand how their actions affect their organization's success. The more important point here is that an educated workforce does not respond well to strict forms of control. Educated workers want and need more input into and control over their work processes. As companies moving to teams discovered, if educated workers are placed in the right conditions, they can manage their own work. Companies can then downsize their unneeded managers. Although ISE's manufacturing workers were not highly educated, they were well educated. Almost all its workers had high school degrees, and some had college experience. They were trained and experienced and knew how important their role was for ISE's overall success. They certainly knew enough to welcome new ways of working better, faster, and smarter.

The last powerful social force that shapes our ways of organizing is the growing diversity of the U.S. workforce (e.g., Deetz, 1995; Stohl, 1995). The United States is a diverse country, and its workforce is increasingly mirroring its differences. Such growing diversity requires an organizational system with work conditions that enable us to rise beyond our differences. Participative organizations provide us with work situations in which we have to figure out how to get along with one another and how to work together productively. When we participate, we have to focus on a project, rather than on competition within a hierarchy. As our diversity grows, our need for participative environments becomes more intense.

Although not always successful, we can generally create positive ways of working together in diverse organizations that practice participation. (I will explore some of the ways that we gain this ability to work together in participative teams later in the book.) As discussed above, ISE's manufacturing workers were a very diverse population. Jack needed a way to capitalize on that diversity, to make it work for the company's success. He saw self-managing teams as meeting this need, and ISE's team workers were reasonably successful in learning how to work together.

To summarize briefly, the last few years have seen four key social forces (increasing technology, global competition, education, and diversity) coalesce into a powerful irresistible force that goads both organizations and their leaders toward making dramatic changes in the way they operate. Participative methods of organizing, with self-managing teams being the most popular participative innovation, are prevalent now because they appear to meet the adaptation need created by this irresistible force. Contemporary managerial rhetoric asserts that strongly bureaucratic organizations, which emphasize supervision, are not as useful as they once were. What works instead, according to today's rhetoric, are organizations with high levels of participation. The next step beyond bureaucracy is actually an age of worker participation.

The rise of the participative organization brings with it dramatic changes in how we think, feel, and act in relation to our work. This change from supervisory to participatory structures means that workers in a participative, self-managing team will experience day-to-day work life in ways vastly different from workers in a traditional management system. One of the ways that this change can be seen is in how we think about management and leadership these days. Presently, we often, and unfortunately, see management discussed as something of a devil term. The rigid and stodgy image of a "manager" does not fit with the rhetoric and, subsequently, with our perceptions of how participative organizations ought to work. Participative manifestations, such as total-quality-management philosophies and team-based restructuring configurations, have been breaking down the familiar superior-subordinate relationship, which for so long has demarcated the manager from the managed in organizations.

Words such as *leader, coach,* and *facilitator* are in vogue now because, as we are led to believe, workers in more participative organizations respond better to leaders, coaches, and facilitators than they do to the old supervisor. Along with this trend, popular organizational futurists such as Peter Drucker (e.g., 1992) regularly call for radically new and improved methods of management, leadership, and organizational structuring that will fit with the perceived needs of highly participative organizations. Thus, as our organizational realities change, our ways of thinking about those realities change, too.

Jack Tackett, in his radical change to teams, wanted to take advantage of all the new realities promised by participative work, and he shaped ISE's change according to the popular rhetoric of participation. Arguably, Jack was successful, very successful. ISE converted to teams and became highly productive in the process. But ISE's success did not come free of charge. Certainly, we can learn much from ISE's success with teams, but we can also learn much from understanding the price its workers had to pay for that success. If we understand this price, we can take a necessary step toward understanding the mysterious *what* that the trend of participation is goading us toward.

LEARNING FROM ISE'S EXPERIENCE

ISE's radical, but successful, change made it the sole survivor in that lonely industrial park. But the odds were not stacked in Jack's favor. For all its contemporary popularity, a conversion to self-managing teams is a very difficult task for a company to complete successfully. Many organizations with senior managers just as capable and just as firm in their beliefs as Jack have failed in their attempts to implement teams. In fact, these days we often see articles in both popular and scholarly managerial literature that address the problems, pitfalls, and failures of team innovations.

ISE stands as a model of how to make teamwork work, and we can learn a lot about making teamwork work by studying ISE's experience. Scholars would want to learn why ISE's teams work so effectively. Managers and participants would want to learn how ISE's experience could positively influence the practice of teamwork in their organizations. As an example of successful radical change, ISE's story offers a rich and unique experience from which to learn. It is a story that can inform and influence the practice of teamwork and other forms of participation both now and in the future.

How Does the Culture Work?

But studying ISE's "success" is not my task in the present book. I want to look at ISE's experience from a different perspective. I want to consider ISE's story as a story of *how a team-based organization works culturally.* From this perspective, ISE's experience becomes a story of how the team members created a system of collective knowledge for doing good work that subsequently functioned to control their behavior in such a way that the company became successful. Given this, the *character* of ISE's new work culture (e.g., what the teams' cultural knowledge "looks" like, how it works, and its manifest and latent consequences) becomes of keen interest to the rest of us facing the prospects of participation. Rather than a story portrayed through quantitative success, ISE's cultural tale is told by the voices of its team workers in their day-to-day work practices, group interactions, and mundane conversations.

The need for all of us to learn from such a rich and unique experience is particularly relevant today. The omnipresent impulse toward more participative organizational forms, as reviewed in the previous section, means that our contemporary world of work is caught up in what my coauthor Phil Tompkins and I have called an era of "organizational anxiety" (Barker & Tompkins, 1994, p. 223). All around us our once safe and secure organizations are undergoing rampant changes forced by technology, globalization, and increasing diversity and worker education: downsizing, restructuring, right-sizing, technologizing, diversifying, centralizing, and even closing down. Workers and managers are united in their anxiety about the future. Maybe our job will be there tomorrow and maybe it won't. We just don't know. The world of work seems to be moving too fast for us to keep up.

ISE's story is more than the success of one company's radical change in response to today's anxieties. Rather, the company's experience illuminates how organizations react to those anxieties on a cultural level. ISE's story shows us how team members participate together in an intensely meaningful environment and how they mold disparate individual behaviors into functional, collective team interaction. It is the story of how a team-based organization creates a work culture and how that culture becomes functional, that is, how the culture works as a social phenomenon so that the organization can succeed.

Our understanding of how our organizations respond to this era of anxiety and change too often focuses on economic effects, such as the move of a manufacturing plant to Asia, the loss of income from downsizing, or the general effect of global economics on our own nation's economy. We are very tempted to see ISE's success with participation only in terms of productivity. But today's movement toward participation also has a powerful effect on us at a social level. We spend much of our lives working and living in organizations with other people. The social fabric of our organizations is very powerful and very important to us. It shapes us in both rational and affective ways. We are not just anxious about the security of our jobs. We are also anxious about what our work lives might become.

Our concern about the social nature of work today is particularly keen because, as discussed above, the primary response of organizations to their turbulent environments has been to ask their workers to become more participative and more involved in the success or failure of the company. Jack Tackett certainly asked this of his manufacturing workers. Teamwork is so popular today because we perceive worker participation and collaboration as *the* way that our organizations can survive this era of anxiety. And ISE is an example of just such survival. Its participative culture "works," and we can learn how it works.

What Are the Social Consequences?

But the move to teamwork and other participative forms does have a price. In particular, participative organizations must ask their workers to give more of themselves to their work: to give more time, to give more energy, to identify strongly with the goals and needs of their organization, and to learn how to collaborate effectively with coworkers. The renowned researcher and consultant Susan Mohrman has called this era of participation a "grand social experiment" in which we participative workers are being pushed to the limit to see how much of ourselves we are willing to give to an organization to ensure its success.[5] We will calculate the price of this experiment in social terms. ISE's experience with teams and the social consequences of this experience give us a good cost-benefit analysis of the social price we will have to pay for participating together at work.

From ISE's experience, then, I want us to learn more about how this trend toward participation affects us as social human beings. All ways of working, all ways of controlling behavior in an organization, from the harsh taskmaster to the unforgiving assembly line to the cold, impersonal bureaucracy, exact a social price. All our ways of working shape and affect who and what we are as social creatures. Out of ISE's story, we can gain much-needed insights into the social consequences that arise from participative work.

To summarize, ISE's story is the story of how a *participative work culture* continuously creates meaningful knowledge about "how to do teamwork" that its members use to guide their day-to-day work behavior. It is a story of *social consequences,* both positive and negative, that arise when organizations are converted into more participative forms. From studying these consequences, we can gain much insight into the complex intricacies of how humans participate together in today's demanding organizations:

- How do humans work in teams on a social level?
- How does that work shape and affect us as humans?
- How can we make teamwork "good" for workers, managers, and organizations?

We all need to know those consequences if we are going to make good decisions about the usefulness of self-managing teams in particular and of worker participation programs in general. This knowledge is the most important information that we can learn from ISE's experience. Uncovering and articulating that knowledge is my goal for this book.

CONFESSING MY AGENDA

The questions I set forth and the issues I raised in the preceding section indicate that I have an agenda here. Before the book ends, I will turn our discussion toward ways that we can make our social lives in teams "better." Because I have openly acknowledged having such an agenda and before I take up the specifics of my study, I need to offer you, the reader, an account of how I became interested in the social consequences of teamwork, why I am seeking to improve participative work, and how I gained access into ISE. I believe that readers ought to know something of my reasons for engaging in the particular sort of study that follows. The time has come for me to confess.[6]

My Own Experience

My account begins in the mid-1980s. Back then, I worked for a large, nationwide trucking company as the "leader" of a self-managing team. In an effort to stay competitive during the wild and crazy perturbations of industry deregulation, my company had dramatically transformed its work culture by changing from what is now called "traditional management structure" (the old supervisor-subordinate work system) to self-managing teams. The company's executives expected that this change would make the firm more efficient, leaner, productive, and an all-around better place to work.

When the change came, the senior managers placed most of the workers (e.g., customer service representatives, salespeople, operations people, and terminal managers) into teams of about 15 each. Our new teams were responsible for all company sales and service operations in our own particular geographic regions.

I was named the "leader" of the Pacific Northwest team and charged with coordinating, not supervising, the team's work. Although we performed different tasks, we were still peers, and we all learned to do each other's jobs so that the team could function as a single unit. We had no formal supervisor, and, by converting to teams, the company actually had eliminated three levels from the old hierarchy.

Faced with the uncertainty of a new supervisorless culture, our team developed a number of communicative patterns, such as informal hierarchies, particular power relationships, and team norms that helped us to make functional sense of our work lives. For example, I found that, because I was the "leader," both my team members and our immediate boss (an old middle manager that now oversaw several teams) expected me to be a decision-making authority figure and to direct the team through tough situations. Gradually, and in a tragically ironic paradox, our team created a context of communicative patterns and expectations that, at the time, did not appear much different from the old, hierarchical work culture. Although we did work much differently than we had before the change to teams, we had a leader, me, who felt compelled to function as a de facto supervisor. We also had sets of norms that functioned as work rules, and we had the general feeling of resignation that often pervades bureaucratic work environments. We had suffered some social consequences from our new-found teamwork.

For all the change our new team culture had wrought, somehow our work experience appeared to remain the same. Our culture had changed without changing, and I found myself often musing over why things turned out the way they had, and I became keenly interested in what contemporary organizational theorists call the "enduring problem of control." To state the problem briefly, any organization continually faces the problem of balancing individual autonomy and collective needs so that the organization can effectively achieve its goals over time.

In contrast to much of today's popular writing, *control,* when applied to organizational studies, is a *neutral* term. All organizations must control the behavior of their individual members in some way. What we do not readily realize is that control needs to occur differently in different types of organizations. In a team environment, worker behavior is supposed to be controlled in a much different and "better" way than in traditional, hierarchical firms. But such a change seemed only superficial among the teams at my trucking company. What had actually happened to us? I very much wanted to know. Thus, my own participation in a self-managing team would give me a unique perspective from which to analyze ISE's new team-based culture in terms of organizational control.

Finding ISE

With my conflicted team leader experience in hand, I made a career change. I left the trucking company and returned to graduate school with a desire to figure out what had happened to my team's erstwhile postbureaucratic company, and I kept this desire in the back of my mind as I looked for an opportunity to work on it. I did write a few papers about my experience early in my doctoral studies, but I really hoped to find a work organization in the process of converting to teams in which I could launch a formal research project.

Basically, I wanted to find out two things. First, I wanted to discover whether my experience with the trucking company's change to a team culture was an anomaly. Second, probably because I did not think that my experience really was an anomaly, I wanted to find out why our teams, when given the opportunity to free ourselves from the shackles of supervision, re-created a new system that still powerfully controlled our work.

I came upon an ideal research setting, almost by accident, when I received an invitation to an alumni reception sponsored by the local chapter of my old social fraternity. I had not had anything to do with my fraternity for a number of years, and I debated whether or not to go, finally deciding to attend. This turned out to be a most fortunate decision.

About halfway through the reception, I found myself sitting next to a casually distinguished-looking man about 15 years or so older than me. He wore glasses and had a slightly thinning head of half-gray hair. He was dressed in a nice wool jacket, fabric tie, and cowboy boots. He introduced himself as Jack Tackett, from the Iota Chapter, 1965. We struck up a conversation on the usual, slightly uncomfortable, almost forced topics that quickly turn to "what we did for a living."

I told him about my career change and return to graduate school. He told me about being the vice president of a nearby manufacturing company, ISE Communications. Next, I told him about studying work teams and cultures. He said that his company was undergoing a major culture change. Sensing my opportunity now, I told him my story about working in the trucking company, its culture change, and my desire to study teams. He said, "Well, why don't you come down to the company and look at what we're doing?" I eagerly consented, and we agreed to arrange a time for a meeting. In early February 1990, I made my first visit with Jack and spent half a day touring ISE.

Entering ISE

I spent that first visit getting to know Jack and walking around the ISE plant. I briefly explained the kinds of research that I wanted to do and that I would want to analyze and describe how ISE's new team-based design had developed, what the consequences of this change had been, and what would happen to the teams in the future. I also said that I wanted to identify both the good points and problem areas associated with the change to teams. Jack was very interested in my doing research at ISE and very open to and supportive of me coming in, observing work, and doing interviews with the team members. He also introduced me to several of his key support personnel who had been involved in planning and implementing ISE's conversion to teams.

I sensed that Jack had his own agenda for wanting me to do research at ISE. First, he made clear his belief that a team structure with its focus on worker participation was a qualitatively better way of working than the traditional supervisory hierarchy. Jack impressed me as a manager who genuinely cared about the "humanistic" quality of work life at ISE. Second, Jack believed that the academic world, particularly business schools, taught students how to be competitive authoritarians and not how to cooperate and work together. His hope was that a university student's writing about teams would help to bring the need for workplace cooperation and participation into academic education. Finally, in his spare time, Jack had developed a lucrative consulting operation in which he helped other firms learn how to convert their work structures to teams. Jack saw my research as giving him more information that he could use in his consulting practice.

At the end of this first meeting, Jack offered me the opportunity to do research at ISE. I felt the need to negotiate an agreement with Jack regarding how the research would proceed, so I arranged another meeting a couple of weeks later. At this meeting, Jack and I established several basic ground rules. I could roam around at will as long as I was safe and respected people's need to work and anyone's desire not to have me watch or talk to them. I would not publish any proprietary company information. I would not identify individuals by name or write material that would be personally embarrassing to any employees.[7] I did agree to brief Jack from time to time about what I was finding and help provide or plan teamwork-training sessions for the workers. These ground rules were, essentially, everything I could have wanted. I had free rein of the place, and I could write what I thought needed to be written about ISE's experience with teams.

STUDYING ISE'S CULTURE

With the above background information in mind, I now want to discuss how I went about studying ISE's teams and structuring the analysis described herein. I studied ISE's teams for a 3-year period in the early 1990s. What follows in the present book are my analysis of ISE's experience with teams and my discussion of what we should learn from that experience. Although there were many ways that I could have approached studying ISE's team-based culture, I did make particular choices in how I investigated, analyzed, and now present ISE's experience as a case study. And, like my background agenda, I need to tell you, the reader, something about those choices. My story of ISE represents "an empirically-grounded consideration of every-day team workers' meanings that serves the interests of a larger critical enterprise" (Barker & Cheney, 1994, p. 32): the analysis and explication of how a participative culture functions to control behavior in an organization and of the consequences and implications attributable to this new system.[8] Let me explain.

An Ethnographic Character

To begin, my story of ISE's teams has an *ethnographic* character. That means that I collected my empirical data in a manner most often associated with ethnographic organizational culture studies (e.g., Adler & Adler, 1991; Kunda, 1992; Watson, 1994). Such studies begin with the assumption that organizational reality is in large part a socially constructed system (i.e., constructed through collective symbol use) whose meaning lies in the cognitions and actions of its members (Allaire & Firsirotu, 1984, p. 221). An organization's cultural reality (or symbolic meaning context) is actively created and maintained through the symbolic practice of the organization members (Putnam, 1982, p. 200).

Such an ethnographic standpoint also assumes that researchers, through careful analysis of their observations and the accounts of their subjects, can learn, understand, and explain an organization's socially constructed reality. This assumption, which has a long sociological heritage, addresses the researcher's ability "to know and understand the broad range of social meanings by which members of a social scene organize their attitudes, behavior, and ultimately, their social world" (Adler & Adler, 1987, p. 12).[9] Learning, understanding, and explaining the social world of organizational actors *and* the social and rhetorical forces that influence or constrain their world, then, becomes a central focus of interpretative-based, ethnographic organizational studies (see Tompkins & Cheney, 1985, p. 205).

Gathering the data necessary for understanding the socially constructed world of the organization and its members requires the researcher to become immersed into the everyday activity of the firm. Researchers most often accomplish such an immersion through the use of observational and interviewing methods common to anthropology and qualitative sociology (Adler & Adler, 1987). In this tradition, researchers adopt some type of membership role in the organization, usually, but not exclusively, as a participant observer (Jorgensen, 1989). The researcher, as observer, collects extensive notes and naturally occurring documentation[10] of activity in the organization and usually conducts a number of in-depth interviews with the organization's members. The goal of ethnographic methods here is to gain "some understanding of the language, concepts, categories, practices, rules, beliefs, and so forth, used by members of the written-about group" (Van Maanen, 1988, p. 13), which is necessary for reaching a valid interpretative understanding of the organizational members' work lives. In addition, researchers often supplement ethnographic data with other information sources, such as survey data produced by either the organization or the researcher.

Collecting Data

After gaining access through Jack Tackett, I began a long process of gathering data.[11] I initially began to immerse myself into ISE's culture by just hanging around the manufacturing shop floor, meeting people, reading bulletin boards, and just "getting a feel for the place." The team workers were, quite naturally, somewhat uncomfortable at first with my presence. They were not really suspicious, just unsure of how to take me. It took several months for the team members to "get used to" me and to feel comfortable with my being around the shop.

As they became comfortable with me, I started collecting data through a number of formats: observations of team activities; informal and formal interviews with team members, team leaders, coaches, and managers; collection of team notes and papers; and any other sources of information that seemed relevant to teamwork at ISE. To paraphrase the distinguished rhetorical and social critic Kenneth Burke, I "used all there was to use." Although I collected a lot of different kinds of data, I primarily stuck to the standard formula of mixing observations and interviews. For example, I would sit in on a team meeting or watch a team solve a problem and then ask the team members why they did things the way they did. I found this method of soliciting team members' accounts to be highly useful as a means for me to understand and analyze the team members' social world.[12]

Given the many possible options for gathering, analyzing, and reporting data, all researchers must make particular choices and assumptions at the beginning of their research project. And I need to explain a few of my choices and assumptions for you. First, as described before, I entered ISE already motivated by certain specific interests and with some preformed questions and perceptions about participation and self-managing teams. In a sense, I could not avoid having a preformed agenda as I had, for some time, been a student of organizations and how organizational reality becomes socially constructed, and I had been a participant in a self-managed team. However, in the spirit of ethnographic methods, I did not start with a specific *theoretical* agenda, just the agenda of questions I discussed above.

I set out to observe and gather information and, based on my intuition, to let the particular patterns and consequences of ISE's experience with teamwork emerge from this information. That is, I inductively tried to allow themes and connections to emerge from the data collected rather than deducing theoretical questions prior to the research (see Adler & Adler, 1987; Jorgensen, 1989). By practicing the ethnographic methods discussed above, I was able to observe and infer the subjective and collective meanings held by ISE's team members. According to Van Maanen (1988), these meanings would represent the apparent "truths" that ISE's team members had constructed about the organization's new system of control and the verisimilitude with which its members constructed these truths through their day-to-day interactions. Such a method of data gathering allowed me to find and to explore both the nuances that are particular to ISE's experience with structural change and the connections that their experience has to other organizations that have similarly changed to teams.

Finally, while I collected my data, I assumed that I could find the clearest and most explanatory understanding of ISE's new teamwork system by assessing work interaction at the lowest levels of the organization. This "shop-floor perspective" (Thomas, 1989) is particularly important when studying, as I did, how ISE's team members socially constructed a new system of teamwork and control. Thus, I concentrated my data gathering on the organization's first-line employees. However, I still included representatives from a variety of hierarchical levels in the organization to ensure that I had sufficiently assessed the differing sources of information in the organization (see Tompkins, 1987).

Analyzing Data

As time passed, I quickly began to amass a lot of data that needed to be analyzed. To analyze ethnographic data, researchers closely examine all the information they have collected and look for any meaningful patterns or relationships that seem to emerge and then compare and contrast these patterns or relationships with any other patterns or relationships that they know about or have discovered. Jorgensen (1989) explained this process of "sorting, sifting, constructing, and reconstructing":

> The analysis of qualitative data is dialectical: Data are disassembled into elements and components; these materials are examined for patterns and relationships, sometimes in connection to ideas derived from literature, existing theories, or hunches that have emerged during fieldwork or perhaps simply common sense suspicions. (p. 110)

Such a process yields an analytical understanding of the organization's social world, a picture of the socially constructed reality of the organization's members and the effects, or consequences, of this reality on the organization and its members (Van Maanen's apparent "truths," as discussed above). Organizational ethnographer Michael Pacanowsky is fond of saying that this picture represented "the goods, the bads, and the uglies" of day-to-day work in the organization.

I began my data analysis by reviewing the information I had collected, while asking myself some necessarily general research questions:

- What was the day-to-day experience of work like at this company?
- How did the team members think and feel about working in teams?
- How had ISE's work system changed, and what were the manifestations of the change in the daily experience of work?
- How did the emerging control system at ISE differ from, or appear similar to, what I expected from both literature I had read and my own experience working with teams?

As more time passed and I did more sorting, sifting, constructing, and reconstructing of my data, I would continually refine and develop the questions I would ask in analyzing my data.

For example, after about 6 months or so of analysis, I found myself studying my data in a different way. Now I was asking such questions as

- What are the differences in the way that separate teams control member behavior?
- How do the teams react to changes in their work environment?
- How do the original team members react to new members being hired onto their team?
- What kinds of behaviors does it take for a team to function effectively?
- What are the behavioral expectations that the team members have of one another?
- How have the relationships between the teams and management changed or not changed since the conversion to teams?

Now I was immersed in a dialectical process of continually collecting and analyzing data and then collecting and analyzing more data. Occasionally, I would pause from my analytical work and write academic papers on teamwork, team culture, and team control.[13] Although I stopped collecting data on ISE in late 1992, my analytical process did not end there.[14] I continued to write papers based on ISE's experience with teams and to analyze and refine my thinking about ISE's story as I compared my findings with available research on the experiences of teams in other companies. Over the following years, I also began to do work with teams in other kinds of organizations, and I naturally compared and contrasted my analysis of ISE with these other examples of teamwork.

My analysis of ISE's experience with teams now culminates with the present book. "We," ISE's experience and me, have been through a lot over the years, but now it is time to bring about a sense of closure. Suffice it to say, all of my sifting and sorting, constructing and reconstructing, comparing and contrasting of ISE's story has been done to ensure the veracity and verisimilitude of the story found in the following chapters. The renowned ethnographer Patti Adler once told me that doing a good ethnography would take *a lot* of time. She was not joking.

A Rhetorical Character

Along with its ethnographic focus, my story of ISE's teams also has two other influential characteristics: a *rhetorical* character and a *critical* character. These two characteristics address the "attitude" I have taken in my data analysis and, more important, in my presentation of ISE's story. These characteristics also represent points at which my particular account of ISE's teams diverges from traditional interpretative ethnographies.

By taking a "rhetorical attitude," I have focused my analysis on how ISE's team members "used" language to do things together. The traditional study of rhetoric concerns how people use language to create persuasive messages, such as in the familiar political stump speech. Although not quite as apparent as a speech, the modern organization is nevertheless a rhetorical site for the continual exercise of persuasion.[15] In the case of organizational activity, the organization, normally represented by its management, uses language to persuade its members to act in ways functional for the organization. When a shift supervisor approaches an assembly worker and says, "Look, the Acme company is our best customer, and we have to ship their order today. Could you work overtime to help us get this order out?" persuasion is occurring.

As I mentioned earlier, I have a particular interest in how team members control their collective work behavior. Team members control themselves by using language to persuade each other that they need to set aside individual wants and needs and work together for the good of the organization. The ways that the team members talk, argue, negotiate, complain, and collaborate with each other are all ways that the members are using language to persuade. Out of these persuasive interactions will emerge a system for controlling behavior on the team. When a team schedules regular meetings to discuss and plan their work schedules, they have rhetorically developed a system for controlling their behavior so that they can work in ways functional for the whole organization.

Thus, by taking a rhetorical attitude, I focused intensely on the empirical use of language by team members: how they used language to do things together, especially to create shared meanings. Though I was certainly sensitive to the traditional interpretative focus on meaning interpretation, I was primarily interested in the empirical indicators of such meanings. These empirical indicators, the expressed experiences of the team members, constitute the varied ways in which the team members used persuasive language to control their own activities such as team meetings, spontaneous problem-solving sessions, disciplinary confrontations, and even mundane social discussions on the assembly line. All organizational activity is rhetorical, and language is the tool of such rhetoric, especially in team-based organizations. Team members use language persuasively to control their own behaviors in ways functional for the organization, as we shall see vividly later.

The rhetorically focused researcher needs to create a "text" out of these empirical indicators of meaning. Such a text serves the organizational critic in the same manner as a politician's speech would serve as a text for the traditional rhetorical critic. My data analysis and subsequent presentation here involved creating rhetorical texts[16] of the different forms in which team members used language (e.g., transcripts of team meetings, detailed observations of spontaneous problem-solving sessions, accounts of disciplinary sessions, etc.). These texts represented evidence of how the team members persuaded themselves to act in ways functional for their team and their organization. As with a speech criticism, the chapters that follow describe how a team-based culture works (as a systemic text of team members actively using language to control activity) and the effects of that culture on the team members themselves.

There is one last element involved in taking a rhetorical attitude. The traditional study of rhetoric has always sought to establish very practical knowledge, such as how to make good, effective speeches. Moreover, the ends of rhetorical criticism have an inherently humanistic quality generally directed toward finding positive ways for us, as a democratic people, to use persuasion as a means of doing things together. For example, we use persuasion civilly to argue and then decide whether a city council should spend additional funds on highway repair, whether a neighborhood association should resist adjacent commercial development, or even such mundane items as which of the latest crop of new movies is the best to see.

To take a rhetorical attitude in organizational studies means to accept the belief that the organization and its members can find mutually beneficial ways of working together through the creative use of language to solve organizational problems. In ISE's story, we will see the team members, together with ISE's management, using language to invent (borrowing the term from traditional rhetoric) new and creative ways of working together as team members. But the new and creative use of language by people in organizations can have a malicious undercurrent. The rhetorical critic of organizations certainly practices what Linda Macdonald called a "reluctant humanism." While the rhetorical critic is dedicated to cultivating better ways for people and organizations to work together, he or she is also dedicated to pointing out the foibles of their journey, which brings me to the third characteristic of my story.

A Critical Character

Finally, my story of ISE's teams has a *critical* character. To take a critical perspective generally means to do three things. First, the critic examines some aspect of the *social world,* such as teamwork in an organization. Next, the critic analyzes the *consequences* of individuals' participation in that social world. Finally, the critic tries to bring about some type of *change* in that social world.[17] The use of *consequences* here refers to an analysis of the effects that participation in a particular social world has on the individuals involved. For example, an organizational critic might discover that if team members do not participate in the development of a company's mission statement, they will feel unfairly left out of such a vital organizational process and will resist shaping their work behaviors in accordance with the company's mission.

The use of the term *change* above means that the critic actively tries to create new and different forms of interaction that fix the problems resulting from the consequences of social activity; that is, the critic has a political agenda. The critic wants us to change how we interact in the social world, and the critic wants us to make this change in a *particular* way. These changes may take a variety of forms, ranging from fomenting radical reformations of the way organizations operate in relation to their individual members (which makes ISE's Jack Tackett something of an organizational critic!) to altering our theories of organizations to account for new perspectives or simply to changing the way we think or feel about our participation as individuals in the organization.

Historically, the critical enterprise has always been on the fringes of organizational studies, due in no small part in the United States to the necessary association of organizational criticism with Marxism. For example, we traditionally think of "organizational criticism" as an exercise directed toward freeing workers from the oppressive constraints of organizational control, such as the Marxist critical aim of freeing the working class from the oppressive forces of capitalism. Thus, as a fringe element, organizational criticism has taken on the role of guardian of the individual in the constant clash between individual autonomy and the needs of the all-powerful organizational collective.

In recent years, however, the thrust of organization criticism has evolved away from fomenting radical confrontation with the oppressive organization and moved toward the analysis of how patterns of discourse or language use create oppressive or overly constrained systems in organizations. In short, the practice of critical theory in organizational studies is becoming more rhetorical. Many contemporary critical scholars see their mission as one of revealing the manifest and latent consequences of language use in organizations and describing how these consequences unduly constrain the possibilities for individual and collective action in the organization. Today's critic tries to answer the question, How do the consequences of our language use in organizations prevent us from being "all that we can be"? The contemporary critic seeks to alter our thinking about the possibilities of organizational participation and to goad us to action in new and creative ways.[18]

Contemporary critical analyses are also turning more toward the "shop-floor" perspective that I discussed earlier. These critics are focusing more and more on *how* we use language and *how* language use affects us. The methodological writings of Foucault (1980) in particular have served to focus our critical attention on the lowest level of the organization, that is, the level of ongoing discursive interaction. As Foucault wrote,

> Let us not, therefore, ask why certain people want to dominate, what they seek, what is their overall strategy. Let us ask, instead, how things work at the level of on-going subjugation, at the level of those continuous and uninterrupted processes which subject our bodies, govern our gestures, dictate our behaviors etc. . . . We should try to discover how it is that subjects are gradually, progressively, really and materially constituted through a multiplicity of organisms, forces, energies, materials, desires, thoughts etc. (p. 97)

By studying language use at the level of day-to-day interaction, at the level that we are "constituted" as organizational citizens, we can discover and effectively criticize our participation in organizational activity. Thus, I have focused my study of ISE at the level of the day-to-day interactions of the team members.

In summary, my story of ISE's teams is a critical analysis, and it has a political agenda. In the chapters that follow, I examine the social world of ISE's self-managing teams, analyze how culture and control work in self-managing teams, identify the consequences that occur in a team-based culture, and, finally, seek to change our thinking about these consequences so that we can make teamwork *work* better for both the organization and the team members. By taking such a critical perspective in my account of ISE's teams, I have again diverged from a "pure" interpretative perspective focused solely on explaining the subjective meanings of ISE's team workers.[19] However, I have not diverged from certain analytical trends in organizational studies, particularly those that examine the rhetorical and historical dynamics of work activity.[20] Yet, in taking this critical approach, I have had to balance a need for understanding ongoing, everyday organizational activity with a desire to critique this activity. As Barker and Cheney (1994) explained,

> To engage in critical analysis with ethnographically generated data requires that we strike a balance between and among critical, interpretive, and empirical traditions in our field. We assert that an interpretive spirit with its concern for actor's interpretations and meanings, combined with an empirical concern for getting at concrete phenomena in the social world points us, as researchers, toward accounts of what it is that actors actually think, say, and "do." (p. 32)

Such is the focus of an ethnographic, rhetorical, and critical story of participation.

Thus concludes my introductory description of how I have constructed ISE's story as an empirically grounded consideration of everyday team workers' meanings that serves the interests of a larger critical enterprise. In the chapters that follow, I present my analysis of the hows, the whys, and the consequences of ISE's participative, team-based culture. Any full understanding of how an organization's culture works must seek out and critique all parts of the culture (Pacanowsky's the goods, the bads, and the uglies). ISE's story has plenty of goods but also a few bads and uglies that are essential parts of its team-based culture. My tale of ISE's teams will provide you with plenty of food for thought about how we can make the team experience more positive for both the organization and its workers.

A NOTE FOR THE READER

To make a good critical, rhetorical, and ethnographic argument requires me, the researcher, to convince you, the reader, that I have done a valid job of sorting, sifting, constructing, and reconstructing my data into a story that is meaningful for you. Such a task is an exercise in persuasion on my part, *my rhetoric* of culture and control in participative teams. And the remainder of the book certainly presents an argumentative story about the reality of work in team-based organizations, which I have explicitly designed to be persuasive. I am not asking that you completely or partially agree with my analysis, but I am asking that you honor my argument by thinking about and reflecting on what I have to say in the pages that follow.

What I am asking of the reader, then, is for your *engagement* with my story of ISE's teams, with my claims and arguments about the character and consequences of teamwork. As you read my analysis of ISE's experience with teams, I ask you to ask yourself whether my claims make sense to you, whether they seem real. I ask you to judge my claims mostly against your own experience in organizations and, perhaps, as a team member yourself. The ultimate validity of ethnographic work rests with the reader, and I offer the remainder of the book for you to judge. The "proof," as the old adage goes, is in the pudding, and how it tastes is up to you.

NOTES

1. This number represents the number of manufacturing team members ISE employed when I completed my fieldwork in 1992.

2. Just in Time is a manufacturing method that emphasizes low inventories, first-line decision making, and fast, effective employee action.

3. For a highly penetrating study of worker participation with a focus on workplace democracy, see Cheney (1995).

4. General and specific discussions of the trend toward participation are available from a variety of sources. A selection of such examples includes Barley (1996), Barley and Kunda (1992), Drucker (1994), Hammer and Champy (1993), McLagan and Nel (1995), Quinn (1992), Stohl (1995), and Womack, Jones, and Roos (1990).

5. Personal communication, May 1997.

6. See Van Maanen's (1988) discussion of "confessional" tales.

7. Throughout the present book, I have taken great pains not to reveal individual identities and to conceal the name of the company. To that end, I have had to make a number of limiting choices in my presentation. For example, I was quite tempted to discuss how ISE has fared since I ended my data collection. However, if I did that, I would unintentionally, but necessarily, provide many clues to the company's real name and to the identities of my informants. Although I could have added to the richness of my story by including some of these details, I would have threatened the trust that ISE's workers placed in me to protect their anonymity.

8. Also see Barker and Cheney (1994, pp. 32, 39-40) for more detail on the critical-analytical perspective I am describing here.

9. The academic term for this process of interpretative understanding is *verstehen*. I will not pursue the long history of the term here, but the interested reader can use the reference in Adler and Adler (1987, p. 12) as a starting point.

10. For example, these methods may include collecting stories or accounts about the organization and action within it, examining documents produced by the organization, constructing field notes from observations, and orchestrating focus groups to discuss issues in the organization.

11. For a detailed account of how I gathered and analyzed my data, see Barker (1993b). For a complete "confessional tale" (Van Maanen, 1988) of my experience at ISE, see Barker (1993a).

12. For a discussion of the usefulness of accounts, see Tompkins and Cheney (1983).

13. Published works based on my analysis of ISE's experience with teams include Barker (1993b), Barker and Cheney (1994), and Barker and Tompkins (1994).

14. I was able to review a set of data collected at ISE in 1994 by David Diamant. David was conducting a follow-up qualitative study to my own, and he graciously consented to let me review his raw data.

15. For discussions of the rhetorical perspective on organizational studies, see Cheney (1991, Chapter 1 in particular) and Cheney and McMillan (1990).

16. For a discussion of how rhetorically focused organizational researchers create and use texts, see Cheney and Tompkins (1988).

17. For a useful discussion of critical practice, see Fay (1987).

18. For an example of a recent "discourse" criticism, see Cheney (1997); also see Deetz (1995).

19. The epistemological issue in making this divergence is one of balancing emic perspectives (stories told from the participants' point of view) and etic perspectives (stories told from the researcher's point of view). Although I have tried to balance these perspectives in my account of ISE's teams, I must, as a critic, necessarily privilege the etic perspective. For an informative account of balancing etic and emic perspectives, see Barley (1996, pp. 414-415 in particular).

20. See, for example, Barker, Melville, and Pacanowsky (1993), Brown and McMillan (1991), Christensen (1991), Dahler-Larsen (1991), Smith and Eisenberg (1987), Stewart (1990), and Willmott (1991).

chapter 2

Reading Organizational Culture as Generative Discipline

You know, if we could only get disciplined, then everything would be OK. Tackett would be happy, and we would be happy because we would be getting our work done. Discipline, that's the key.

Lee Ann, a long-term ISE team member

A RADICAL PERSPECTIVE FOR A RADICAL CHANGE

All analysts of organizations necessarily view the object of their study through some type of filter or lens. We use this filter as our conceptual framework for making sense out of what we see and then for articulating that "sense" to the reader. And you, as the reader, need to know something of the framework that grounds my version of ISE's story prior to engaging in it. My framework extends from the critical and rhetorical characteristics of my study that I discussed in the preceding chapter. Because ISE's story is a story of radical cultural change in an organization, my framework will present a somewhat radical perspective from which to view organizational culture. I begin with the assumption that organizational culture is not something an organization has or is. Instead, organizational culture is something an organization *does*.

Contemporary Perspectives on Organizational Culture

Two dominant perspectives have framed much of the writing on organizational culture.[1] The first is a *functionalist* perspective that presents organizational culture as something that an organization *has*.[2] From this perspective, organiza-

29

tional culture constitutes an objective reality of values, artifacts, and meanings that scholars and managers can readily quantify, measure, and correlate with a number of other important organizational measures. They use these measurements to "manage" culture much as they would any other organizational process.

The second dominant viewpoint is a *symbolic* perspective that presents organizational culture as something that an organization *is*. From this perspective, an organization's culture constitutes a subjective reality of rites, rituals, and meanings that cannot be easily quantified and measured. Rather, scholars and managers should seek to understand and appreciate an organization's culture for what it is. An organization's culture is something that should be studied holistically and engaged in much the same manner as an anthropologist would engage an alien society.

These two perspectives on organizational culture have held sway for a number of years. Today's business scholars and practitioners alike normally will have some appreciation for culture as a potent determinant of the success or failure of their organizations. More recently, however, knowledge about organizational culture has grown more complex, and managerial philosophies have become more focused on managing meaning in organizations. The result is that now more complex understandings of organizational culture and how culture functions as a force that shapes and affects both organizational activity and the members of the firm themselves are needed. Both the functionalist and symbolic perspectives fail to explain the fluid and dynamic processes used to create meaning in an organization.

What scholars call "organizational culture" is more than the collection of shared meanings in an organization. Any organization's culture constitutes a creative force of shared *discursive* processes that is used to construct, reconstruct, and even "destruct" collective meanings (Gray, Bougon, & Donnellon, 1985, p. 83). This view of organizational culture as both a creative process that we use to create meanings and a force that affects us as members of the organization has given rise to a third perspective.

The third perspective presents organizational culture as something that the organization *does*. What we call "organizational culture" actually represents a system of generating meaning in the organization that is inherently persuasive (i.e., rhetorical). An organization's culture aggressively, and rhetorically, seeks to shape work activity so that its members will choose to act in ways that appear functional for the organization as they negotiate everyday life at work. An organization's culture is active and alive. But, despite some outward appearances, this is not a chaotic process. An organization's culture *must* weave together the firm's goals, symbols, and member activities so that the organization can do whatever it is that the particular organization does.

Within this third perspective, we focus our attention on the subtle and often not readily apparent processes involved in constructing, reconstructing, and destructing meaning. We consider our ability to understand these processes of meaning construction as being more useful than simply understanding the meanings themselves (e.g., Coombs, Knights, & Willmott, 1992; Dahler-Larsen, 1991; Willmott, 1991). Constructed meaning in organizational interactions is fleeting and useful only at the moment its members need it, as Gray, Bougon, and Donnellon (1985) explained,

> Even if action is initially predicated on coincident meaning, unanticipated consequences of the action or new circumstances often force reinterpretation of past experiences, thereby destroying past meaning and constructing new, and not necessarily coincident, meaning in its place. As a consequence, the degree to which meaning is coincident among its members is constantly in flux and thereby problematic. (p. 84)

The problem in understanding meaning generation that Gray, Bougon, and Donnellon described above illustrates this third perspective's concern for viewing organizational culture as an inherently inventive and formative process. Christensen (1991) further clarified the issue of understanding meaning construction as a formative process:

> [C]ulture, however, is not determined by established significations. It leans on them, draws on them and confronts them incessantly in a process, which is not only functional, but at once complementarian and antagonistic (Morin, 1984). Rather than being defined by meaning as such, that is as a coherent and univocal pattern of significations, culture presupposes the *problem* of meaning, which give rise to a number of organizing processes at the level of the individual, the organization, and society. (pp. 2-3)

These "organizing processes" are what the culture "does," and they are the object of interest within the third perspective.

Culture as Discursive Formations

Thus, organizational culture, from this third perspective, is not so much an underlying structure of knowledge from which members interpret meaning or a set of variables to be correlated with other variables but is rather a formation of knowledge discourses,[3] or *discursive formations,* that an organization's members call on to guide their interactions. Watson (1994), whose study of a company called ZTC Ryland exemplifies a relatively recent cultural analysis drawn from this third perspective, described the term *discourse* as it applies here:

> Thus, we saw in the culture-building efforts in ZTC the production of what I called a *rhetoric;* a language or *discourse* designed to persuade people to *"work together," "developing"* themselves in the process of helping develop the business. . . . A *discourse, in this sense, is a connected set of statements, concepts, terms, and expressions which constitutes a way of talking or writing about a particular issue, thus framing the way people understand and act with respect to that issue.* (pp. 112-113)

Christensen and Cheney (1994) provided a similarly instructive view of discourse. They described discourse as referring to "a prevailing way of thinking about an action within the world: in a sense, paradigm plus practice" (p. 231).

To summarize, an organization's culture, from this third perspective, is better understood as a set of *discursive formations* that create an "environment," which arises to inform and influence ongoing action by providing the social forms necessary for interaction to occur in the organization. To interact collectively, an organization's members need an influencing "form" from which to base their interactions (i.e., simultaneously interpret meaning and act), a form that is flexible, malleable, and full of possibilities, not a rigid, constraining structure. From this view, an organization's culture is not a structure so much as it is a fluid formation of possible meanings, available to members through discourses that they use to enable their interactions.

As an example, say that Joyce and Bob are on their coffee break when Joyce looks at her watch and exclaims, "Oh my god, it's five past ten. Toni [her boss] will have a fit." As she is saying this, she sets her cup down and runs back to the office with a wave to Bob, who says, "See you later." As this short example unfolded, both Joyce and Bob called on cultural knowledge to "negotiate" their interaction. When Joyce noticed that she was late, several discourses of cultural knowledge began to play in her and Bob's interaction environment: Joyce was late on her break; she had to get back because being late was "wrong" in this company; her boss would react negatively to her being late. These are cultural knowledges, particular to Joyce and Bob's organization, that influenced the possibilities of their interaction.

This third perspective, which presents organizational culture as a fluid and dynamic set of discursive formations, extends from the work of Michel Foucault (see, specifically, 1972).[4] Discourse was central to Foucault's view of the systemic structure of knowledge. Foss, Foss, and Trapp (1991) described the link between discursive formations and culture by arguing that discursive formations "might be thought of as a cultural code, characteristic system, structure, network, or ground of thought that governs the language, perception, values, and practices of an age" (p. 216), or an organization in this case.[5] Discursive knowledge formations, according to the authors, are composed of various statements that are sets "of signs or symbols to which a status of knowledge can be ascribed. It is a type of utterance that, because it follows particular rules or has passed the appropriate tests, is understood to be true in a culture" (p. 217).

The Epistemic Quality of Discursive Formations

Discursive formations are relevant as an organization works through its ongoing process of constructing useful meanings and destructing meanings no longer useful. During this process, an organization's members appropriate certain knowledge that becomes useful for them. This knowledge *follows particular rules* or *passes particular appropriate tests* and then becomes understood by the organization's members as an apparent *truth* that they can reconstruct as they need in future interactions. In this and future contexts, I will use the term *truth* to refer to what workers would perceive as an accurate conceptualization of their organizational life, such as the "right" way of working or a correct way of acting with other members. Their apparent truth is their perception, with a good degree of verisimilitude, of how their organization works and how they should act within it (see also the discussion of apparent truths in Chapter 1). In the example above, Joyce's concern about her boss's anger at her being late reflects a particular symbolic discourse between Joyce and her boss in which they had ascribed cultural knowledge ("If I'm late, I'm in trouble.").

From this Foucaultian view, an organization's culture, as a set of discursive formations, is epistemic by nature;[6] it enables an organization's members to ascribe knowledge in a discursive form (essentially, assign meaning to their own activity) that then provides the necessary "environment" for social interaction in the organization. Together as a discursive formation, these apparent truths influence and guide organizational meaning interpretation and action as the organization's members call on them to guide their interpretation and action. Organizational culture as discursive knowledge formations becomes a flexible and dynamic knowledge process (or system) that members use, *as needed,* to form their social interactions. What we call organizational culture is in actuality a discursive formation of knowledge that helps us to create useful meanings in the organization. This is what organizational culture *does.*

The Inventive Quality of Discursive Formations

Let me briefly summarize here by describing two key assumptions that mark the view of organizational culture as discursive formations. First, *an organization's culture is essentially a persuasive argument about what constitutes knowledge in the organization and how that knowledge should be used.* We use these discursive knowledge formations to persuade ourselves and each other about how to think, feel, and act in the organization. However, this perspective does not assume that action is completely fixed or constrained. To the contrary, the discursive perspective emphasizes the role of the traditional rhetorical canon of *invention.* Cultural discourses provide certain possibilities and parameters for our action, and then we *use* this knowledge in day-to-day activity to create (invent) a shared, collective organizational reality.

For example, let's say that a self-managing team meets each morning for 15 minutes at the start of the workday. Each meeting is facilitated and directed by the team's leader. But one day, the team leader calls in sick and is not present at the start of the meeting. What will happen? Odds are the team meeting will still take place because the team has a discursive formation that persuades them that the meeting is necessary and that they should conduct the meeting in a particular way. The team may spend a few minutes trying to figure out how to get going, but then they will invent a solution that fits with their culture. Perhaps one of the team members will step up and run the meeting in the same manner as the missing team leader.

Although discursive formations make possible our ability to create shared meaning in an organization, they do place constraints on the possibilities of our creativity. The second key assumption of the discursive perspective is that *we essentially use discursive knowledge formations (the organization's culture) to control ourselves.* As seen in the above example, the morning meeting *had* to take place. Someone had to step up and lead the meeting. Again, discursive formations do not completely constrain our behavior; perhaps two or even three people could have emerged to lead the team meeting. But, as the essential knowledge about living in the organization, these formations shape and direct ("persuade," to use Watson's, 1994, words) us toward behaviors that are functional for the organization. The team members all *knew* that the morning meeting had to take place for the team to be effective. All organizations have goals and objectives; thus, all organizations need their individual members to act in ways that enable the organization to be effective and successful. We should not be surprised that organizational culture represents knowledge of, for, and about control. What is instructive, though, is *an understanding of why organizational culture and control are so necessarily intertwined, especially in organizations that use teams.*

Today, we generally assume that team-based organizations control worker behavior in ways quite different from the traditional bureaucracy. Among teams, control arises from the team members' own negotiated and persuasive discourses about how to do good work for their organization, essentially, the team's discursive formations. The team members themselves act in *concert* with each other to create a mechanism for controlling their own behavior, which represents the "using culture to control ourselves" point I discussed just above. Hence, the name given the *type* of control that occurs in team-based, or otherwise partici-pative, organizations is *concertive control.*

CONCERTIVE CONTROL AND THE TEAM-BASED ORGANIZATION[7]

Control has been a central concept in organizational theory since the time of Weber and remains perhaps the key issue that shapes and permeates our experiences of organizational life. Barnard (1938/1968, p. 17) best stated the importance of control when he wrote that a key defining element of any organization is the necessity of individuals to subordinate, to an extent, their own desires to the collective will of the organization.[8] For individuals to achieve larger goals, they must actually surrender some autonomy in organizational participation. Because of this basic tension, control is always problematic in any organization.

To work through this problem, an organization's members—managers and workers alike—must create an effective discourse about how they should control behavior in the organization. To draw on Coombs, Knights, and Willmott's (1992) words, the organization's members must engage in ongoing formal and informal "processes of negotiation in which various strategies are developed . . . [that] produce particular outcomes" (p. 58) for the organization. Herein lies the essence of control as it becomes manifest in organizational activity. For any organization to move toward its goals and purposes, its "particular outcomes," its members must interactively negotiate and implement some type of strategy that effectively controls member activities in a manner functional for the organization.

Edwards's Three Strategies of Control

Edwards (1981) has identified three broad strategies that evolved from the modern organization's struggle with controlling its members' activities. First is *simple control,* the direct, authoritarian, and personal control of work and workers by the company's owner or hired bosses, best seen in 19th-century factories and in small family-owned companies today. Second is *technological control,* in which control emerges from the physical technology of an organization, such as in the assembly line found in traditional manufacturing. Third and most familiar is *bureaucratic control,* in which control derives from the hierarchically based social relations of the organization and its concomitant sets of systemic rational-legal rules that reward compliance and punish noncompliance.

A pivotal aspect of Edwards's model is that the second and third strategies, technological and bureaucratic control, represent adaptations to the forms of control that preceded them, each intended to counter the disadvantages of the previous form. Technological control resulted not only from technological advances in factories but also from worker alienation and dissatisfaction with the despotism too often possible in simple control. But technological control proved subject to such factors as worker protests, slowdowns, and assembly-line sabotage. The stultifying effects of the assembly line, with workers as just cogs in the machine, still produced worker alienation from the company. The bureaucratic form of control, with its emphasis on methodical, rational-legal rules for direction, hierarchical monitoring, and rewards for compliance such as job security, was already existent in the 19th century and was further developed to counter the problems inherent in technological control. The bureaucracy and bureaucratic control, which become manifest in a variety of forms (Perrow, 1986; Riggs, 1979), have matured into the primary strategy available to managers to control work effectively in the modern organization. But, as with its predecessors, this strategy of control, too, is problematic.

Bureaucratic Control and the Iron Cage

Weber (1978) articulated the bureaucracy as the dominant form of modern control, in both the positive and negative senses. Although the bureaucracy offers the fairest and most efficient method of control, its system of rational rules may become troublesome, as seen in the infamous "red tape" that constrains and slows the bureaucracy, making it unresponsive to environmental changes. Also, as Weber warned us, in our desire for organizational order and predictability, we tend to focus too much on the rationality of the rules in and of themselves, overintellectualizing the moral and ethical values critical to our organizational lives. When that happens, we begin making decisions according to the rules, without regard to the people involved (Kalberg, 1980, p. 1158). We become so enmeshed in creating and following a legalistic, rule-based hierarchy that the bureaucracy becomes a subtle but powerful form of domination.

This notion of the inevitable, highly rational, but powerfully oppressive bureaucracy refers to what Weber (1958, pp. 180-181) called the "iron cage." Weber saw the bureaucracy and bureaucratic control as an irresistible force of high rationality that would commandeer and consume all other forms of control. According to Weber (1978), we would, out of our desire for order, continually rationalize our bureaucratic relationships, making them less negotiated and more structured. These structures ultimately become immovable objects of control: "Once fully established, bureaucracy is among those social structures which are the hardest to destroy. Bureaucracy is *the* means of transforming social action into rationally organized action" (1978, p. 987). As bureaucratic rationalization processes increasingly saturate our organizational activity, they concomitantly increasingly constrain us. A rule requiring a customer service representative to have all refund decisions approved by someone two hierarchical levels above may impede the representative's ability to meet a customer's demands for a quick response. A rule that apparently benefits an organization's effectiveness (getting managerial approval and oversight of refunds) also constrains its effectiveness (slows down response). In Weber's (1978) words, the individual organizational actor in a modern bureaucracy "cannot squirm out of the apparatus into which he has been harnessed" (pp. 987-988).

Weber's image of how we become trapped in an iron cage of bureaucratic control suggests that control, as it becomes manifest as organizational activity through Edwards's three strategies, has become less apparent, or not as readily personal. These days, our methods of control are almost imperceptibly imbedded in the social relations of organizational members (Barker & Cheney, 1994; Tompkins & Cheney, 1985). Control in the bureaucratic organization becomes impersonal because its authority rests ultimately with the system, leaving organization members, in many cases, with what Weber (1958) called "specialists without spirit, sensualists without heart" (p. 182). Whereas the 19th-century mill owner overtly controlled workers, ordering, directing, and firing them at will, the bureaucracy's rules are more indirect. The bureaucracy controls workers by shaping their knowledge about the "right" ways to act and interact in the organization, which constitutes a powerful set of discursive formations. A worker seeks supervisory approval for a decision because that is *what the worker is supposed to do.* The "apparency" of control becomes hidden in the bureaucracy's seemingly natural rules and hierarchy. Thus, bureaucratic control leaves us in a paradoxical situation. The same rational activities that enable collective organizational interaction eventually come to constrain that activity in ways often difficult for us to perceive, much less comprehend the consequences and ramifications. Our bureaucratic rules ultimately confine us as solidly as if we were in a cage bound by iron bars.

Concertive Control as a Fourth Strategy

Almost since the beginning of modern organizational study, influential theorists have argued that decentralized, participative, and more democratic systems of control offer the most viable alternatives to the bureaucracy's confining routines and rules (e.g., Follett, 1941; Lewin, 1948). This continual push toward participation and a flat organizational structure has become an obsession in the managerial literature of the last decade or so (Eccles & Nohria, 1992). Contemporary writers have unleashed a flood of literature announcing the "coming demise of bureaucracy and hierarchy" (Kanter, 1989, p. 351). These authors detail the dawn of a postbureaucratic age in which control emerges not from rational rules and hierarchy but from the concertive, value-based actions of the organization's members (Ogilvy, 1990; Parker, 1992; Soeters, 1986).

Characteristic of this movement are influential business consultants such as Tom Peters (1988) and Peter Drucker (1988) who have urged corporate executives (Jack Tackett certainly felt the urging) to debureaucratize their firms and adopt more ideologically based designs drawn around unimpeded, agile authority structures that grow out of a company's consensual, normative ideology, not from its system of formal rules. By cutting out bureaucratic offices and rules, organizations can flatten hierarchies, cut costs, boost productivity, and increase the speed with which they respond to the changing business world. Here, we again see today's powerful impulse toward participatory organizational structures that I discussed in Chapter 1.

Tompkins and Cheney (1985) argued that the numerous variations these authors have offered on the postbureaucratic organization represent a new type of control, "concertive" control,[9] which extends Edwards's three traditional control strategies. This form represents a key shift in the locus of control from management to the workers themselves, who collaborate together to develop the means of their own control, as we see in team-based or participative organizations such as ISE. Workers achieve concertive control by reaching a negotiated consensus on how to shape their behavior according to a set of core values, such as the values found in a corporate vision statement. In a sense, concertive control reflects the adoption of a new substantive rationality, a new set of consensual values, by the organization and its members.

This negotiated consensus creates and re-creates a value-based discourse that workers use to infer and deduce "proper" behavioral premises: ideas, norms, or rules that enable them to act in ways functional for the organization. For example, a newly concertive company may have a vision statement that states, "We are a principled organization that values teamwork." This value may lead one of its members to create a discourse that calls out the premise that "to be principled and value teamwork, we all must come to work on time." The actors can then deduce a method of acting (e.g., coming to work promptly at 7:00 a.m., not at 7:30) that is functional for the organization and does not require a supervisor's close direction. Thus, concertive control becomes manifest as the team members act, discursively, within the parameters of these value systems and the discourses they themselves create. These new collaboratively created and value-laden premises (manifest as ideas, norms, and rules) become the supervisory force that guides activity in the concertive-control system. In concertive control, then, the necessary social rules that constitute meaning and sanction modes of social conduct become manifest through the collaborative interactions of the organization's members. Workers in a concertive organization create the meanings, the discursive formations that, in turn, structure the system of their own control. Rule generation moves from the traditional supervisor-subordinate relationship to the actors' negotiated consensus about values.

A second and more important difference between the concertive-control model and its bureaucratic predecessor lies in the locus of authority. In the concertive organization, the locus of authority, what actors see as the legitimate source of control to which they are willing to submit (Whitley, 1977), transfers from the bureaucratic system and its rational-legal constitutive rules to the value consensus of the members and its socially created generative rules system. Under bureaucratic control, employees might ensure that they come to work on time because the employee handbook prescribed it and the supervisor had the legal right to demand it. But, in the concertive system, employees might come to work on time because their peers now have the authority to demand the workers' willing compliance.[10]

Concertive control develops from the value-based discourses of workers in highly participative organizations, such as team-based companies. And because concertive control represents a highly persuasive discourse of collective values, norms, and rules, it becomes a very powerful force within the organization. In fact, concertive control is actually more powerful and has a greater ability to control than the bureaucratic system it replaces.

For some time now, theorists have warned that concertive control could become a stronger force than bureaucratic control. Tompkins and Cheney (1985, p. 184) asserted that concertive control would increase the strength of control in its system, and Tannenbaum (1968) proposed that if management would give up some of its authority to the workers, it would, in turn, increase the effectiveness of control in the firm. Tannenbaum wrote that participative (self-managing in our case) organizations could not be productive unless

> they have an effective system of control through which the potentially diverse interests and actions of members are integrated in concerted, that is, organized behavior. The relative success of participative approaches, therefore, hinges, not on reducing control, but on achieving a system of control that is more effective than that of other systems. (p. 23)

This "more effective system of control," in terms of participative teams, comes from the authority and power teammates exercise over each other as peer managers and from the grounding of their discursive formations in their commonly shared values for doing good work together.

Concertive control, then, serves as an *ideal type* for describing control in participative organizations. "Ideal type" refers to a conceptualization of social phenomena that can then be used for descriptive and analytical purposes. Simple, technological, and bureaucratic are Edwards's ideal types for describing and analyzing control in organizations. Here, I have added concertive control to this typology. One caveat with ideal types is that they are general rather than exact types. An ideal type will vary in appearance and manifestation in differing circumstances. For example, a military organization and a business will share many *general* characteristics of a bureaucracy, but their *exact* controlling mechanisms will vary. Concertive control, as an ideal type, gives us a general understanding of the form of control marking participative work; however, the exact manifestation of concertive control will vary from organization to organization.

Concertive control, as an ideal type, presents a general conceptualization of the complex ways through which we become willing participants in and creators of a system that controls our own behavior. It is a powerful and persuasive system that demands our obedience, and we obey because the system reflects our own work values. The implication here is that because team members work in concertive environments, their work culture—their discursive formations—will have a very powerful effect on them. The team members will create their own discursive formations, they will identify strongly with them, and the formations will persuade them to create meanings that will very effectively control their own behavior.

GENERATIVE DISCIPLINE

In establishing my analytical framework so far, I have argued for two essential assumptions. My first assumption is that what we call "organizational culture" actually represents a creative set of *discursive formations* that we use as needed to help us make our work life meaningful, sensible, and rational. As I discussed above, an organization's culture is essentially a persuasive argument about what constitutes knowledge in the organization and how that knowledge should be used. My second assumption is that we use these discursive knowledge formations (the organization's culture) to create a *systematic mechanism* that will effectively control our behavior. In participative organizations, such as ISE's team-based structure, we call such a systematic mechanism *concertive control* because it represents the organization's members acting in concert with each other discursively to control their work behavior. When we put these two assumptions together, when we mix organizational culture and control, we get a *generative discipline.*[11]

I am emphasizing *generative discipline* here to divert attention away from the common, strictly punitive connotations of the term *discipline,* as in "the boss disciplined the worker with a 1-day suspension." Instead, I want to focus consideration on the connotation of discipline as a means for producing regular, recurring, functional behavior, as in "the team worked together as a highly disciplined unit and was very productive." Perhaps a better example of this connotation of discipline would be a good marching band. The band members all know their places and their relationships with each other, their inter-dependencies with each other, and how they need to support each other. Because they are disciplined, they can work *in concert* to perform intricate maneuvers while still making beautiful music. They are "good." Thus, I am drawing a purposeful distinction between what we might call "little d" discipline, the punitive variety, and "big D" discipline, the more systematic, regular, and social variety.

I also want us to understand *generative* here within two denotations for the term. The first, and more common, is the use of generative to mean something that produces, something that causes other forms to come into being. Thus, a *generative discipline* is potent and creative, just as a disciplined marching band is able to navigate complex, difficult music and maneuvers. The second meaning is a more loosely held denotation. I also want us to consider generative similarly to the way that we apply the term to "generative grammar." Particularly, I am referring to the manner in which we consider generative grammar as a system of rules that, when applied, create "well-formed" sentences and "good" language use and that rely on both deep (the knowledge we carry with us) and surface structures (our behaviors). With these two ideas in mind, a generative discipline becomes a potent, creative, and powerful social force, difficult for us to resist.

Thus, I am using the term *generative discipline* here to refer to the mechanism through which an organization's discursive formations and system of control (as described above) become manifest in actual day-to-day organizational activity as a method for doing good work in the organization. That is, the organization's discursive system of discipline teaches us what we need to know to be a productive contributor to that organization. Furthermore, the discipline also trains us so that we can be such a productive contributor over time.

In a participative organization, the team members will act in concert with each other (concertive control) to create knowledge about how to do good work on the team (a discursive formation). When team members act in accordance with their concertively developed norms and values for doing good work, they are being disciplined. Generative discipline, then, refers to the mechanisms we use to act as good people in the organization. As I use the term *discipline* in the remainder of the book, I am referring to the concept of generative discipline that I have developed here. First, however, I want to explore the theoretical implications of such a view of discipline in greater detail.

Foucault and the Concept of Discipline

Foucault (1972, 1976, 1980) argued that, whereas we originally thought of discipline in only its overt forms (e.g., the prison), we must now understand that discipline in contemporary times, particularly in the modern organization, becomes embedded in the various means by which we "shape" ourselves. Through this process, we necessarily surrender some of our autonomy (become "docile," in Foucault's terms) to the will of the organization. To illustrate, many organizational disciplines undoubtedly are overt and tangible (e.g., the clear knowledge, power, and rule reflected in a strong order from a supervisor: "You either make your quota or you're fired.").

Most times, however, disciplines work beyond the perception of an organization's members (e.g., the members of a work group all show up for a daily meeting even though their group leader is on vacation and not there to "order" them to have the meeting). We surrender our autonomy in a number of ways that appear to us as natural occurrences. In today's modern organization, we normally do not attend to the fact that the organization and its discourses are disciplining us (see also Deetz, 1992, 1995).

To be meaningful, an organizational discipline must be discernible. That is, the discipline must enable the organization's members to differentiate clearly between what is good, or expected behavior, and what is bad, or undesirable behavior, in the organization. The organization's members must be able to understand how the discipline is supposed to work and readily be able to act in accordance with the discipline. They must be able to "read" the disciplinary culture. To meet this need for discernibility, disciplines in team-based organizations reflect a particular relationship between discursive formations and concertive control.

Power Relationships, Knowledge, and Rules of Right

A generative discipline, as a structure of discursive formations, arises from a set of power relationships, ascribed knowledge about those relationships, and rules that reinforce the knowledge and power relations (see Barker & Cheney, 1994, pp. 22-24). In the social world, we define our relationships and how we should behave in relation to each other in terms of power differences and similarities. Power is a very useful tool that facilitates our ability to work together.[12] For example, in a concertive organization, the team members may all share decision-making power, and they make decisions either by voting or by arguing out a consensus. However, the team will have some power differences. One team member may be a good leader, another more adept at a vital team function. Perhaps a few team members have worked at the organization since its beginning and enjoy a higher status than newer team members.

Further, power relationships are more complex than one person having power or status over another. In organizations, we also form power relationships with nonhuman entities such as goals and values. For example, if we work hard to ensure that our organization makes a profit, then we have ascribed a power relationship to the value of profitability. If we say that our team values a high level of customer satisfaction and we behave in a way that supports that value (e.g., working overtime to meet a customer deadline), then we have socially constructed a power relationship with that value. If, on a team, we decide that all team members should learn to do all the jobs required by the team and I learn how to do several other jobs because "that's what we decided to do as a team," then we have also constructed a power relationship.

Each team will have its own unique power relationships, and each team member will have a set of ascribed knowledge about those power relationships. That is, the team members will know how to behave in relation to the power relationships. A new team member may know to ask a more experienced team member for help in solving a difficult problem. The team members may look to the "good leader" among themselves or to the teammate with a reputation for problem solving to offer advice to help the team move forward on a decision. A team member who is a chronic poor producer can expect the team to react in some negative manner.

The term *knowledge* here also pertains to the individual's relationship with both the organization's and the team's power relationships. For knowledge to "work," to be ascribed as meaningful, the individual must know the knowledge (i.e., have been socialized by peers into the values, goals, and other discursive formations of the team) *and the individual must accept the knowledge as being true and meaningful.* The individual must readily *identify* with the organization's (and, by extension to a concertive organization, the team's) discursive knowledge formations. The need for individual identification puts the organization into something of a quandary. The organization (and again by extension, the team) can easily "speak" its important discursive formations: "Our company has to fill 700 customer orders a week or we will go broke." But getting the worker to identify and comply with these formations is another issue. The organization is very aware of this problem and has a mechanism in place to help ensure identification and compliance. We commonly call such mechanisms *control.*

Organizational control hinges on the knowledge we have about how to act in accordance with the power relationships that affect us. To ensure that we "behave" according to our knowledge of power relationships, we discursively create what Foucault called "rules of right" (1980, p. 94). Rules of right are just that: rules that spell out the right way to act in the organization according to the power relationships, as George Cheney and I (Barker & Cheney, 1994) argued,

> Rules of right typify and legitimize power relationships. They are the discursive "mechanisms of power" and "effects of truth (knowledge)" that function to normalize and control individual and collective behavior (Foucault, 1980, p. 90).

Rules of right are seemingly "natural" rules and norms that enable the exercise of power and allow for the regular governance of individuals' actions. Religious doctrine, national constitutions, and the taken-for-granted powers of "the boss" (e.g., in the U.S., the long-upheld principle of "at will" employment) are a few examples of rules of right. But perhaps we find the best example in the simple statement, "That's the way *we* do things around here." (p. 24)

From this perspective, a discursive formation forms a fragment of organizational rationality ("On our team, we all come to work on time because we all have agreed that being on time is a vital team value."). *Discipline,* then, is the practical arm of this rationality. A discipline is the social force that enables the discursive formation to become manifest in organizational activity (in the words of a "disciplined" employee, "I always tidy up my work area at 5 p.m. because the company and my peers expect me to have a clean area.").

Disciplines become the method for "teaching" us how to do good work in the organization in regular and recurring ways. Again, as George Cheney and I (Barker & Cheney, 1994) asserted in our analysis of Foucault's views on discipline,

> Foucault's concept of discipline was meant to capture those micro-techniques of power in use that rationalize and normalize not only individuals but also collective, organized bodies (Clegg, 1989). Discipline also referred to a general tendency in modern society to expand the subtle means of control over the individual even as coercion becomes less prevalent. Consistent with Foucault's concept of discipline and his archaeology of modern institutions, we emphasize three meanings of the term "discipline" found in the *Oxford English Dictionary* (1989): as a noun (a) a system or method for the maintenance of order or for conduct, and (b) the orderly conduct of action which result from training; and as a verb, (c) to train habits of order and subordination, to bring under control (p. 416). Discipline is thus *both* a set of activities and an outcome. And, it becomes clear that attempts to "rationalize" the world, the workplace, and relations (e.g., through an obsession with efficiency) have a disciplining effect on human experience. (p. 21)[13]

As the practical dimension of discursive formations, disciplines reinforce the organization's knowledge base (or cultural context) with "additional stamina" through various tactics of control (see Tompkins, 1985, p. 129) such as the forms of simple, technological, bureaucratic, and concertive control discussed earlier in this chapter. To take an example from bureaucratic control, the famous "organizational chart" that delineates the formal network of power relationships in an organization serves as a strong discursive discipline affecting the actions of the organization's members. In a bureaucracy, a worker who knows "I can't go over my boss's head" feels the normative force of discipline and, in Ray's (1986, p. 287) terms, becomes "ensnared" in a discursive iron cage.[14]

Discipline and Concertive Control

As also discussed in the above section on control, concertive systems, such as those found among ISE's teams, have the potential to create powerful mechanisms for controlling behavior because their discursive formations are rooted in shared core values enforced through peer pressure. This line of reasoning holds true for disciplines as well. Barker and Cheney (1994, pp. 27-31) argued that disciplines were most powerful when they were based on collaboratively generated and enforced shared values that emerged through the natural work activity of the organization's members, a point later confirmed in the works of Papa, Auwal, and Singhal (1995, 1997).

To summarize briefly, discursive formations are sets of power relationships, knowledge about those relationships, and rules for the right way of behaving in terms of the power and knowledge.[15] Discursive formations are sets of possibilities that we use to create a workable shared meaning in the organization. Disciplines present us with specific arrangements of these possible meanings, a behavioral template that instructs us how to act, regularly and recurrently, in ways functional for the organization. Disciplines operating in a concertive system are exceptionally strong and robust because the team members themselves create and subsequently enforce the disciplines. The concertive system disciplines us, and, because we are a part of that concertive system, we willingly accept, even welcome, that discipline. After all, we do want our organizations to be successful, and we value our ability to do good work for the organization.

There is a tendency in the above discussion to misperceive *generative disciplines* as being rigid methods of control, but in a concertive organization, such as ISE, this is not the case. Certainly, generative disciplines teach, push, and constrain us to act in particular ways, but a discipline is an inanimate force. Disciplines do not use us. We use disciplines rhetorically to create particular kinds of realities in regular and recurring ways. An organizational discipline sets the conditions, contexts, constraints, and parameters of our ability to work together in an organization, but we members of the organization fill in the blanks by interacting together in terms of the discipline through our shared work lives. A discipline is not the final product of our activity, but it certainly is a powerful rough draft for that activity.

A METHODOLOGY FOR LIVING
IN THE ORGANIZATION

The social critic Kenneth Burke (1964) wrote of culture as being a "rough draft for living" (p. 155). A culture confronts us with "a bundle of *judgments* as to how things were, how they are, and how they may be" [italics added] (Burke, 1984, p. 15), and we have to figure out how to use that rough draft to create a meaningful reality, to find a useful and productive way of getting along with each other. What a culture *does,* then, is present us with possibilities for creating shared meaning in any collectivity: a group, a dyad, an organization, or a society. In line with this perspective, an organization's generative discipline presents us with a well-formed, but not final, discursive "rough draft" of apparently "truthful" possibilities for working together productively. Generative disciplines certainly have a sense of persuasiveness and purposefulness.

Generative Discipline as Methodology

With this thought in mind, a generative discipline represents a "rough draft" *methodology* for *how* to live in the organization.[16] A generative discipline is not the final product, but it moves us toward a final product both in particular directions and within particular constraints. A methodology, as in a methodology for doing something, is an instructive or teaching device. In academic terms, we use the word *methodology* to refer to "how" we go about learning new knowledge about the world. Methodologies guide how we collect data on a phenomenon, how we analyze that data, and how we act on the results of that analysis. A methodology is rigorous and thoroughgoing. A methodology leads us to the truth. That is, a methodology, when applied correctly, will lead us to an accurate assessment of everyday life, just as a scientific methodology will lead us to an accurate assessment of an experiment.

Generative disciplines, as discursive, social methodologies for action, are formulas that we follow to ensure that we act in the way the organization needs us to act, which, for the organization, *is* the truth. Christensen and Cheney (1994) also described disciplinary discourses in this "methodological" manner:

> By making distinctions, setting boundaries, and highlighting certain aspects of experience, discourses provide "subtle and covert prior structuring" (Cooper & Burrell, 1988, p. 102). Conceptualized this way, discourses do not determine

individual meanings, but they do suggest a range of possibilities within which individual meanings will be constructed. (p. 231)

A Methodology With a "Rough Draft" Quality

Again, recalling Burke's ideas, disciplines, though certainly a methodology for organizational activity, still have a "rough draft" or generative quality. They enable us to generate an organizationally useful method for controlling our own behavior. Certainly, I do not wish to give the impression that organizational disciplines fully determine our actions. Disciplines allow us to be creative in our work together; however, we are compelled to be creative within the parameters of the disciplinary methodology.

As discussed above, discursive formations and disciplines are not static but instead are fluid and dynamic, just as our day-to-day construction of meaning in a concertive organization is fluid and dynamic. As members of the organization, we create actual meanings only at the particular point in time when we need to do something, just as Joyce in the earlier example "created" a meaning with Bob to explain her need to rush back to her work. The fluid and dynamic character of organizational life is a nasty little problem that greatly confounds and vexes us academics and organizational members alike. We tend to get caught up in trying to understand or predict exactly how an organization's members will create meaning (e.g., make particular decisions) in specific and constant situations. We want our generative disciplines, as methodologies, to produce perfect behavior in every instance. We focus in on culture as something that the organization is or has because understanding culture as something the organization does is too abstract, conceptually slippery, and difficult. What should we do about this problem?

My solution has been to direct my attention on how our organizational generative disciplines work as methodologies for action or, in the case of ISE, as methodologies for the daily activity of teams and team members. If we are to gain a rich understanding of the social consequences of life in participative organizations and if we want to offer practical suggestions for how we can shape and influence the way that we create shared meaning in organizations, then we must be willing to move from the relatively secure study of the outcomes of organizational activity to the loose, intangible, and even unsafe territory of disciplines, discursive formations, and concertive control. But taking that step requires us to grasp the intellectually difficult concept of visualizing generative discipline as a methodology in "rough draft" form.

A rough draft contains all the core and central concepts that are needed to create a final product. We use that rough draft to help us, to guide us, and to instruct us on how we should go about making something final. The rough draft shapes and influences what will be. A methodology does the same thing. As a source for "how" to do something, it shapes and influences "what will be" ontologically. We do not know what will happen for certain when we apply a methodology. But we know that if we apply the methodology correctly, we will find the apparent truth of everyday organizational life, a workable reality with a high degree of verisimilitude. To fully appreciate the inherently creative process of constructing meaning in an organization, we need to keep in mind the "rough draft" quality of our disciplinary methodology for creating meaning.

A further element that we need to remember is that a generative discipline is not a neutral methodology. A discipline pulls us toward certain sets of meaning possibilities and away from others. Organizational disciplines are persuasive forces that "teach" us the right and good ways of creating meaning at work. When we make these kinds of choices—when we "choose" to let an organizational discipline guide us and when we choose not to let the discipline guide us—consequences will arise. Again from the earlier example, if Joyce had "chosen" not to hurry back to work, she certainly would have been in even more trouble than she already was. When we choose to work overtime to meet a customer order at the expense of time with our families, social consequences, both good and bad, arise. Thus, we need to gain a rich understanding of how we create and use disciplines in team-based organizations, and we need to gain an equally rich understanding of the consequences of this activity and its effect on us as social human beings. Now we must take that step into the uncertain world of the cultural methodology, into the world of discursive formations, concertive control, and generative discipline. It is a step that we need to take if we are to understand what we have gotten ourselves into with today's impulse toward participation.

Analyzing How Generative Discipline Works

In the chapters that follow, I will explore how we use disciplines as methodologies to influence, shape, constrain, and even make possible our collective activity in an organization. ISE's team members did not solve every problem the same way. They did not make every decision in the same manner. However, their solutions to problems, their decisions, and their other activities take on consistent patterns with consistent consequences. ISE's workers were working off of a set of methodologies for living and working together. They did have a consistent foundation, a foundation from which they could construct useful meanings (e.g., solve their problems, make good decisions, etc.), which is their generative discipline at work. I wrote in the preceding chapter that our essential need now is to understand the social consequences of work in participative, team-based organizations. These social consequences are found in the analysis of how we use generative discipline to create useful meanings. An analysis of ISE's team members' methodologies in practice will produce a useful understanding of those consequences and their implications.

In ethnographic research, some manifestations of a generative discipline are reasonably readily apparent. I could observe a team meeting at ISE, which followed a set agenda each day, and easily deduce the discipline behind how and why the meeting unfolded as it did. I could also fairly easily deduce the consequences of this discipline. Perhaps the meeting made the team more productive, but the team took so much time in getting through the meeting that their increased productivity was compromised.

Understanding and analyzing the discursive formations and the effects of concertive control that underlie the deeper structures of generative disciplines are more difficult undertakings, however, and require no small amount of ethnographic detective work. My tactic here was to rely on interview accounts that the team members gave me,[17] on the artifacts that the teams and the organization created, and on my intuition as an experienced team worker.

In constructing my account of how discipline works in a team environment, I have organized my findings around the three elements of discursive formations: power relationships, individual knowledge of the relationships, and rules of right for enforcing the relationships. For example, Chapter 4 discusses how the teams negotiated power relationships in a concertive setting, how disciplines took shape from these negotiations, and the manifest and latent consequences of the teams' formation of power relationships.

Following this procedure enables me to answer the three key questions I have developed in this book so far: How do generative disciplines work in team-based organizations? What are the consequences of our use of disciplines in team-based organizations? and How should we respond to these consequences? Before doing this, however, I need to spend some time discussing ISE's change to teams and the aftermath of the change. Essentially, we cannot understand how ISE's new generative discipline works without understanding how its team-based system of concertive control formed, developed, and matured. So begins my story of ISE's experience with participation, teams, and the generative discipline of concertive control.

NOTES

1. My purpose in this section is not to summarize the vast organizational culture literature but to review, very superficially, the most essential assumptions of the two dominant perspectives. I direct readers interested in detailed reviews of organizational culture literature to the articles by Allaire and Firsirotu (1984), Barnett (1988), O'Donnell-Trujillo and Pacanowsky (1983), Ouchi and Wilkins (1985), Pacanowsky and O'Donnell-Trujillo (1982), Putnam (1982), Sackmann (1990), Schein (1990), and Smircich and Calas (1987) and the anthologies edited by Frost, Moore, Louis, Lundberg, and Martin (1985, 1991).

2. See Smircich and Calas's (1987) discussion of culture paradigms.

3. Essentially, here, knowledge discourse refers to the unique language that members use to talk about themselves, their organization, and their activity in the organization.

4. For compatible views of organizational culture, see Coombs, Knights, and Willmott (1992) and Knights and Morgan (1991). Also see the discussions of discursive formations in Barker and Cheney (1994), Deetz (1992, 1995), and Foss, Foss, and Trapp (1991).

5. In his earlier work, Foucault used the term *episteme* in the same manner as he used *discursive formation* in his latter work. Foss, Foss, and Trapp (1991) explained Foucault's motivation to change terms:

> With the publication of *The Archaeology of Knowledge,* Foucault [1972] replaced the term "episteme" with "discursive formation," and he abandoned his former label. One reason for this change in terminology may have been Foucault's belief that he was not a structuralist and did not use the methods, concepts, or key terms of the structuralist movement. (p. 217)

6. I use the term *epistemic* here advisedly because of Foucault's aversion to structuralist explanations (see Barker & Cheney, 1994, p. 39). Still, the point is instructive, as Foucault viewed an episteme as a "cultural code, characteristic system, structure, network, or ground of thought that governs the language, perception, values, and practices of an age" (Foss, Foss, & Trapp, 1991, p. 216). Foucault's perspective here directly implies the view of organizational culture as a discursive formation that influences and shapes language, perception, values, and practice in an organization.

7. Portions of the following section are excerpted from Barker (1993b).

8. For an in-depth discussion of the evolution of control practices in organizations, see Sewell (1998).

9. Elaine Tompkins first coined the term *concertive control.*

10. See Papa, Auwal, and Singhal's (1997) discussion of self-imposed constraints in a concertive-control system.

11. Linda Macdonald coined the term *generative discipline.*

12. See Foucault's discussion of power in society (1980, pp. 92-94). For related discussions, see Daudi (1986) and Mumby and Stohl (1991).

13. For other discussions of discipline and teamwork, see Ezzamel and Willmott (1998) and Sewell (1998).

14. The conceptualization of discursive formations and disciplines that I have developed here is consistent with other lines of thought in contemporary control theory. For example, organizational disciplines, as described above, are congruous with the social force that Tompkins and McPhee (1985, p. 9) have called "microhegemonies" within the organization. Hegemony, in the

broad sense, refers to "a process of education carried on through various institutions of civil society in order to make normative, inevitable, and even 'natural' the ruling ideas of ruling interests" (Lentricchia, 1985, p. 76). Hegemony suggests a purposeful aspect to the culture or society as a whole. In an organization, "microhegemony," then, refers to the purposeful nature of organizational activity: how an organization's structures, policies, strategies, and processes become normative, accepted, and "commonsensical" for its actors in day-to-day practice—essentially, what Barker and Cheney (1994) called "organizational disciplines."

15. Readers may note some parallels between my discussion of *discipline* and Giddens's (e.g., 1984) theorizing on how we structure society. Although I could have delved more into the connections to Giddens's ideas, I have purposefully taken a more Foucaultian view. I considered Foucault's concept of discipline a more useful means for illustrating how participative organizations work and the consequences of our participation together. For a recent analysis using Giddens's perspective, see Scott, Corman, and Cheney (1998).

16. Though not using the term *discipline,* Burke discussed cultural reality in much the same way I have in the preceding sections. Burke's (1984) term "orientation" fits very well with the way I have presented Foucault's term *discipline.* Also see discussions of Burke's social theory as applied to organizations in Perinbanayagam (1985, p. 79 in particular) and in Carrier (1982, p. 51 in particular).

17. See my discussion of the usefulness of accounts in Chapter 1.

chapter 3

Creating a Generative Discipline[1]

> Jack was the major convert in this whole process of changing to
> teams. Jack got really excited when he saw the application of team
> concepts to the factory. In fact, he became quite the zealot.
>
> *Jonie Ross, ISE's vice president of human resources*

IN THE BEGINNING . . .

One day, about 3 years after ISE's transition to teams, I found Jack
Tackett, ISE's vice president of manufacturing, sitting in his cubicle with his
feet propped up on his desk. I asked if we could talk for a bit, and I found him
to be in a reflective mood. Jack said that he had been thinking about how things
had changed at ISE since the start of teamwork, particularly about his role:

> You know, I used to have my office on the other side of the building. I had a big
> window that overlooked the air force base. I used to sit in there and watch the
> jets take off and land. No more of that now.

And he laughed.

When ISE changed from a traditional manufacturing design to a team-based
structure, Jack had moved his office from the "executive wing" to a small space
adjacent to the large manufacturing floor. Jack and a few of his support staff now
occupied this space with small, cubicle offices. Jack wanted to be close to the
action, close to where his teams were doing their work. Jack's 6-by-6 cubicle
was a far cry from his former spacious office, but it very much symbolized how
he had changed his managerial style. For Jack, ISE's radical "conversion" to
self-managing teams had been literal. He had become more than just the leader
of the change. He had become the apostle. He had seen the light.

Jack began his tenure at the future ISE in 1980. He was working as the production manager for another high-tech firm in the same metropolitan area when Bob Sullivan, who would become ISE's president, invited Jack to help him start a new circuit board production division for a very large telecommunications corporation.

In early 1979, the large corporation had chosen Bob to build and start up a new production division, which was a bold move for this company because it previously had focused only on telecommunications service. After a year of planning, Bob chose the future ISE site as the place to start the new division. He moved to the area and began hiring the necessary personnel to get started. Bob brought in Jack to plan and develop the entire manufacturing aspect of the division.

Jack, who holds an advanced electrical engineering degree and has had a number of years' experience in production management, immediately began designing the new plant. After a year of preparation, he started a prototype production operation in late 1981 with six workers in the factory.

From 1980 to 1984, the larger corporation was in a period of turmoil and transition, marked by three presidents during these 5 years. In 1983, the corporation's senior executives began to recognize that they did not want to be in the manufacturing business and decided to close the new division. They made this decision even though the division had become profitable that year, with a business volume of $8 to $10 million.

The division's management team, which included Jack, began to negotiate buying the division themselves. They set about raising the buyout money and eventually located a willing venture capital group on the East Coast. With this group's funds, the management team's chief financial manager was able to present a leveraged buyout plan to the large corporation in the summer of 1984. The management team had been able to retain controlling interest in the new company. The large corporation agreed to the plan in September 1984 and immediately became a customer of the new firm. ISE was born.

ISE's manufacturing plant continued to function as it had before the buyout. Jack, now the vice president of manufacturing, structured and operated the plant in the same manner as most other manufacturing companies: through hierarchical supervision and assembly-line production. As Jack told me, "Then, it was the only way I knew how to operate a plant. That's the way I was brought up. It seemed like a good idea at the time."

Jack had organized the plant according to the activities involved in assembling circuit boards. Workers assigned to the drop-in line were in one area of the plant assembling all the boards the company produced. Another group soldered all the boards in a different location and touched up any mistakes. Another group tested all the boards to ensure that they worked properly. Another repaired all the defective boards, and so forth. Four hierarchical levels extended below Jack: plant manager, manufacturing manager, shift foreman, and line or area leads. In addition, Jack had five managers on his support staff: plant manager, production control manager, purchasing manager, test engineering manager, and manufacturing engineer manager. ISE's manufacturing department operated with this configuration until the change to teams in 1988. After the change to teams, ISE's workers referred to the original assembly-line setup as "traditional," as in "traditional manufacturing." Rick, who was one of the first ISE workers, provided a shop-floor perspective on the original structure and how it worked:

> At that time, we were very traditional in our organization. We had assemblers that worked on the drop-in line. They were considered first assemblers. Then we had second assemblers that did touch-up to the product. We had a separate group that we called testers. Everything was very, very traditional and very split as far as responsibilities went. If you looked at our job at that time, each operation was tracked. Every single operation was tracked. When you worked, you were assigned to a particular station and someone tracked your work at that station. People came in, they went to their assigned seats, and that was the job that they did all day long. If you were an assembler, you might have been on the drop-in line. You were probably doing that for years unless an opportunity opened for someone to move up into second assembly because that was the direction you would have gone into. If you were a first assembler, there was a monetary increase if you became a second assembler. When jobs came open, they would post it in-house. And then, of course, you would go through an interview process, and you would be selected.
>
> The other opportunity was in the wave solder area [the workers who soldered the circuit boards together], which was considered a process operator. That was another grade level higher, paywise. If you looked at them as grade level 1, 2, and 3, the process operator was a grade level 3, and that was an avenue or direction assemblers could go in to gain more experience, to move up in jobs. And then, of course, there were the lead positions, which were a grade 4 at that point in time.

Everything and everyone was ordered. Everything was in its place, and everyone had his or her place. It was a "traditional" manufacturing plant.

Though the *structure* of the direct work functions at ISE seemed stable, the management team had quickly seen the necessity for change. During the buyout process, they began to realize that they could not operate in the same way they had when they were part of the large corporation. They had no deep financial pockets, no established customer base, and no guarantee that the large corporation would remain as their leading customer. Jonie Ross, ISE's vice president of human resources and a member of the original management team, described their situation:

> We [the management team] had been talking about doing something. We had to change our big-company mentality. When we were a part of the big company [ISE's former owner], we used to have procedures and policies. There were bookshelves of policies and procedures on how we did things. You didn't necessarily have an environment where you were awarded for risk taking or responsiveness. People basically did whatever they did, and it took as long as it took, and they weren't particularly customer-oriented. And we started to say in telecommunications, it is going to be a very competitive market. The Bell companies were deregulating. We thought there was a lot of opportunity, but there was also a lot of competition. So from a strategic standpoint, we felt that in order for us to be competitive, we needed to change our corporate culture. We needed to have a culture that reflected a small company, not a big company.

The management team felt that they had to develop a new way of operating if they were going to be successful with their new company.

During the buyout process, the management team had gotten to know each other very well. They realized that they were a diverse group with different personalities. They did not have the facilitation skills to work together as a team. They also recognized that they needed to quicken their ability to make collective decisions, develop more efficient managerial work processes, and establish a level of competitiveness in a tough market. Again Jonie Ross detailed their quandary:

> So we started reading books. We went to a couple of different conferences, brought back some information, and kind of worked together. We created, you probably have seen it hanging on the wall, something called the "pledge to excellence." And that was our first attempt at changing corporate culture. What we did was we drafted it, we wrote it among ourselves, we hung it on the wall, and we expected the culture to change—which was extremely naive, but I guess we aren't the only ones to ever make that mistake. So we hung it on the wall and we waited for something to happen, and we looked around about 6 months later and nothing had happened. Gee, what a surprise.
>
> So we got more aggressive, and we decided we probably needed some help in changing corporate culture. Our view before that was, we have a lot of people

with master's degrees and Ph.D.'s and we're extremely intelligent, and we can do this ourselves. And that has kind of been our whole mentality all along. I mean we don't use a lot of outside consultants. We do a lot of things ourselves. And sometimes that's good, and sometimes that's not so good. But the view has always been that this is a more cost-effective way for a small company to do things. But we realized that we really hadn't made any changes.

The management team felt that they needed help, help they could not provide for themselves; they now realized that they needed a consultant. Bill Farmer started coming to ISE in 1985 and began training the executive group in managerial teamwork and collective decision making. He even took them to a local ski resort for a weekend retreat to learn all about working together. Farmer's retreat included a strong and persuasive dose of team philosophy. Jack called it "going to the mountain to hear the wisdom." The more important result of their work with the consultant, however, was that the management team began to understand that change was good and that they needed to significantly change the way they operated ISE.

THE APOSTLE OF TEAMWORK

During this first experience with Bill Farmer, Jack underwent something of a conversion experience regarding self-managing teams, getting what Kunda (1992) called a new "managerial religion" (p. 5). Through the buyout process, Jack and the others in the executive group had become very astute students of new managerial philosophies and strategies. Most of the management team had read the then currently popular works of Crosby, Peters, Drucker, and other consultants. In fact, they had taken the name ISE from Peters and Waterman's (1982) *In Search of Excellence.*

Motivated by his strong desire that the new company be successful and by the words of Bill Farmer, Jack began studying a number of radical manufacturing concepts. He started examining the Just-in-Time (JIT) production philosophy[2] and managerial concepts such as self-managing teams and cellular manufacturing. Jack came to believe that these new concepts would make ISE more competitive in its marketplace. Again, Jack described his thoughts at the time:

> I had been reading things by Tom Peters and the Leadership Alliance and others. And I was seeing what was going on in other companies: how they were working with reducing cycle times and increasing customer service and things of that

nature. Besides, [the larger corporation] was reducing its supplier base, so there was no guarantee that they would stay with us. Our production quality was not so good, neither was our customer responsiveness. I said that we are not going to make it unless we make some major changes, or that the trauma created in the company [from loss of customers and the possibility of going under] is going to be so dramatic that nobody is going to like anybody much.

Jack's solution, inspired by his conversion at the mountain retreat with Bill Farmer, was self-managing teams.

Jack Tackett was and is a man of determination with no small amount of business smarts. In taking stock of ISE, Jack could tell that he had an ailing organization on his hands. Sure, things were not too bad at the time, but Jack and the others could forecast the market. They could see the specter of change looming in their future. They saw rough weather ahead. Partly what they were sensing was the growing trend toward participative organizations. In practical terms, then, what the dramatic shift toward participation meant for Jack and the rest of the management team was that they had to create a new corporate culture, a new set of knowledge for how to *do* work and do it well. To survive, they had to turn ISE into a participative organization. ISE had to find a way of working harder, faster, and smarter. After hearing Bill Farmer's sermon on the mount (even if it was only a retreat at a mountain resort), Jack now knew that self-managing teams were the way, the truth, and the light. He would create a new culture, a culture of self-management.

Jack faced another problem. Phil Tompkins (1993, pp. 185-186) wrote persuasively that an ailing organization must be fixed in three ways:

1. There has to be a change in leadership;
2. the new leadership has to possess new and engaging characteristics, such as trust and a sense of value for participative organizations; and
3. the organization must undergo a "redemptive praxis," that is, the organization must symbolically leave its past behind and move on to something new, essentially creating a new culture.

The change to self-managing teams could serve as ISE's redemptive praxis, but Tompkins's points one and two posed real dilemmas for Jack. He was not about to leave. Jack's solution to the need for a change in leadership was to change himself. He came home from the retreat a changed man, a true believer in teams. He firmly and honestly came to believe that, on a humanistic level, self-managing teams represented a fundamentally better way of working. In a later conversation, Jack told me of his feelings:

> I knew that we had to change and that I had to change fundamentally. Sure, I was worried about the bottom line. We had to make money. But I firmly felt that we could work better. We could create a more humane way of working out there on the line. I believe that teams are the way to go; they are a qualitatively better way of working. With teams, we can make money and make a better working environment.

Jack, then, was both a calculating manager and a sensitive humanist. His dual focus on making ISE's teamwork both more productive and more humane would guide the change as it became manifest.

As with any conversion experience, Jack's transformation was not superficial. He had become a different person, a different leader. Jack's colleagues readily saw the difference, as Jonie Ross explained,

> Now Jack was probably one of the most traditional managers I had ever seen. I've told people before that he was probably one of the most strongly Theory X[3] managers around. He would pound on the table, and he would yell. I've even seen him throw things. But it is a much different Jack Tackett that you see today. I think he realized that you didn't need to take that approach [Theory X]. You didn't need to handle things in that way to be successful. And it was probably more healthy for him and his blood pressure not to approach things that way. And that is probably what he saw through the training with Farmer.

Jack had his own reflections on his sudden change:

> I believed that we had a national problem in terms of productivity. And it really hurts when I read about Japanese executives saying that we [in the United States] don't have a work ethic. But the fact of the matter is that there's a lot of truth in that statement, and the truth hurts. I think that the empowerment issues, the cultural transformations we go through are, for me, the answers for that charge. Cultural change creates motivation, drives out laziness, drives out mediocrity, creates an ethic to perform and to meet a market demand and to feel good about doing it. That's the key. And if we can help others to pass that ethic along, then some day the Japanese are gonna eat their words, because I think that we can turn around and clean their clock. When the American worker sets his mind to something, there's no one in the world that can stop him. It's the management structure that has held him back. And now you see more managers saying, "We

have to change," but I say, "Don't tell me that we have to change, I have to change first." It all starts with me. If I didn't make the decision to change, the rest of my organization would not have changed. And that's where it starts. It starts with the man in charge saying, "I'm willing to do things differently."

Jack did what it took to save ISE, and that meant reinventing himself as a leader and as a person. Such a conversion was necessary for Jack to make the radical change to teams. Jack certainly became ISE's apostle of self-management as a qualitatively better way of working, but he was also certainly a pragmatist.

JACK'S RADICAL CHANGE

By mid-1985, Jack had made his resolute decision to radically change the plant. He had decided that ISE's very survival depended on converting to self-management and doing away with its old traditional, bureaucratic production model. Echoing the environmental forces pressuring ISE toward teamwork, he told me of how his plans took shape:

> I thought that if we did things the same way all the time, we were headed for disaster. We could not meet customer demands anymore. Hierarchy insulates people from the customer. The traditional organization cannot know the customer. They are in the dark about what goes on around them with the manager making all the decisions. You can't succeed with that anymore. The demands of the market are too dynamic for a company to be controlled by a handful of managers. The whole company needs to be focused on customer needs, and I needed to marshal the resources of the whole organization, not just a few.

Jack now began to form the plans for changing his production area to self-managing teams. In bringing about this change, he had two key allies on the management team: Jonie Ross, the vice president of human resources who strongly believed that ISE's culture had to change, and Bob Sullivan, the president. Bob had given Jack the green light to plan and make the changes. Bob, like Jack, was a believer in the need to change the company to make it more competitive, and Jack had a strong track record of making good decisions. Jack recalled their relationship:

> I was fortunate in my relationship with him as [Bob] is very open to new ideas and in supporting what I wanted to do. We have done a lot of nontraditional

things here, and we've raised some eyebrows. But as long as we have been successful, he's gone along with it. He has a desire for excellence and a desire to grit his teeth when things don't go well.

Bob gave his approval to Jack's bringing JIT and self-management concepts into ISE's manufacturing department.

With his two allies helping sway the other executives, Jack now concentrated on selling his idea to his own management staff and to the production department. By 1986, Jack was ready to pitch to his staff his plan for implementing JIT and self-managing teams at ISE. Jack convinced many of them that the change to teams was absolutely necessary for ISE to survive (which, for most of them, meant giving up their management jobs, although Jack did arrange lateral moves for them within ISE), and he recruited them to help him institute the change. Some thought that the change was a "stupid idea." But Jack was adamant that self-management was *the* way to revitalize the company. He was so adamant, in fact, that his zeal caused his Theory X side to reappear occasionally:

> I had it firmly set in my mind that this was the way we had to go and these guys [the reluctant supervisors] were going to come up to speed or I was gonna get rid of them. And this team process was the natural opportunity to give people the chance to either get on board on their own or to fall by the wayside.

And the change proceeded.

Jack now began a process of collective planning for the change to teams and teamwork training for his workers. He formed what he called a "steering committee" of about 10 workers and managers to help him prepare for the change. He also brought Bill Farmer back in to conduct teamwork training. The cost of having several all-day training sessions in a row was prohibitive, so Jack arranged with Bill a series of 1-day sessions every other month. Jack's plan was to stretch the transition to teams out over several years.

SPREADING THE WORD

The teamwork training began in 1987. By this time, Jack and his group had, as Jack recalled, "planned the thing to death." They had all their ideas in place for how to physically change the manufacturing environment. They had organized all the team-building material and planned the training sessions.

Again, they originally wanted to do things in small doses, with training from Bill every 60 days and with in-house application meetings in between to work on his team-building material.

However, although Jack had enough power to overcome resistance from his subordinates, he did have a difficult time with other members of the management team. Flush with his growing success in changing the manufacturing section, Jack now became convinced that not only his manufacturing area but the *whole* organization needed to follow his lead. So he began to push the other areas of the company (e.g., finance, marketing, engineering, etc.) to convert to his managerial religion. Jack's apostle's zeal was wearing thin on some of his colleagues. Joanne, one of Jack's subordinate managers at the time, described the tension:

> Well, I don't think anyone outside of manufacturing understood what was going on. Nobody had sat down and said, "Hey, what's going on," but, yes, there was a general feeling of confusion and resentment. It was like there were large walls between manufacturing and the rest of the company in a lot of cases, and we were accused many times, and there was some truth into it, of being elitists. You know, especially engineering, they would think that we were walking around, "We've been through this team-building training and aren't we special. We're different from you and, therefore, we are better than you," or whatever, at least that was the perception.
>
> In engineering, a lot of it manifested itself through Jack's actions: getting up on the soapbox and preaching rather than participating in a meaningful discussion. Sometimes he was unwilling to listen to other people's input. He had turned the rest of the company or the rest of the executive staff off of what he was trying to do because of this. In essence, it became manufacturing against everybody else. Manufacturing had vision; we even came up with our own vision statement. It was said many times by Jack that we are going to do what we need to do, and screw the rest of them. There are better ways of doing it than the way he did it, like working on having a whole company buy in or at least a communicated understanding of what is going on, rather than doing it and telling them about it later.

Jack could tell that his plans for the company were not working out as he thought they would. As Jack recalled,

> Many of them [the other members of the executive management committee besides the president and human resources] thought it [JIT and self-managing teams] was a wild goose chase. They could not see the value in it. They did not

have access to the indicators that I was using to measure success: basic productivity indicators, cycle times, inventory levels, which told us if we were getting better. Their resistance came in the fact that I was trying to force other parts of the organization to act as we [in production] were acting. "See how good we are. Wouldn't you like to be like us?" It created a lot of animosity, just in the tension that was created any time anything relative to culture issues came up.

Engineering, finance, marketing [the other vice presidents on the executive committee besides the supportive human resources vice president] resisted it. They chose not to do team training. The consultant would spend a day training with manufacturing and then be available for the other divisions [e.g., marketing, engineering, finance, etc.], but no one else took advantage of it. They thought that we were elitist and had created barriers, saying, "Engineering, why can't you make it right? Marketing, why can't you forecast right? You're making our life miserable." It took me a while to recognize that you can't deal with other folks like that.

For me, I had to back off and realize that I couldn't make others look small because they weren't taking advantage of the same things we were. This lack of success made me realize this; I was not achieving anything with them. I decided that I cannot force them to change. They will have to change themselves.

In the face of resistance from ISE's other departments, Jack turned inward to manufacturing, to his people, determined to do what he believed needed doing to make his department successful and to create that "more humane, better way of working." And, by this time, he had surrounded himself with a core group of loyal workers and managers equally determined to see the change through. Jack had charged this group with bringing about the transformation to teams, JIT, and cellular manufacturing. This group consisted primarily of several supervisors, including Joanne, whose jobs would be eliminated or changed after the transformation, and a few of the line workers who were especially interested in the prospects of teamwork. The supervisors' participation in this transformation is, in part, a tribute to Jack's enthusiasm for and leadership of the project, to Jack's persuasive arguments that *something* had to be done if the company was to survive, and to Jack's determination that "this is going ahead, with you or without you."

After more than a year of planning and training in teamwork skills,[4] which included drafting and distributing the manufacturing area's vision statement, Jack and his advisory group started one self-managing team on a trial run in early 1988. Jack selected Juli Patterson, one of his managers and a former line worker, to oversee the pilot team. He still planned to slowly convert the entire production department to teams over the course of 2 more years.

THE PLAN COMES TOGETHER

Juli Patterson had rapidly worked her way up from the assembly line to become one of Jack's immediate subordinates. Juli had no problem with taking the initiative:

> I started in 1981, back before we were even ISE. I came in as an assembler, so I worked in the production environment. I started out building products on the line, but very quickly I moved through the ranks. I worked on the line and then the position for what was called a utility worker, which was much like a lead position. And I became that within about 4 months after I joined the company. Then we expanded over time, and I became the lead on first assembly. Then we expanded again, and I moved into the test area for a while. It was very separate. There was another supervisor over the assembly side of the organization, and then there was a supervisor over the test side of the organization as we expanded.
>
> There was some squabbling going on at that time, and I ended up in the test area organizing things. I wasn't really exactly in the lead position, although I still held the title. I was doing a lot of material handling issues in keeping the test area organized. And then in 1982 as the assembly side expanded, I moved back into assembly. I became the lead in the second assembly area where they did the touch-up of the product. I did that for over a year or so. I was a lead in second assembly when we moved into this new facility and became ISE, although I really had responsibility for first assembly and second assembly.
>
> I had been a lead for about 5 years and a position was posted for manufacturing engineering assistant. That individual would have been responsible for doing processes and procedures for the production area or working with the manufacturing engineering group. You did not need to have an engineering degree because you were an assistant; you were helping put together procedures. I went for that job at that time because I had been a lead for a few years myself, and there was nowhere for me to go as an individual. I needed to move on. I had started back to school for my education at that time, and I was going for my degree. I felt that would allow me to gain more knowledge and give me an opportunity.

Juli became the manufacturing engineering assistant and began learning all she could about her new role. And the role quickly created the opportunity she wanted.

Jack's plans for the conversion included more than the change to teams. As mentioned above, Jack was also instituting Just-in-Time inventory control practices and cellular manufacturing techniques, which is an assembly process that lends itself to team environments. This three-part change was a fortuitous decision on his part as conversions to self-managing teams normally require a corresponding change in the fundamental way that the organization does its work (Barker, Melville, & Pacanowsky, 1993). What Jack needed, though, was an expert in JIT and cellular manufacturing design. Juli was a natural choice:

> I was working with manufacturing engineering and doing processes and proce-
> dures, and they were talking about getting someone in-house that could help
> facilitate the Just-in-Time process, in getting Just in Time into our organization.
> They did post the job, but it was at a higher level than I could do. I didn't go for
> that job at the time because it required a degree, and I didn't have the qualifica-
> tions. I don't think they ever really did fill that position because they [Jack and
> Frank Duggan, Jack's plant manager at the time] soon asked me how would I
> like to become involved in the process. They would send me to a local training
> school that taught Just in Time.
>
> Since I was really enjoying learning work procedures, I would love to have
> that opportunity. I think they picked me because I knew the organization. I had
> the background because I was familiar with the processes on the floor. I
> understood the overall JIT concept, and I was a good employee. I think they felt
> that I could handle it. I also had the background knowledge since I had been with
> the organization by the time about 6 or 7 years.

Juli proved to be an operational catalyst for Jack's grand design. First, she organized a group of assembly workers into the pilot team and created a work space for them in a corner of the manufacturing area. As she learned more about JIT procedures, she began to work them into the pilot team's operations and into other areas of the plant. Bonnie, another long-term ISE employee, volunteered for the pilot team. The manufacturing workers knew that something big was going to happen to the shop floor, and they knew that this something involved a new way of working. But Jack had been talking about teams and Farmer had been doing team training for some time now. Jack's big change seemed a long way off. Bonnie wanted to get things going:

> For the longest time, we were taking very, very little steps at a time. It seemed
> like a very, very slow, slow process. Even when they announced the pilot team,
> it was at this little meeting. Most of the people, as soon as they got home, stopped
> thinking about it. Just very, very little at a time. Slow. People still didn't really
> take Just in Time as a big deal when they did that [started the pilot team] because
> they thought, "Oh, that's just another process for trying to do something better,
> and it usually blows over and nothing is ever made of it." And that's about how
> I felt.

Even when Juli got the pilot team going, progress still seemed slow, as Bonnie again explained,

> We set up the pilot team in one of the assembly and configuration areas. And it wasn't really a team at that time because what they did is they started very slow. We started learning how to do all the team processes and the JIT system, the pull system instead of the push system.[5] So that's how basically we started out, learning the pull system, instead of shove 'em [circuit boards] through, shove 'em through. It took a while, but then we began to work OK.

After working through some difficulties, learning how to use JIT procedures, and learning how to work together, the new team soon began to perform better than Jack, Frank, Juli, or anyone else had expected. By August 1988, Juli, now the transition process expert, knew that the time had come to convert the whole plant:

> I knew that Jack wanted to get this implemented, and there was kind of a push to get it going from the [pilot] team members. But not everybody knew what needed to be done. There was a lot of confusion out there, too. Some senior people were just plain screwing it up. Like, our plant manager [Frank] would walk in and say, "Well, I want you to do this with the floor, and I want you to put JIT over here, and we're starting up this new product, and I want some JIT to go on this new product." That kind of jumping around was really messing us up.
>
> Frank happened not to be there on one particular day, and I went over to one of the areas that he told to do some JIT, and I said, "No, you can't do that." And they said, "Frank is going to be mad because he told us to go ahead and do this." I said, "No, you can't do it because you are taking this [the JIT philosophy], and you are fragmenting it all over the place. It's not going to work." We'd [the pilot team] been struggling to meet our production schedule, and it hadn't been working because our area was relying on somebody else to supply us with products. They couldn't meet our needs because they weren't on Just in Time. And the other departments weren't on Just in Time either. So I said, "No, you can't do that," and they said, "Well, we're going to get in trouble." And I said, "No, you won't. I'll take responsibility for it because I'm telling you not to do it."
>
> Well, Frank wasn't too pleased on Monday when he came back in, but he understood what I was saying. I said, "Look, I've put this plan together over the weekend. I sat down and I thought about what we needed to do if we are really going to make this work. We have to stop fooling around in one area. We have to go ahead and move this into the entire organization. We're a small enough organization and that is what we need to do. We need to make the commitment to say we are going to do it." I had put it all together, a new plan for a quick

changeover. I showed it to Tackett and to Frank, and they said, "OK, let's go with it."

Actually, I knew what I was doing. I had gone through the training at the JIT Institute. I had watched our struggles of trying to get this implemented, and it didn't seem to be working as well as I knew it could. I said we have to go and make a commitment and go ahead and do it. Basically, my plan was to organize the teams on the production floor, assign a product to them, and assign people to them. Then we could start in training them in Just in Time, the team concept, and what we wanted to do with it.

Jack recounted his perspective on the decision:

Juli came to me and said, "This is going pretty good, and we are not going to get any more information from them [the pilot team]. Let's change it over. We can't get any further with the pilot program, we have to move ahead. We have to see more independent results." So she planned the changeover. She took my nice 2-year plan[6] and condensed it down to 1 weekend. I wasn't wild about it because it was *my* plan that was being scrapped. They [Juli and the other planning group members] could see short range, while I was looking out long range. They got real anxious to see results. They could sense the potential of JIT and cellular manufacturing, and we had been sending people to the JIT Institute.[7] So they said, "Let's get on with it! If we screw it up, next weekend, we'll put it back. It's [the production equipment] all on wheels anyway!"

Bonnie was ready, too:

Juli was our chief facilitator [on the pilot team], and she decided the best thing to do was to stop talking about it. We'd talked enough about it. We'd done piddily things enough about it. Like I said, most people thought, "Oh, it's just going to blow over." Well, at that time, a lot of people thought, "They'll forget about it [the change to teams]. They'll just go back to the mountain for another retreat, and we'll be off on something new." But Juli said that the best way to do it is just to do it and start it. You know, forget this little piddily stuff that we've been doing all the time. Just turn around and do it.

Over the next weekend, Juli and the rest of the planning group completely reorganized the manufacturing area. They remodeled the production space and set it up for three self-managing teams (originally called red, white, and blue, they were supplemented by silver, green, and aqua teams in 1991). The group moved machines, worktables, and other equipment around to form three distinct and self-sufficient work areas. They gave each team all the necessary equipment it needed to produce the types of circuit boards that the new teams would build. The work areas had separate sections for circuit board assembly, testing, repair and touch-up, troubleshooting, and packaging and shipping, all the key tasks required in making a complete circuit board.

On Monday, Jack divided the workers into three teams and assigned each team to manufacture or configure two or three particular types of boards (the teams did not make the same types of boards). Jack described his complex selection process:

> Monday everyone came in, stared around, "Where do I go now?" I put all the names in a hat and drew them out and said, "You go here, you go here, find your chair, and here's your product." Juli put name tags on their chairs, and they got going.

Jack's dream of a radical change at ISE was now a reality.

Now that Jack's plan for teamwork was in effect, a new, participative way of working, a new culture, began to spread among the teams. Over the next few years, a new *generative discipline* enabling teamwork to work began slowly to emerge, develop, and mature among ISE's teams. ISE's new generative discipline of concertive control (which I will refer to as a *concertive discipline* for short) was born of the drama and turbulence of the abrupt change to teams, and it carried the workers through many difficult times that were to come.

THE CONCERTIVE DISCIPLINE EMERGES

The immediate consequence of the abrupt change to teams was chaos. Though the workers knew that the change was coming, they still walked into a whole new experience on Monday morning. Brenda, another original team worker, described the scene:

> Well, it was mass confusion. Nobody knew where they were sitting, what team they were on. They had an idea of what was going on at that point and what the team aspect was all about. But as far as details, no idea! So, basically, everybody was just kind of like *wow,* this is kinda fun! Because everything was different, it was wonderful in a way, the atmosphere had changed. It was fun to see who you were going to be sitting with, what team you were going to be on, and what you were going to be doing. For me, it was like, what board am I going to be working on? 'Cause before, I had a certain board that I had worked on from the beginning [of her tenure at ISE], and I still wanted to be working on it.

TABLE 3.1 Structure of ISE Before and After the Change to Teams

Before the Change	After the Change
Four levels of managerial hierarchy between the vice president and the manufacturing workers	Managerial hierarchy extends directly from the manufacturing teams to the vice president
Manufacturing assembly line organizes the plant; workers manufacture boards according to their individual place on the line	Teamwork areas organize the plant; teams are responsible for complete fabrication, testing, and packaging of their assigned circuit boards
Line leads and shift supervisors form first managerial link	Teams manage their own affairs and elect one person to coordinate information for them
Workers have little input into work-related decisions; managers make all decisions and give all directions	Team members make their own decisions within guidelines set by management and the company vision statement; teams have shared responsibility for their own productivity
Management supervises workers	Team members supervise themselves
Management interviews and hires all new workers	Team members interview, hire, and fire their own members

Claudine, another original team worker, had a similar experience:

I remember walking in and saying, "What the hell is going on here? Where is everybody?" And it was funny because the only way people knew how to find where they were supposed to sit is that Juli put names on the backs of their chairs. It was really funny. We'd all sit there, look around and say, "Who's going to be on my team?" It was kind of like choosing teams for a game. I was pretty surprised that they did it [made the change so fast]. I could sense some fear on the part of a lot of people. I was kind of scared myself, a little bit. But I wanted to keep my mind pretty open to new things. I said to myself, "OK, let's try this and see if it works."

In Table 3.1, I have summarized the differences between ISE's operations before and after the change.

To help mediate the effects of the chaotic change, Jack assigned three former managers—Juli, Joanne, and Sam—to coach each of the teams for 6 to 9 months until they got used to managing themselves. Jack instructed these coaches, who had themselves been key players (and believers) in the transition to teams, not to overly direct the teams but to let them learn how to manage themselves. The coaches saw their roles primarily as preventing disasters and helping the teams keep production flowing. Joanne saw her coaching role as mostly being there to assist the new team members as they experimented with teamwork:

> I just tried to be supportive, listen to them, and help them get things done. I never interfered unless they were about to have a serious problem, and that was only once or twice early on. At that time, I had more knowledge of the whole process [than the team members did], so I tried to share that with them until they got their feet on the ground. With a supportive environment, it didn't take them long to figure out how to do their own work.

Joanne accurately described the initial challenge for the teams immediately after the change: learning how to work together and supervise themselves functionally. They had to learn how to get a customer's order manufactured and out the door. To do this, they had to merge, or consolidate, a variety of differing perspectives on how to do good work. They had to lay the foundation (essentially, begin constructing discursive formations) for a concertive discipline to emerge. For example, the new team members knew the separate activities involved in circuit board production, but they did not know how to control their individual efforts so that they could complete the whole process themselves. They knew how their former supervisors valued good work, but they lacked a means of articulating this value for themselves. They had to create some sense of shared meaning for how to do good work as a team. To meet this need, the team members began developing their own value consensus about what constituted, both collectively and individually, good work for the teams and patterns of behavior that put this consensus into action. Jack had already provided the foundation of this consensus in the vision statement that he had written for his new teams.

Recall that when ISE began converting to self-managing teams, Jack, along with several others, crafted a vision statement that articulated a set of core values and goals, which all employees were to use to guide their daily actions. ISE's seven-paragraph vision statement now began to function as a socially integrating myth that merged basic human values and "day-to-day [employee] behavior with long-run [organizational] meaning and purpose" (Peters & Waterman, 1982, p. 282). Within this context, ISE's vision statement gave Jack a formula for creating his new concertive organization that centered on all the new team members working together in concert under the guidance of shared values rather than the old ISE managerial hierarchy. The vision became the foundation for the concertive discipline that would follow.

ISE's vision contained the familiar elements of high-quality production, customer service, and profitability that we see in many such statements.[8]

However, the vision statement's fourth paragraph detailed the essential values that the teams would draw on during their initial work as teammates:

> We will be an organization where each of us is a self-manager who will:
>
> Initiate action, commit to, and act responsibly in achieving objectives
>
> Be responsible for ISE's performance
>
> Be responsible for the quality of individual and team output
>
> Invite team members to contribute based on experience, knowledge and ability

The values expressed here, such as personal initiative, responsibility, commitment to the team, and quality of individual and team contributions, along with Jack's directive for all to be self-managers, provided the necessary and legitimate preconditions for the teams to draw their value consensus, an essential characteristic of a concertive-control environment. The vision provided the fundamental "truth" on which the team members could begin building their methodology for doing good work. It was a catalyst that moved the teams to identify values useful for ISE. I will return to the character of this apparent truth in Chapter 4.

Early in my research, I saw a framed copy of the vision statement near Jack's desk and asked him what he saw as its purpose. He replied, "The vision provides the company with a guiding light for driving day-to-day operations for each of the teams." The goals and values in ISE's vision statement served as the nexus for consolidating the teams' material reality—how work gets done—with their ideational reality—their values (Jermier, Slocum, Fry, & Gaines, 1991, p. 172). When ISE converted to self-management, Jack distributed copies of the vision statement to all team members. Framed copies soon appeared in each team's area and in central locations like the break room. This led the new team members to talk with each other individually and at team meetings about the vision, particularly its fourth paragraph, and how it related to their work. Out of this talk came the functional patterns that allowed the teams to work together.

I readily noticed the results of this process. The team members talked openly about initiating action, taking ownership of their team's success, taking responsibility for satisfying ISE's customers' needs, emphasizing team quality, and expecting member contributions. The teams had learned to direct their work through planned and ad hoc team meetings run by a peer-elected coordinator who did just that—coordinated information such as production schedules, parts supplies, and companywide memos. At the start of the workday, all the teams met formally for about 15 minutes to plan the day and solve any known problems. When serious problems arose during the workday, such as an un-known parts shortage holding up production, the teams would meet briefly and decide how to deal with the problem.

During team meetings, workers would spend some time talking in adminis-trative terms about the work they had to do and in abstract terms about values expressed in the vision: responsibility, quality, member contribution, and com-mitment to their team and the company. The most prevalent example of these discussions occurred when team members had to decide whether to work overtime to meet their production schedules. My illustration comes from one of many such situations the blue team found themselves in while I was tracking their decision making during the fall of 1990.

Early Friday afternoon, Lee Ann, the coordinator, was anxiously await-ing word from the stockroom that a shipment of circuit potentiometers had arrived. The vendor, about 800 miles away, had promised that the ship-ment would arrive that morning, and the blue team had to get a customer's board order out that evening. Jim, from the stockroom, came running down to the blue team's area about 12:30 to tell Lee Ann that the potenti-ometers had just arrived. She then called the other 11 members of the team together for a short meeting.

She looked at the team. "We've got the 'pots' in, but it's gonna take us two extra hours to get this done. What do you want to do?"

Larry groaned, "Damn, I've got plans for 5:30!"

Suna spoke up, "My daughter's school play's tonight!"

Johnny countered, "But we told Howard Bell [their customer] that we would have these boards out today. It's our responsibility."

Terry followed, "We're gonna have to stay. We have to do this right."

What followed was a process in which the team negotiated which values and needs (individual or team) would take precedence here and how the team would work out this problem. The team decided to work late; they valued their commitment to a quality product delivered on time to their customer more than their individual time. Lee Ann volunteered to coordinate for the late shipment and to tell Jack Tackett that they would be working overtime (they could do this without his approval). Another team member went to arrange for the building to stay open for them. Larry said that he could postpone his plans for 2 hours. The team agreed to let Suna leave, but she promised to work late the next time they were in a bind.

This vignette depicts how the teams concertively reached a value consensus that, in turn, controlled their individual and collective work. They brought the abstract values of the vision statement into concrete terms. The team agreed on the priority of their commitment to the team's goals and responsibility for customer needs, and they acted based on this value consensus. These points of agreement were a discursive formation that would also set a strong precedent for future action. The blue team's agreement to work overtime to meet customer needs was not a onetime quick fix; it became a pattern that they would follow as similar situations arose. In a conversation some time after the above meeting, Diego described for me the continuing power of the blue team's value consensus regarding personal responsibility: "I work my best at trying to help our team to get stuff out the door. If it requires overtime, coming in at 5 o'clock and spending my weekend here, that's what I do." Diego was becoming disciplined. He was working from an internally held methodology for how to do good work on his team.

Although there were slight differences, this value consensus and these decision premises emerged as a powerful and remarkably consistent discursive formation across the new teams. Early in 1991, I was sitting with Wendy watching her work with the blue team. I asked her how she reacted to missing a customer requirement:

> I feel bad, believe it or not. Last Friday we missed a shipment. I feel like *I* missed the shipment since I'm the last person that sees what goes to ship. But Friday we missed the shipment by two boards, and it shouldn't have been missed. But it was, and I felt bad because it's me, it's a reflection on me, too, for not getting the boards out the door.

Over time, the teams faced many situations that called for them to reach some sort of value consensus. Other values, not explicitly stated in the vision but influenced by its general thrust, began to appear in the team members' talk and actions and began to take on the character of discursive formations. These values helped them unite, learn how to work together, and navigate the turbulence of the change and the possible failure of the company. Team members like Wendy talked about taking ownership of their work, being committed to the success of their team, and viewing ISE as a family and their teammates as family members. Debbie, another original team member, told me about this new feeling of ownership: "Under the old system, who gave a hoot if the boards shipped today or not? We just did our jobs. Now, we have more buy-in by the team members. We feel more personal responsibility for the product."

Other values included the need for everyone to contribute fully. The team members called this "saying your piece" at team meetings so that the team's decision would be better (and its consensus stronger). Another part of this value was the need for all team members to learn all of the jobs required by the team so that they could fill in and cover for each other. ISE's team workers were beginning to piece together the discursive formations they needed to build a useful and readily discernible concertive discipline.

This was also a time when ISE was struggling desperately and almost went under. In mid-1990, layoffs reduced the teams from three to two. The power of their values, as discursive formations, helped the teams navigate this difficult period. One of my most vivid memories of this time comes from Liz, who became one of my primary key informants. In August 1990, when the workers did not know if ISE would survive the quarter, she told me how she thought of ISE as a family and how she "spends more time with these people than my real family." She told me that if ISE closed down, "I'm gonna turn the lights out. I love this place and these people so much, I've got to be the last one out. I've gotta see the lights go out to believe it."

The teams' value-based talk and action during this phase were essential elements that enabled their discursive formations to form and the new generative discipline to emerge. The reason why shared values necessarily had to be the basis of the teams' discursive formations is found in the work of the famous sociologist Max Weber. Weber would have called the discursive formations that the teams were creating here a new *substantive rationality*. The team members had committed themselves "first and foremost to substantive goals, to an ethic" (Rothschild & Whitt, 1986, p. 22) that overrode all other commitments. Substantive rationality, in this context, extends from what Weber called "a unified configuration of values" (Kalberg, 1980, p. 1164) held by a collectivity of people, in this case ISE's team members. This value configuration, or consensus, is intellectually analyzable by the members; they use it to make sense of and guide their everyday interactions. For example, in an organizational situation, a consensus about values informs and influences members' outlooks on and processes of work activity, such as decision making. In doing this, the members place a psychological premium on themselves to act in ethical ways in terms of their values (Kalberg, 1980, p. 1165; Weber, 1978, p. 36).

These values, as discursive formations, *are morally binding on the team members* (a point I will return to in Chapter 4) because they represent the will of the teams and were arrived at through the democratic participation of the team members (Homans, 1950, pp. 125-127; Rothschild & Whitt, 1986, p. 50). In

Weber's terms, the old rationality and ethic of obeying the supervisor had given way to a new substantive rationality, the value consensus among the teams, and a new form of ethical rational action, working in ways that supported the teams' values. Wendy's taking personal responsibility for her team's failure, Debbie's buying in to her team's success, Johnny's reminding his team of their customer commitment, and Diego's willingness to come in at 5 a.m. all illustrate this point. The teams' discursive formations now had power. They could shape and direct team action. A generative discipline was beginning to emerge.

These examples also point out another significant aspect of Weber's theory of substantive rationality and its effect on organizational action. The ethical rational action spawned by a value consensus will take on a methodical character (Kalberg, 1980, p. 1164). That is, the teams will develop behavioral norms that put their values into action in consistent patterns applicable to a variety of situations, just as they applied their norm of working overtime to meet customer demands to a variety of situations requiring extra work. Thus, the teams could turn their value consensus (discursive formations) into social norms or rules (generative discipline). The teams had manifested the essential element of concertive control: Their value-based interactions were forming a methodology that controlled their actions, as seen in Larry's willingness to forgo his plans to work overtime for the team. Authority had transferred from ISE's old supervisory system to the teams' value consensus. These norms of ethical action, based in consensual values, penetrate and subjugate other forms of action by the team members. As this occurs, these norms take on a "heightened intensity" (Kalberg, 1980, p. 1167); they become powerful social rules among the team (Hackman, 1992; Hackman & Walton, 1986). This process played a pivotal role as ISE's concertive discipline further developed.

Four key points characterize this period when the team members at ISE were concertively forming their initial discursive formations and their team-based generative discipline was beginning to emerge:

1. The teams received ISE's vision statement, which framed a value system for them.
2. The teams began to negotiate value consensus on how to act in accordance with the vision's values.
3. A new substantive rationality spread among the teams that filled the void left by the former supervisors and the formal rationality associated with following their directives; the teams' values now had authority.
4. The teams began to form normative rules that brought this rationality into social action.[9]

The initial foundations for a concertive discipline at ISE emerged from the discursive formations of a core group of longtime ISE team workers committed to the company and to teamwork. The employees had developed a consensus about what values were important to them, what allowed them to do their work, and what gave them pride. And they would both adhere to and guard this consensus closely.

THE CONCERTIVE DISCIPLINE DEVELOPS

ISE did survive through 1990. In early 1991, the company began to prosper, and a large number of new workers had to be integrated into the teams. These workers were unfamiliar with the teams' value consensus, which posed an immediate challenge to the power relationships that the longer-tenured employees had formed. Furthermore, when ISE began to hire new workers, it hired them on a temporary basis and let the teams decide who to hire on as full-time workers. ISE also added four new teams to the two remaining original teams, for a total of six—red, blue, a new white, and green, silver, and aqua. Jack had to place some of the older, more experienced workers on these new teams to help them get organized, and the teams had to integrate their new teammates into their value-based social order, essentially to socialize the new workers into the team's developing discipline. As the team's value consensus and particular work ethic began to penetrate and subjugate the new members' individual work ethics, this process took on a heightened intensity. The substantive rationality of the teams' values gave them authority, which, in a concertive-control environment, they would exercise at will.

Members of the old teams responded to these changing conditions by discursively turning their value consensus (which, as discussed in Chapter 2, was essentially a set of power relationships and knowledge about those relationships) into normative rules of right that the new workers could readily understand and to which they could subject themselves. By rationalizing their value-based work ethic, the new team members could understand the intent and purpose of their team's values and norms (e.g., why it was important to work overtime to meet a customer need), use the norms to make sense of their daily work experience, and develop methodical patterns of behavior in accordance with the team's values (Hackman, 1992; Miller & O'Leary, 1987).

The longer-tenured team members expected the new workers to identify with (they called it "buy into") the teams' values and act according to their norms, which illustrates the "knowledge" aspect of generative discipline at work. By doing this, ISE's teams were asserting concertive control over the new workers, and the new members began to take part in controlling themselves. Slowly, the value-based norms that everyone on the team once "knew" became objective, rationalized rules that the new members could easily understand and follow.

Between March and April 1991, I began to notice that the way the team members talked, both informally and at team meetings, had changed. They did not talk as much about the importance of their teamwork values as they did about the need to "obey" the team's work norms. Team meetings began to have a confrontational tone, and the new workers' attitudes and performance became open topics for team discussion. When the longer-tenured team members saw someone not acting in accordance with their norms, such as not being willing to do whatever it took for the team to be successful, they said something about it. Liz, an original team member, told me of the old team workers' feelings:

> We've had occasions where we've had a person say, "I refuse to sit on the [assembly] line." And we had to remind him, "Hey, you are a part of the team and you go where you're needed and you do it."

Team meetings became a forum for discussing norms and creating new rules. Team members could bring up anybody's behavior for discussion. Again, Liz clarified their feelings: "If you notice that somebody's not getting anything done, then we can bring it up at a meeting, you know, and ask them what the problem is, what's causing them not to be able to get their work done."

The new team members began to feel the heat, and the ones who wanted to be full-time members began to obey the norms. The teams' value-based concertive control began to penetrate and inform the new workers' attitudes and actions. Stephi, who was a temporary employee at the time, told me how she personally tried to conform to the values and norms of her team:

> When I first started, I really didn't start off on the right foot, so I've been having to re-prove myself as far as a team player. My attitude gets in the way; I let it get in the way too many times and now I've been watching it and hoping they [her team] will see the change in me so I can prove to them that I will make a good ISE employee.

Stephi's words indicate that concertive control at ISE now involved the human dignity of the individual team workers. The team members rewarded their teammates who readily conformed to their team's norms by making them feel a part of the team and a participant in the team's success. In turn, they punished teammates who had bad attitudes, like Stephi, with guilt and peer pressure to conform (Hackman, 1992; Hackman & Walton, 1986; Mumby & Stohl, 1991). The power of the teams' concertive work ethic, as reflected in their discursive formations, had taken on its predicted heightened intensity as their concertive discipline became more developed and refined.

A pivotal occurrence during this phase was the teams' value-based norms changing from a loose system that the workers "knew" to a tighter system of objective rules. This transformation most often occurred when new members were not acting according to their team's work norms, such as coming to work on time. Danny told me how easily this change came about:

> Well, we had some disciplinary thing, you know. We had a few certain people who didn't show up on time and made a habit of coming in late. So the team got together and kinda set some guidelines and we told them, you know, "If you come in late the third time and you don't wanna do anything to correct it, you're gone." That was a team decision that this was a guideline that we were gonna follow.

The teams experienced the need to make their normative work ethic easy to understand (and to reward and punish), and they responded by making objective guidelines. They could feel a need for discipline—not just punitive discipline but the need to make their "good" team behaviors regular and recurring.

The team members' talk turned toward the need to follow the rules, to work effectively in concert with one another. In mid-1991, I found Ronald, a technician and my key informant on the green team, angrily cleaning up a mistake made by a new technician who had not followed the rules:

> All this should have been caught 3 months ago, and I'm just now catching it. And upon looking into it, it was because the tech wasn't taking his responsibility for raising the flag or turning on the red light when he had a problem.

Later that day, I was sitting with the silver team when I saw Ryan confront a newer team member who was working on four boards at a time instead of one, which the team had discovered increased the chance for error. Ryan stood above the offender and pointed at him, "Hey, quit doing that. You're not allowed to do that. It's against the rules."

By turning their norms into rational rules, the teams could integrate new members and still be functional, getting products out the door on time. The "supervisor" was now not as much the teams' value consensus as it was their rules. You either obeyed the rules and the team welcomed you as a member or you broke them and risked punishment. This element of concertive control worked well. As Danny, a temporary worker at this time told me, "If you're a new person here, you're going to be watched."

Even the coordinator's role and responsibilities became more objectified during this phase. The three managers that Jack had originally appointed as team coaches had begun to withdraw from the teams after about a year. The teams were able to do more of their own supervision, and they were able to figure out how to do "good" work by themselves. Juli, Joanne, and Sam returned to support roles on Jack's reduced staff. The coordinator role then evolved to suit the changing needs of the teams. As the coaches withdrew, the teams struggled with having the coordinator role rotate across the team members. They found that they needed to maintain some leadership consistency if their new concertive discipline was going to emerge effectively. At first, the teams made the coordinator position a 6-month role rather than the original 1 month, and they selected strong leaders (such as Liz) from among themselves to be coordinators. Before the initial 6 months had elapsed, the teams decided to make the coordinator role semipermanent, with the coordinators filling in the role until they wanted out.

As the coordinator role continued to evolve, the teams started to articulate specific responsibilities for the person in the role. Some teams agreed on five specific tasks for the coordinator to do, other teams had seven. The coordinator role began to take on the aura of a supervisor. People began to look to coordinators for leadership and direction. Lee Ann, a coordinator at this time, told me one day, "Damn, I feel like a supervisor, I just don't get paid for it."

The second pivotal occurrence during this phase involved how authority worked among the teams. After the initial emergence of a concertive discipline, authority had moved from the former supervisory system to the new value consensus of the teams. But as the teams' disciplinary culture continued to develop, the old team members, all full-time employees, became the keepers of this new system. They identified strongly with it and expected new members to demonstrate their worthiness to participate with them in the concertive process. They began to use rewards and punishments to encourage compliance among the team members. Temporary workers either obeyed the rules and became integrated into this system or they found the door. The teams' interactions left little room for resistance. This placed strong pressure on the temporary workers to conform to their team's rules. Anthony, a temporary worker then, explained the pressure:

> Being temporary, you could come in any day and find out you don't have a job no more. So, that's kind of scary for a lot of people who have, you know, kids and a lot of bills to take care of. So they tend to hold it in, what they want to say, to the point where they can't do it anymore and they just blow up, which causes them to lose their job anyway.

Before the change to teams, the line supervisors would generally tolerate some degree of slackness among the workers and allow someone many chances to screw up before taking drastic action. But now the team members exercised their newfound authority with much less patience.

In June 1991, the red team was experiencing a problem with one of its temporary workers, Phil. In the last week, Phil had become romantically involved with Sandy, who worked on the white team. Consequently, Phil had been finding excuses for going into the white team's area, for lingering at Sandy's workstation during breaks and lunches. In the last few days, a team member had had to go fetch him from the white team's area and remind him that the team had work to do. Phil had made the mistake of "resisting" the team's value consensus, and as Martha, the red team's coordinator at the time, told me later, "We just couldn't let it go. We had to take action before he got himself into real trouble."

Martha saw that Phil was late, again, getting back to work from a break. She got up from her work on testing, said something to Marty and Diego, two longer-tenured workers on the team, and went to the white team's area. She caught Phil's attention and beckoned him to come. She waited for him just behind the red team's area. Marty and Diego joined her. I was off to one side but still within hearing range.

Phil started, "I was just coming back. It's no big deal."

Martha interrupted, "Look, Phil, we don't like the pattern you're setting here. You've been late getting back and you're going to get yourself in trouble."

Phil started to say something, but Marty cut him off. "You're a member of our team. We expect you to support all of us. When we start back to work you have to be here. You can't be hanging back."

Diego followed, "You've got to support us. We all support each other. When you're late, the rest of us have to work harder."

Martha then said, "That's not fair for any of us."

Phil started to challenge them. "Now, look . . ."

But Martha held the floor. "No, you look. This is a bad pattern you have going here. When you work, you do a good job. But if you are not going to do what we need you to do, if you are going to cause problems for the rest of us, then we will have to do something. Don't make us do that."

Phil looked at them, then looked away. "OK, OK."

Martha continued, "We don't care about your personal life, what you do on your own time. We don't mind you visiting Sandy every now and then. But you've started to cause problems. We're worried that we can't depend on you."

"You're a part of the team. You have to support us when we're at work. Outside of work, you can do what you want," Diego said.

"Do you understand us?" Martha asked and looked at Phil directly.

"Yes, I understand. I'll watch myself more. I'm OK," Phil said.

Martha, Marty, and Diego nodded, and the meeting broke up.

Though peer pressure may be essential to the effective work of any team (Larson & LaFasto, 1989, p. 96; Walton & Hackman, 1986, p. 186), the dynamics of ISE's teams during this phase go much deeper. The above episode was not a simple case of the full-timers beating up on the temporaries. What seemed to be peer pressure and power games on the surface were in fact a manifestation of the generative discipline of concertive control. Authority here rests in the team's values, norms, and, now, rules. Team members rewarded themselves for compliance and punished themselves for noncompliance. They had invested their human dignity in the system of their own control (Mumby & Stohl, 1991; Parker & Slaughter, 1988). As participants in concertive control, the team members had begun a process of functionally constructing both their work activity and their own identities (Cheney, 1991) within the context of their new generative discipline.

This occurrence represents a natural progression of the value-based substantive rationality that marks the teams' concertive disciplines. Each team demystified its value consensus for new members by making it intellectually analyzable. The norms of the first year or so of teamwork now became guidelines or rules, increasingly objectified and clarified for the team members, which allowed for effective interaction. The values forming the teams' substantive rationality, their discursive formations, provided the boundaries of action and interest within and among the teams (Kalberg, 1980, p. 1170). However, the control of actions and interests in the teams is not stable; it has to be fixed at particular points in time. The emergence of rational rules during this developmental phase served this function. These rules made concertive control concrete, almost as tangible as their old supervisors' book of job descriptions. It was the locus of authority resting with the teams themselves, however, that gave the rules their power. It empowered the teams to enable certain activities and constrain others. The locus of authority made concertive control work for ISE's teams.

Four key points characterize this developmental period of concertive discipline at ISE:

1. The teams had to bring new members into the particular value-based social systems they had created after the initial formation of teams.

2. To meet this need, the teams began to form normative rules for doing good work on the teams, creating what Hackman and Walton (1986) called a team's "core norms" (p. 83). Longer-tenured team members expected the new members to identify and comply with these rules and their underlying values.

3. The rules naturally began to take on a more rationalized character.

4. Concertive control functioned through the team members themselves sanctioning their own actions.

The influx of new members may have served as a catalyst for the development of disciplinary rules on the teams, but the rules came about through the natural progression of the team's value consensus into what Weber called a "methodical way of life" on the organizational/team level (Kalberg, 1980, p. 1164). This was how the new members could learn their team's discursive value consensus and participate in their new form of control. Furthermore, these particular tensions between full-time and temporary workers were not enduring. What did last was the impact of rationalizing the rules and the fact that authority rested with the peer pressure of the teams.

THE CONCERTIVE DISCIPLINE MATURES

By mid-1992, two key events had happened. First, ISE began to stabilize and turn a profit. A large number of temporary workers had been integrated into the full-time pool during this time, which resulted in the number of temporaries falling from a high of almost 50% at times in 1991 to as low as 10% during 1992. Second, the teams' rules of right became more and more rationalized: Their value-based substantive rationality was giving way to rationalization (Cooper & Burrell, 1988, p. 93). The teams' new generative discipline had matured into a social force that shaped and directed the activity of the workers. The effects of concertive discipline now were readily perceptible. New members on the teams could rapidly understand the discipline and know that they had to behave accordingly. What were simple norms 2 years ago ("We all need to be at work on time") now became highly objective rules similar to ISE's old bureaucratic structure ("If you are more than 5 minutes late, the team will write an official warning and place it in your company file"). On the surface, day-to-day control looked much different from when ISE had traditional supervisors, but, on a deeper level, this control seemed hauntingly familiar and much more powerful.

The most noticeable change occurred in the coordinator's role. From my first days at ISE, I had tracked a continual pressure to make the coordinator's duties clearer and more specified. Thus, the coordinator's work gradually had become more formalized. If the team members needed something from the human resources department, they would ask the coordinator to get it. If Jack needed information about a team's work, he would ask the coordinator for it. As we saw earlier in this chapter, the coordinators began to take on more specific tasks: scheduling, tracking production errors, holding regular meetings with each other, and so forth. In early 1992, the role was once again reformalized into a new permanent position, now called "facilitator." The teams nominated workers for the six positions, and a committee of workers and managers (including Jack) interviewed the nominees and selected the new facilitators. These six workers received a 10% boost in their hourly wage to signify their new importance. They also drew up a list of duties for the role, which really just formalized what the old coordinators had already been doing. Lee Ann, who became the green team's facilitator, recognized this process, too, as she told me about a month after assuming the new role: "It's more formalized acceptance that somebody is gonna be the one to answer the questions, and you might as well have someone answering the questions of the team and of management. And I get paid for it, too." For me, the most interesting aspect of the change in the coordinator role was that the workers wanted it, not so much to reinvent hierarchy on the teams but because formalizing their work life seemed so natural to them. The mature discipline was taking hold of their work lives. They were "living" with the generative discipline of concertive control.

Formalizing the aspects of their work appeared to give the teams a sense of stability that would insulate them from the turmoil of the past year, and so rules proliferated in all aspects of the teams' activity. As Brown (1978, p. 368) suggested, the rules were taking on their own rationality and legitimacy. What was once an abstract value, such as "a team member should be able to do all the work roles on the team," had now become a set of specific guidelines for how long a new member had to train for a specific function (assembling, testing, repairing, etc.) and how long a team member would have to work in assembly before rotating to a new team job, such as repair.

As the concertive discipline further matured, I saw the teams' social rules become more and more rigid. The teams seemed to be trying to permanently fix their rules. Two examples stand out for me. In mid-1992, I was talking with Liz, who had also become a facilitator, about how the teams directed each other's actions now as opposed to 3 years before. Liz told me that her team had been talking about drafting a "code of conduct" for team members that spelled out the behaviors needed to be a good team member. She began to get very excited about the possibilities of making these actions clear and concrete. She said,

> If we can just get this *written down* [emphasis hers]. If we can just get our code of conduct in writing, then everyone will know what to do. We won't have so many problems. If we can just get it written down.

I found the second telling example when I visited ISE again 2 weeks later. I had been following how the teams were dealing with attendance and how their rules for coming into work on time were becoming more specific. A team member who came in 5 minutes late or later would be charged with an "occurrence" and considered to be absent for the whole day. If a worker accumulated four occurrences in 1 month, the team facilitator would place a written warning in that person's company file. A worker who came in between 1 and 4 minutes late received a "tardy," and seven tardies equaled one occurrence. Though I knew that all the teams had some kind of attendance policy, what I found this day truly surprised me. When I walked into the red team's area, I saw a new chart on its wall. The chart listed each team member's name down the left-hand side and had across the top a series of columns representing days of the week. Beside each name were color-coded dots that indicated "on time," "tardy," or "occurrence." The team had posted this board in plain sight for all team members to see, and the team updated its board each day. I found a similar chart in use by the other teams.

Three thoughts went through my mind. The first was the powerful insight of some of the team members who, since the development phase, had been telling me that they felt "watched" by the rest of their teammates. The second was that this policy seemed uncannily similar to something I would have expected to find in the old supervisory system. The third was that the teams had now created, in effect, a nearly perfect form of control. Their attendance behavior (and in a way their human dignity) was on constant display for everyone else on the team to monitor; essentially, it was a total system of control almost impossible to resist (Foucault, 1976). The transformation from values to norms to rules had gained even more heightened intensity.

The fact that the teams were creating their own rational rule systems was not lost on all the team members, but they expressed the feeling that these rules were good for them and their work. As Lee Ann told me at this time,

> We are making a lot of new rules, but most of them come from, "Well, see, because so and so person did such and such, well, we're not gonna allow that [concertive control at work] anymore." But the majority of the rules that we are putting in are coming from what the old rules were [before the change to teams]. They had a purpose. They did stop people from making, like, expensive mistakes. . . . With more people on the teams, we have to be more formal. We have 17 people on my team. That large amount of people moving is what's causing the bureaucracy to come back in.

Lee Ann's use of "bureaucracy" perplexed me. Had ISE's teams reinvented a bureaucratic system of control? Certainly, the substantive rationality and its focus on value consensus, which characterized the emergent phase of concertive discipline, now had become blurred with a new formal rationality that focused on making rules. Such a blurring appeared to fit with Weber's prediction that "a *multiplicity* of rationalization processes . . . variously conflict and coalesce with one another at all societal and civilizational levels" (Kalberg, 1980, p. 1147), to include ISE's teams. Certainly, much of the pressure toward formalization came from the teams' need to be productive and efficient for ISE to survive in its competitive market (Kalberg, 1980, p. 1163). But as I later reflected on Lee Ann's comment and my experience at ISE, the nature of this blurring of substantive and formal rationality in the teams' concertive discipline became clearer.

The progression of the teams' value-based work ethic from norms to rational rules indicated that the workers had created a generative discipline that rationalized their work behaviors to make them purposeful, functional, and controlled (Barker & Cheney, 1994; Foucault, 1980). Recall that *generative discipline* refers to a willingly accepted social force that rationalizes organizational work to ensure normalized and controlled individual and collective action. A readily detectable generative discipline matured when the teams developed formalized rule systems out of the normative ethics of their original discursive value consensus. These disciplinary systems enabled the teams to work effectively, integrate new members easily, and meet their production demands. The team members willingly accepted the concertive discipline because they themselves had created it. Moreover, the discipline appeared to work. As already mentioned, ISE became profitable again. ISE's top management believed that the change to teams was one of the key reasons (along with other key changes in engineering and marketing) for the company's success. Jack had the hard fact of his 25% cut in factory costs since the change to teams.

But the teams' formalization of their value system and norms did not mean that they had re-created a bureaucracy. Authority in ISE's concertive system rested with the teams and their interactions with each other. The character of ISE's concertive control was still much different from when it operated under bureaucratic control. As they integrated more temporary workers into the ranks of full-time members, the team members still held authority over each other. They still expected each other to follow the rules and, as evidenced by their attendance charts, still monitored each other's behavior carefully. The team members themselves still rewarded or punished each other's behavior. They did not give this function to the new facilitators; they kept it for themselves.

Close to the end of my data collection, Liz told me of an incident that had occurred a few days before involving Sharon, a single mother who had some difficulty getting to work at 7 a.m. The team had been sensitive to her needs and had even given her a week off when one of her children was sick. The day before the incident, enough time had passed for Sharon to drop one of her many occurrences. (Sharon's team had a policy that an occurrence would be taken off of a team member's attendance record after 30 days.) She even announced this to the team by making a joke of it: "I just dropped one occurrence, so that means I can have another." The next morning, one of her children was sick again and she was late. And the team remembered her "joke" the night before.

When Sharon showed up, the team reacted in the same way a shift supervisor in ISE's old system might have. The team confronted Sharon immediately and directly. They told her that they were very upset that she was late. They bluntly told her how much they had suffered from having to work short-handed. Stung by the criticism of her peers, Sharon began to cry. The team's tack shifted to healing the wounds they had caused. They told her that they had not meant to hurt her feelings but that they wanted her to understand how her actions had affected them. They asked her to be certain to contact them immediately when she had a problem. The episode closed with the team telling her, "We really count on you to be here, and we really need you here." When I checked a month later, Sharon had not recorded another occurrence.

Within a mature generative discipline, the team members still kept the authority to control each other's behaviors; concertive control still occurred within the teams. In many ways, the formalization of the teams' normative rules made this process easier, as seen in the incident with Sharon. The teams had created an omnipresent "tutelary eye of the norm,"[10] with the team members themselves as the eye that continually observed their actions, ready either to reward or, more important, punish. Being under the constant eye of the norm appeared to me to have an effect on the workers. All of the longer-tenured team workers told me that they felt much more stress in the team environment than they had under the old ISE system. The newer members also complained of the constant strain of self-management. This sense of heightened stress that ISE's workers expressed to me was similar to that found in other team-based organizations (e.g., Grenier, 1988; Mumby & Stohl, 1991). Parker and Slaughter (1988) even called the self-management concept "management by stress."

My key informants also appeared more strained and burdened than in times past. I had watched Liz change from the totally committed team member in 1990 who saw her team as a family to a distant, distracted facilitator in 1992, too harried and pressured to take any enjoyment in her team or to think of it as a family. Lee Ann, in a conversation with me in August 1992, expressed the same feelings:

> After you've been here a while, you're gonna get superinvolved, then you're gonna get burned out. I see this with person after person. You get really involved, you take it home with you, you eat with it, and you sleep with it. You work 12-, 16-hour days and you just burn out. You may step out just a bit, let someone else get superinvolved for a while, then you'll pick it up again. But you won't have that enthusiasm anymore.

The tutelary eye of the norm demanded its observants become superinvolved or risk its wrath, and, critical to this phase, the eye also demanded that its observants demonstrate this involvement by following its rules, its rational routine. That was work life in the eye of the norm, in ISE's brand of concertive control.

But life in the eye of the norm also meant that ISE's team workers had more control over their work lives, which they certainly appreciated. Right after Lee Ann told me the above comment on burning out, I asked her if she ever wanted to go back to the old system:

> No way [laugh]. I've worked damn hard. We've worked damn hard for this. We've made this thing work. Yeah, we get superinvolved. We work the long

hours. But it works. The company works. I'm proud of that, and I don't want to go back [to a traditional management system]. We have self-management here, and I don't want to give that up. No way.

And all the other workers of whom I asked a similar question held the same opinion as Lee Ann. No one wanted a return to the old system. Certainly, ISE was still there, and turning a profit, too. They were all well aware that they had jobs, good jobs. Jack Tackett's radical surgery, with help from Juli, Liz, Lee Ann, Joanne, and all the rest, had become a successful reality.

Four years after the change to teams, ISE's system of control, its concertive discipline (its generative discipline of concertive control), had matured into stable sets of formalized rules that provided a rational and effective routine for the team members' day-to-day actions. This formalization did not move the locus of authority away from the teams but, rather, strengthened the authority held by the teams and their value systems. The team members directed and monitored each other's actions, and concertive control still occurred within the teams themselves. Four key points characterize the maturity of the concertive discipline:

1. Their former normative rules became more objective, creating a new formal rationality among the teams.
2. The teams appeared to "settle in" to the rational routine these formal rules brought to their work. The rules made it easier for them to deal objectively with difficult situations (such as Sharon's coming in late) by establishing a system of work regulation and worker self-control.
3. The team members felt stress from the concertive system, but they accepted this as a natural part of their work. They did not want to give up their feeling of being self-managers, however, no matter how intense the system of control became.
4. The work life at ISE stabilized into a concertive system that revolved around sets of rational rules, as in the old bureaucracy, but the authority to command obedience rested with the team members themselves, in contrast to the old ISE.

So far, my story has covered how ISE's generative discipline *developed* as a system of concertive control founded on sets of discursive formations. But now, with a mature disciplinary methodology in place, I will turn the story toward how the discipline created by ISE's team members *works* as a generative discipline: How does the concertive discipline make manifest a discursive methodology of power relationships, knowledge, and rules of right? How do consequences arise from the discipline? and How should we respond to the effects of these consequences? Such an analysis will help reveal the conditions through which the structure of concertive discipline compels the day-to-day actions of the team members.

NOTES

1. Portions of this chapter have been excerpted from Barker (1993b).

2. To expand on the initial discussion in Chapter 1, "Just in Time" refers to a company-specific manufacturing method that emphasizes low inventories, first-line decision making, and fast, effective employee action (see, e.g., Guest, 1989; Helms, 1990; Sewell & Wilkinson, 1992).

3. Theory X here refers to McGregor's (1960) famous distinction between authoritarian managers, which he called Theory X managers, and humanistic managers, which he called Theory Y managers. Following the logic of McGregor's argument, Theory Y managers would "fit" better in participative structures such as self-managing teams; hence, Joni's use of Theory X to contrast the old Jack with the new Jack.

4. The teamwork-skills training included classes on interpersonal skills, the philosophy of teamwork, and the job skills required for different team functions. After the change, ISE's staff did include team members in the design of additional training programs.

5. "Pull" system refers to the Just-in-Time principle of "pulling" supply parts from inventory onto the assembly only at the moment they are needed.

6. There were still 2 years left to go on Jack's original plan for the conversion to teams.

7. The JIT Institute was a consultant-operated training company in town that trained managers and workers in JIT and cellular manufacturing concepts. As discussed earlier, Juli had already completed its training program.

8. I have purposefully not included the entire ISE vision to minimize the possibility of revealing ISE's actual company identity.

9. ISE's teams developed in ways consistent with traditional studies of small groups and teams, most notably Tuckman's (1965), Homans's (1950), and Lewin's (1948) models of group formation and Walton and Hackman's (1986) model of work-group value and norm development. Though cognizant of the parallels ISE's teams have to these fundamental models, I have sought to situate the story of how the teams developed a new disciplinary form of control within the broader framework of the social forces (rationality, authority, social rule generation, etc.) that shaped the teams' organizational context.

10. I am indebted to Lars Thogar Christensen's coining this phrase.

4

Molding a Community

Demarcation

Yeah, a lot of people talk about us being a family and all, but I think that it's more than that. We depend on each other, and we rely on each other, and all that. But you know we also see things the same way. When it comes to our job, to doing our work, and to working together as a team, we all know what's important. We're all different people, but we share a big part of our lives together, and we know how to do things together. We all understand that. We're all like a little community that way.

Mark, a team member who joined ISE in 1990

MOLD: TO FORM, SHAPE, OR PATTERN;
COMMUNITY: A UNIFIED BODY OF INDIVIDUALS,
A GROUP LINKED BY COMMON POLICY[1]

In Chapter 3, I addressed how the generative discipline of concertive control formed and developed at ISE through the team members' own discursive formations about values, norms, and rules. I also discussed how the teams' rules had become collectively enforced with no small degree of intensity, and I identified some of the initial consequences of concertive discipline. In Chapters 4, 5, and 6, I now turn our attention to how a concertive discipline works on a day-to-day basis as a methodology for appropriate team action. Or, to return to the terms discussed in Chapter 2, I will focus on detailing how the generative discipline of concertive control works in practice; that is, how team members participate together in team-based organizations to create and re-create the regulated, regular, and recurring meanings we saw in Chapter 3. Furthermore, I will also identify the social consequences of that participation.

First, and perhaps foremost, the generative discipline of concertive control (again, a concertive discipline for short) molds a group of diverse individuals into a unified community of teammates who believe in a common set of values, norms, and rules, which we saw ISE's teams create in Chapter 3. As Mark noted in the opening quote, his team understood "how to do things together," and he felt they were "a little community that way." They shared a common set of values, norms, and rules, a shared policy that molded them into a community. They had created what the classical sociologist Emile Durkheim called "a common life" (Collins, 1985, p. 128).

ISE's workers were not born into this community of teamwork. As the definition above implies, they had to be linked together by common policy, which for teams is a discursive substantive rationality. Recall from Chapter 3 that *substantive rationality* refers to a collectively defined, shaped, patterned, and molded set of "substantive goals, to an ethic" (Rothschild & Whitt, 1986, p. 22) that overrides all other commitments on the team. A substantive rationality is a "unified configuration of values" (Kalberg, 1980, p. 1164) that molds the disparate team members into a unified community. The team members used their substantive rationality, as discursive formations, to make sense of and guide their everyday interactions.

Molding a community is not simply the team reaching a consensus on core values. "Molding" refers to an ongoing process. The team is incessantly molding itself as a community, continually trying to figure out what it should value and arranging and rearranging its values into meaningful and workable configurations. How does the team do this as a part of its day-to-day interaction? How does it mold itself as a community?

The answer reveals the first element of how a concertive discipline works. Team members must discursively demarcate (i.e., identify and define through their talk and actions) *power relationships* on the team. As discussed in Chapter 2, the key power relationships for a participative team are not just relationships between people. Instead, the team has to demarcate which of its values and, subsequently, its rules are more important than other possible team values and rules. The team also has to demarcate how these values apply in certain conditions. Team members must negotiate power relationships with each other; these power relationships will then affect, or mold, how they create meaning. Before team members can make their lives meaningful, before they can do things together, before they can be useful together, they have to have a shared sense of which values on their team are more powerful than other possible values. And they must be able to understand these power relationships as a substantive rationality.

Teams demarcate power relationships discursively through their natural interactions. The way they make decisions, the way they handle crises, and the way they instruct new members all demarcate what is and is not important on the team. The first step in being a disciplined team member, especially as a new teammate, is to learn what your peers expect of you and then become molded in their image so that you can become an accepted member of their—your— community. The story of Greg on the silver team vividly represents this community molding effect.

CHECK YOUR WORK

Greg looked up from his work on a board and saw Martha and Grace Anne coming toward him. Grace Anne was carrying a circuit board with her. Greg knew then that he was in trouble. In fact, he already was figuring on getting in trouble sometime that day. Greg was a new worker at ISE on the silver team, and today was Thursday of his first real week at work. He had started as a temporary worker 2 weeks ago and had just finished the mandatory 2-week training program ISE had for new temporary workers. He had mostly learned about how to put together circuit boards, although he had taken a few classes on teamwork. Most times when the subject of self-managing teams came up, the instructors (who were team members themselves) said, "Don't worry about it, we'll teach you how to work as a team with us when we get you out on the floor. All you need is the right attitude, and we can make a good teammate out of you. Right now, just learn how to do the boards." All new team members began their ISE experience doing board assembly, and that is where Greg had started out last Monday.

Greg had learned how to do the boards well enough, but ISE's small classroom was a lot different from actually working on the assembly line. At the beginning of the week, Karen, a more experienced temporary employee, had been working with him and showing him how to do board assembly. Other times during those days, he sat with other team members and learned how to do additional job roles on the team. The silver team's boards were very difficult to build. Two separate boards had to be assembled and then very carefully configured together to make one circuit board. Karen had helped him a lot, but now Greg needed to do his own assembly work.

The silver team assemblers worked in a line of five people. Greg was number two in line. Karen started a new board by attaching several diodes and then passed the board on to Greg. Greg attached more diodes and passed the board to Diego, who was third in line, and so on. Eventually, the board ended up with Grace Anne, who did the final configuration and tested the board to make sure the circuits were OK.

The five assemblers worked in line along a special table that enabled them to slide the boards along a rack as it went from person to person. When Greg got a board from Karen, he first had to check her work (a team rule) and then very carefully install three tiny diodes (about half the size of a paper clip) into a 2-inch by 5-inch board. He then checked his work and slid the board to Diego, who repeated the checking process. Greg was having trouble getting the diodes in right. One, the tiniest and most finicky diode he had to install, was really giving him fits. He was only $1\frac{1}{2}$ hours into the day, and already Diego had to correct several errors that Greg had let slip. Diego was not really angry with him yet. He just pointed out the error and told Greg, "Just keep watching what you are doing and check your work. You'll get it. It takes a while to learn how we do things out here."

Greg's last mistake, which Diego had caught, had been about a half hour ago. But now Greg saw Martha and Grace Anne coming toward him, which could mean only one thing. Martha was the team's facilitator, which meant, for all practical purposes, that she was the team's leader. And Grace Anne did one of the most important team jobs (configuration and testing). Both had been working for ISE for a long time, since before the change to teams. Both, especially Martha, could be forceful and downright harsh when they were mad. Greg sank low in his chair. The other assemblers (all within a few feet of each other) looked up to see what was going to happen.

"Hey Greg," Martha said, "let's talk for a minute." Her voice was not angry, which surprised Greg. He let out his breath.

"Sure."

"Take a look at this board and tell me what's wrong." Grace Anne carefully handed the board to him. He had to hold it on the sides with his thumbs and forefingers. The diodes had not yet been soldered onto the board, so if he tilted it too much, they would all fall out.

Greg looked over the board. That damned little bitty, hard-to-get-right diode, his diode, was in backward. "I put that little diode in backwards," he said after a minute, tilting his head generally toward the board. They knew what the problem was anyway.

"Look," she said, in a coaching voice, "we know that you are just starting out and that you're going to make some mistakes. But you have to do two things." She used her fingers to emphasize the "two." "First, you have to put the diodes in right. That just takes time to learn, and you'll get it soon. But more importantly, you have to check your work. That's what we do on our team. We each check our own work. We're all big believers in that because it keeps us all straight. It takes a long time to fix a messed-up board. Got it?" She looked down at him.

"Yes, I know. It's just hard right now."

"Don't worry. You're learning how we work on this team. We always check our own work. We always check each other's work. That's the thing to remember."

"I'll get it right."

Martha nodded and turned toward Diego.

"Dieeeeegooooo," she called in a mockingly sweet voice. Diego turned toward her.

"I know, I know. I messed up. I should have caught it."

"You don't want to get on my shit list, buddy boy." Martha smiled and began walking back to her workstation. The assemblers all laughed and returned to their work.

Greg took a couple of minutes to recover from the experience. He knew that, although Martha was still letting him learn how to do the work, she would not be in such good humor about future mistakes. Neither would Grace Anne, nor Diego, nor Karen, nor anyone else on the team.

DEMARCATION, POWER RELATIONSHIPS, AND VALUE CONSENSUS

The first element of a discipline's ability to function as a methodology for action in the organization is the demarcation of power relationships in such a way as to mold an organizational community. The above vignette from the silver team reveals one of the primary ways ISE's teams methodically demarcated power relationships (as discussed in Chapter 2). Similar scenes were very common, to the point of practically being daily occurrences. The older members of the team were demarcating power relationships for Greg by illustrating the importance of checking his work, a key team value. Greg had to demonstrate, empirically, that he could put the value into practice. Even longer-tenured team members, such as Diego, occasionally had to be reminded about their team's power relationships.

Power relationships have to be made rational. The team has to be able to understand them and shape their behavior to fit the relationships. In bureaucracies, power relationships tend to be written down and codified into job descriptions and organizational charts. In more participative environments, power relationships get written down less often, but team members still must know them. The team's disciplinary system must, somehow, inform its members of what the power relationships are. The silver team had worked out a discursive but highly effective method of informing its members about their power relationships. That was exactly *what* Greg was learning. He was learning what values were "powerful" in which circumstances. When he was on the assembly line, he *always* had to check his work.

Here is the point at which demarcation becomes essential for a team environment. To be a useful person in such a system, a team member must know the power relationships among the team's values and its people. To do that, the power relationships have to be made known to everyone. As illustrated in the vignette, Greg was learning, through his interaction with the silver team, that the team placed much value on "checking your work." The team members knew that if they checked their work, they would be effective. Thus, the team had a particular power relationship with the value of "checking your work," and Greg was learning to shape his behavior in accordance with that power relationship. Greg was learning the substantive rationality, the discursive common policy that unified the silver team as a community. And Greg had to demonstrate his learning in order for the rest of the team to accept him into their community. They were clearly expecting him to make such a demonstration, not just that day but in all his work. When team members, especially new team members, demonstrate that they understand the power relationships of their team, its substantive rationality, they become accepted members of the team community. They have shown that they are good and effective team members.

Members of a participative team demarcate power relationships through the normal course of team interaction, particularly when they solve common problems. Certainly, ISE's teams had powerful people, as seen in Martha's interaction with Greg. But in the team's particular participative environment, their shared values and the power relationships the team demarcated about those values were more important than any power held by an individual team member. What a disciplinary culture *does* is demarcate power relationships. And the culture has to demarcate power relationships in a way that molds together a community of believers in these relationships. Belief in the power relationships molds the community in a particular way and holds it together as a community.

The team community at ISE arose from demarcated configurations of many different kinds of values. Some were personal values, some were social and democratic values, some came from total-quality-management (TQM) and Just-in-Time (JIT) values, and some were general business values (such as being profitable, doing a good job, and working hard). To make sense out of all the possible values available to them, the team had to demarcate which values held power for them and which did not.

This leaves us with the question, Why do team members demarcate power to some values and not to others? The answer is because they have to. Values and power relationships are necessary for us to reason effective and appropriate ways of acting together. Power relationships have to be, to use Weber's (1978) terms again, "intellectually analyzable." They have to form a substantive rationality. Team members must readily understand the power relationships and easily see how to shape their behavior accordingly. In Chapter 3, I discussed how, over a considerable period of time, the team members struggled to reach a consensus among themselves about what constituted useful values for doing teamwork. Once they had several consensually validated configurations of values in place, the team members naturally began to formulate rules for acting in accordance with the values that they could use to guide their behavior over time. Out of this initial substantive rationality, then, the team members naturally developed a concertive discipline.

Value consensus or configuration refers to a cognitive structuring of different types of values together. One configuration of values was a perception among the team concerning what it took to be a good team member. "Being a good team member" included such values as showing up at work on time, learning all the different jobs on the team, not taking advantage of team members (e.g., staying out too long on breaks), and supporting each other. If someone went on vacation, other team members would step up and fill that void.

As seen in the opening vignette, "check your work" served as a key value consensus among the teams. Interestingly, the teams took the "check your work" value from their early JIT and TQM training. In Chapter 3, I described how "saying your piece" became a key value consensus among ISE's teams. The team members knew that if everyone said their piece, if they said what they thought of a potential team decision, then they tended to make good, well-reasoned decisions. The team members knew that they needed input from all the team members. Furthermore, they knew from past experience that if somebody was not saying anything, was staying quiet, that person was usually upset about something.

Often during team meetings, when the team was faced with a decision, the members would begin a process of saying their piece. One member would start by giving an opinion on the issue. That person would then turn to the next person, who would then offer an opinion. The process would continue until everybody had stated an opinion on the issue at hand. Other times, the team's conversation would be more free-flowing, with only two or three team members doing most of the talking. However, in these cases, someone in the group would play the role of gatekeeper or moderator and make sure everyone got their say. The exact approach would vary from team to team, but the members realized that they needed input and that they would get in trouble if only two or three people made all the decisions. By saying their piece, the team members could identify problems and try to deal with them. Saying your piece was a powerful value because it was connected to the team's ability to be functional and effective.

Other key configurations of value consensus were "we are all in this together," in which the members made known to each other that they all shared in the success or failure of their team, and "the team comes first," which was a signal that the team members expected each other to make sacrifices, such as working overtime, for the good of the team.

Demarcating power relationships from their value consensus was an ongoing process for the team, especially during their first few years together. In general, many team members were aware that shared values were a key part of their work together. Randy, a long-term ISE worker who had done two stints as team coordinator, described how his team continually worked on demarcating power to values:

> When we first got together, we had to decide on the principles that we wanted to support as a team and find out all the common values that everyone had. I mean, everyone believes in honesty. I can't imagine a world that would have principles of dishonesty and distrust there. Laziness, you can't really support those kinds of things. You have to support the principles of industry and integrity, honesty, flexibility, fairness, those types of things. Once we began talking about them [their shared values], we realized that everyone has different understandings. Everyone places a different value on each one of those principles. So, we try to at least choose as a team what works best for us. We try to find what values we should have commonality in and the principles that we are going to live by here, the value systems that we are going to have here on the team. It may or may not be the right values. And we may or may not have the same values outside of work as we have here. But at least we try to decide what works best for us.
>
> Take industry and hard work, the principle of industry and being industrious is something that we want to have in place as a high value on our team. We

discuss those principles, and we realize that everyone looks at things differently. That's where we start building the trust and talk about values. People understand those concepts. We know that things such as industry and hard work need to be presented to the team. And we need to talk about them over and over and over again in open discussion.

Right now, we meet twice a day, and then on Friday, we go out for breakfast and have an hour-long meeting with a set agenda. We talk about long-range and short-range goals for the team that are both production related and not production related. We plan our own training. We talk about trust, principles, and values. We have to do it that way.

The common thread among the teams' value consensus was that the teams developed almost all of their configurations early in the team experience (see Chapter 3) and then demarcated the power of these configurations for new team members (like Greg). As mentioned above, they drew their values from a variety of sources: the ISE mission statement, their training in TQM and JIT, their work experiences, their understanding of what "teamwork" meant (sacrifice, sharing work, etc.), and a variety of social values (fairness, equity, etc.). In fact, ISE's mission statement actually blurred many of these values together (see Chapter 3). For ISE's teams, their truth, their understanding of the right way to work as a team, lay in the value-based power relationships they had demarcated for themselves. By demarcating these power relationships, their disciplinary methodology could lead them to the apparent "truth" for how to work together as a team.

POWER RELATIONSHIPS, VALUES, AND DECISION MAKING

But the need for the team to create a sense of "truth" from their power relationships is more complex than a consensus on values and the subsequent formation of rules to put the values into practice. Certainly, the demarcation of value-based power relationships enables the team to create useful meaning; however, the team also has to reason with their values. They have to use them to guide their day-to-day actions. They have to use the values to solve problems and make decisions.

Teams use their values to solve problems and make decisions in a manner that is not unlike basic deductive reasoning. Essentially, when the team demarcates power to a value configuration, the value becomes a decision premise that the team members will use syllogistically (reasoning from the general to the specific) to deduce appropriate and consistent ways of acting in certain situations. Again, I want to return to Greg's example from the beginning of this chapter. In learning the general importance of checking his work, as a decision premise, Greg was learning how to reason specific behaviors in terms of his team's value configurations. When he finished assembling parts on a board, Greg had to decide whether he should send the board on to the next person on the line. Greg solved this problem syllogistically by reasoning: "My team needs to be successful (a key value configuration). For my team to be successful, my work needs to be error free; therefore, I must check my work for errors before sending the board on down the line."

Greg's thinking reveals the value-based deductive process. In traditional deductive reasoning, we first hold a major premise (all humans are mortal). Next, we apply a minor premise to the major premise (Socrates is a human) and then draw a conclusion (Socrates is mortal). Team deduction gives a slight rhetorical twist to this traditional process. For Greg, the major premise was an essential (or core) value-based power relationship on his team (the team must be successful). The minor premise extended directly from the major premise: Greg needed to do certain things to ensure that the major premise was fulfilled. From these two premises, Greg could easily deduce an appropriate decision. Greg and the rest of the team members used this deductive process continually as a means for reasoning appropriate decisions and ways of acting together.

When the teams demarcated power to a value configuration, the configuration became a decision premise for the team members to use syllogistically. The team members had to learn the appropriate conditions for reasoning with the premises from experience. That was why Martha and the other senior team members were so concerned with Greg's learning to check his work and why Martha "reminded" Diego that he had failed to use the team's syllogism. The key point here is that the team's power relationships become the *source* of their decision premises. They use their power relationships to both organize their lives into meaningful patterns and reason appropriate decisions.

Tompkins and Cheney (1985) have called this syllogistic reasoning method "enthymeme$_2$." Tompkins and Cheney developed their theory of enthymeme$_2$ as a means of distinguishing it from Aristotle's original conceptualization of the enthymeme (a syllogism with at least one premise implicit). As modern-day organizational scholars, they were particularly concerned with the sources of the enthymemes we use in today's world of work. They argued that, in today's diverse society, we are confronted with many different enthymemes from many different, even opposing, sources. In particular, they argued, the organization is a key source of enthymemes in our lives. Enthymeme$_2$, then, represents how organizations can control workers' behavior by shaping the way they reason about work:

> We shall define enthymeme$_2$ as a syllogistic decision-making process, individual or collective, in which a conclusion is drawn from premises (beliefs, values, expectations) inculcated in the decision maker(s) by the controlling members of the organization. One or more parts of enthymeme$_2$ may be suppressed. Organizations offer inducements to the individual in exchange for accepting its decision premises as controlling his or her decisions. Organizationally appropriate decisions, once the premises are inculcated, are motivated by the universal psychological process of consistency maintenance and the individual's desire to "behave organizationally." (pp. 188-189)[2]

Tompkins and Cheney focused their view of enthymeme$_2$ on the organization, and managers in particular, as the source of decision premises for its members. If management tells workers "We have to be profitable this quarter or we will go under," then management has communicated a powerful enthymeme. We could then expect lower-level workers to make decisions that help the company to be profitable (working longer hours, cutting costs, refining production techniques, etc.). In the participative team environment, however, the team members become the arbiters of what is and what is not a valid enthymeme$_2$. As we have seen so far, the team draws values from a number of sources: management, the team metaphor, current practices such as TQM, the broader society, and themselves. A lot of potential and possible value configurations are available, but the team has to demarcate which of these do and do not have power.

With this reasoning process, the teams are creating their own rationality, what March and Olson (1989) would call a "logic of appropriateness" for team activity. Once the teams demarcate their power relationships, once they create their enthymeme$_2$s, they have created rationality both in perception and in fact.

Over time, the teams developed a number of quite similar enthymeme$_2$s, with the differences between the teams tending to be more idiosyncratic than core. For example, once the shop floor became aware that a team had a good idea, the other teams were quick to adopt it. One of the fastest spreading decision-making values was "build the best customer's order first," which I will discuss in Chapter 5. This power relationship helped the team to decide which customer order to build first: When in doubt, build the best customer's order first. The value originated in the green team and, within a couple of days, spread to all the others.

The teams' use of their power relationships as enthymeme$_2$s enabled them to make good decisions and to act appropriately, consistently. In Chapter 3, I discussed how the teams had developed what Weber would call a new "ethical rational action" (Kalberg, 1980, p. 1164). The power relationships they had attached to their values enabled them to act in "good" ways. They knew practical methods for solving problems and meeting their work demands. They could reason well with their value configurations. They had a shared way of believing that transcended their differences. And, as we saw in Chapter 3, they then made their ethical action methodical. If they acted according to their value configuration, they could reach the apparent truth of successful, effective, and useful teamwork.[3]

THE NEGOTIATIVE QUALITY OF DEMARCATION

As I discussed in Chapter 3, once the teams had demarcated power relationships among their values, they became quite methodical in enforcing their values as rules. The teams' values took on what Weber called a "heightened intensity" (Kalberg, 1980, p. 1167). This intensity arises because the team members themselves have created their value configurations, and they have demarcated the power relationships themselves through a long process of day-to-day negotiations about the meaning of doing good teamwork. This day-to-day negotiative quality had a profound effect in linking the teams together with a perception of community and shared ties. Liz, when she was a coordinator, told me how the negotiative quality worked to tie the team together as a community:

> See, teams grow just like families do. Say you're divorced with kids and you get remarried. There's this growth time when you have to learn how to get along together. You have to work at it each day. But after a while, you either find a way of making it work or things fall apart. It takes constant work. Same thing happens with the teams. You figure that you spend 8 to 10 hours a day here, and you only spend how much with your family? We are truly a family here. We are all in this together. We have to make it work together. So, we have to grow together.
>
> We have to learn how to work around each other and work with each other. I have to be in tune with what makes you, what pushes your buttons, and you have to be in tune with what pushes my buttons. All of us have to know what the team needs to do, how we should do it, and how we can help each other get the job done. When I say "we go the extra mile here," I truly mean it. You see more people doing that now. You see more people committed to the team's success and willing to do what it takes for that to happen.

Because they are continually negotiating their power relationships, the team members develop an intense sense of ownership of their way of doing work. We can see more of the complexity inherent in this "heightened intensity" if we examine two key forces that shaped the team: a need for hierarchy and a need for authority.

The Role of Hierarchy

When Jack converted ISE to a participative environment, he also created something of a hierarchy vacuum: The old managerial hierarchy went away and was replaced, ostensibly, by level teams of peers. But organizations, like nature, abhor a vacuum. As we saw earlier in this chapter, the teams acted quickly to demarcate hierarchies among their values. These days, hierarchy is an often-maligned and often-misunderstood concept. Some sense of hierarchy is necessary for us to make meaning out of the world. In fact, hierarchy is more important to us for language use (using hierarchy to make sense out of our environments by placing meaningful things in orders and ranks, such as demarcating one value as more important than another) than it is for division of labor (using hierarchy to create formal separations, such as workers from managers). The teams had to put their values and power relationships in orders and ranks if they were to make them meaningful. While the team is demarcating power relationships, they are also creating a sense of hierarchy for themselves.

The teams naturally developed hierarchies similar to those we might see in a bureaucracy. However, they did exhibit several key differences that reflected their participative character. For example, ISE's teams resembled bureaucracies because they were rule based. But, with few exceptions, they did not have a clear and graded hierarchy of rules. A team member had to know which rules applied to which situations (the demarcated power relationships). Recall that Greg had to know to check his work, but Diego, sitting next down on the line, had to know to check both Greg's work and his own work.

Although team members still had status differences among themselves, these differences were not specifically written down, as would be seen in a bureaucracy. In terms of people (as opposed to the team members' demarcated hierarchy among values), the team's hierarchy reflected who did and who did not have the ability to demarcate power relationships. The people who had the higher positions in this form of hierarchy were the people who had been on the team for the longest time. The teams tended to operate under the assumption that team members who had the longest tenure knew how to do the work well and, therefore, should be listened to and learned from, as we saw with Martha's taking the lead in instructing Greg on how to check his work. Grace Ann clearly saw a specific role for herself in socializing new workers on her team: "If you're new on the team, my job is not to train you as an employee. My job is to incorporate you into the team and to get you sufficiently skilled to be useful to the team."

Long tenure meant that a worker was there when the team's values were created, developed, and demarcated. As we saw in Chapter 3, the longer-tenured team members were the champions of their team's value configurations. They were the ones who had negotiated the values in the first place. They knew which values worked and expected new members, as we saw with Greg, to demonstrate their allegiance and ability to use the values as a condition of acceptance on the team.

A side effect of the complex working of hierarchy among the teams was that the longer-tenured team members also tended to assume both formal (e.g., the coordinator or facilitator) and informal leadership roles on the teams. These people were the true believers in teamwork, and they could readily articulate and model their team's necessary values. Fairly early in my study of ISE, Tony, one of the long-term ISE workers, tipped me off to the "true believer" effect:

> We have a good cross-section of people out there that truly believe [in the teams' values]. You could walk out on this [shop] floor and people will tell you what I've told you. They will tell you the same principles. You'll be surprised.

That is what I did. That is what I found. And that is what I was.

As the "keepers" of their team's values, the longer-tenured team members also led or deflected any movement to change their existing power relationships. Like a bureaucracy, once the teams had power relationships in place and had begun discussing their values as rules, the team members were quite reluctant to make changes. The changes that the teams did make tended to be incremental, such as the evolution in the coordinator/facilitator role that took several years to unfold.

Changes in the teams' power relationships among values occurred most commonly when the teams encountered a new problem that they could not readily solve.[4] When such an occurrence happened, the teams had to invent (referring to the rhetorical definition of invention) a new way of dealing with the problem. ISE's teams faced such an occurrence when their business volume increased about 2 years after the change to teams. Tomas, a member of the green team, described the scene:

> Well, when business finally picked up, we didn't have enough people to handle it, and we had to work a lot of overtime. But not everyone on the team wanted

to work overtime. Maybe a third of us were picking up the slack for everyone else. So you had five or six people working overtime and weekends with the rest not doing their share. And we were getting burned out. We had to do something.

To meet this problem, the team first held a rather confrontational meeting that resulted in a general agreement that everyone had to support the team's new work schedule. Then, they worked out a rotational plan to ensure that the overtime load was relatively evenly distributed.

As discussed above, such occurrences of change among the teams' values were, for the most part, incremental. And the change had to have the blessing of the longer-tenured team members, as in the green team's new overtime schedule. Again, as we saw in Chapter 3, once a workable value configuration was demarcated, the teams were hesitant to change it. Jack's transformation to self-managing teams was enough radical change for them.

Another key aspect of hierarchy in the demarcation of the teams' power relationships appears in the evolution of the team leader role. Again, as we saw in Chapter 3, the leader's role began as an elected "coordinator" serving a 30-day term. After a period of time, the coordinator position became a semipermanent appointment. As the teams matured, the coordinator position evolved into a formal leadership role and was renamed "facilitator." The longer-tenured team members naturally found themselves selected for these positions.

In the hierarchical vacuum that occurred with the change to teams, the team members naturally tried to fill this vacuum with something familiar: a supervisor who could direct their work. Many early team meetings included rancorous arguments focused on the team members trying to get the coordinator to act like a supervisor and the coordinator saying, "Wait, that is not what I do." Such occurrences reveal some of the intricacies of how the teams were using hierarchy to make their new team environment meaningful. What appeared on the surface to be an argument about hierarchical office was in fact a struggle by the teams to demarcate, through an extended negotiation process, a hierarchy of leadership values. Would they invest power in the traditional supervisor role or would they invest power through peer-based leadership? As seen in the evolution of the team leader role, this debate took several years to work itself out.

This issue was resolved as a tenure-based, informal hierarchy evolved on the teams. The people who naturally gravitated toward the leadership roles on the teams were the "true believers" in teamwork, the molders and keepers of their team's values. The team members who became facilitators saw their role as keeping the teams focused on their values and maintaining participation. Although they took on many supervisory functions, they still adamantly played the role of peer leader. Even Liz, who would quickly complain that her facilitator role was too much like a supervisor's, would, in her next breath, say, "But I try to defeat that idea by keeping the team focused on what we are. We work together and solve problems together. I just help them to do that."

With the "first" among the longer-tenured team members moving into the facilitator roles, the teams then had in place a quite stable hierarchy among both people and values. They could make sense of their work because they knew which values were more important than other values. They could demarcate power relationships consistent with their values as the longer-tenured team members led them in that direction. Their new participative hierarchy was working well for them. The teams had negotiated for themselves a workable hierarchy among values and a hierarchical method for keeping their values in place, which had molded a team "community." The generative discipline of concertive control was very much a natural part of their lives.

The Role of Authority

At this point, I need to address why the teams saw their power relationships, their values, and the discipline that arose from them as being legitimate. That is, why did the team members so readily allow their discipline to control their behavior? The answer lies in the concept of authority.

In organizational terms, "authority" is that which the members of an organization legitimately allow to control their behavior.[5] When we join an organization, we bring with us some sense of an exchange relationship[6] with that firm. We make a tacit agreement with the organization that if we are going to be a member of it, we are going to both give something to the organization and get something in return. We will exchange something of ourselves (our work, our energy, our lives) to the organization in exchange for a livelihood, money, satisfaction, meaningfulness, or whatever. Embedded in this exchange relationship is a very tacit agreement that, as a condition of our membership, the organization can control our behavior. The organization and its managers can *legitimately* tell us what to do because we give them the authority to do just that when we join the organization.

The classical sociologist Max Weber (1978) described three types of authority (legitimate forms of control) that commonly occurred in organizations. The first was charismatic authority, which referred to the authority followers give a charismatic leader (e.g., a cult religious leader or a business executive with a high level of personal magnetism such as Sam Walton). The second was traditional authority, which referred to the authority traditionally held by patriarchal leaders (e.g., the pope or the "father" of an old family-owned business).

Weber named the third type of authority "rational-legal." These days people tend to call this form of authority by its better-known name: bureaucratic.

Bureaucratic authority resides in its system of hierarchical offices and formal rules. If you hold an office, say human resources manager, you have legitimate authority to give orders and directives and make decisions for all areas that concern human resources. However, as we saw in Chapter 3, in the team environment, the locus of authority shifts from the bureaucracy's system of offices and rules to the shared values and power relationships of the team members themselves. When Greg joined the silver team, he made a tacit agreement to obey the team's values and rules. Now, to be accepted as a team member, Greg had to demonstrate that he had submitted to the authority of the team. He had to show that he knew to check his work. The team members themselves negotiate authority in a system of concertive discipline as they demarcate power relationships among shared values. Socializing new members into the team's values is more important than the team following a formal bureaucratic procedure. The values and the demarcated power relationships are the source of authority for participative teams.

Given the shift in locus of authority that occurs in participative environments, these environments do not fit well into any of Weber's models of charismatic, traditional, or bureaucratic authority. A different type of authority operates in such environments. Authority in a concertive environment is "communal-rational" rather than bureaucratic, traditional, or charismatic. By "communal," I am referring to the sense of community that team members perceive because of their high level of consensus on key values and the power relationships they have demarcated for themselves. Their community is exceptionally meaningful for them, and they enjoy the feeling of community that they get from working together as a team.

By "rational," I am referring to the underlying system of values, norms, and rules that characterizes concertive discipline. As we saw in Chapter 3, the team's rules are not the cold, impersonal rules of the bureaucracy in which we often can find no clear meaning or purpose. The team's rules are clear and intellectually analyzable (i.e., rational), but they are powerfully connected to the team's shared value configurations. They are rational because the team members have negotiated the rules themselves and because they are functional for the team. The communal-rational authority of concertive discipline legitimizes the team's power over its individual members:

> The value intensive influence of communal[-rational] authority allows the self-managing team to function without the direct supervision that marks bureaucratic

and hierarchical organizations. The value-based communication found in a concertive system provides team members with the parameters they need to manage themselves. This is what allows the organization to accrue the benefits of self-management such as streamlining costs by eliminating supervisory positions, by increasing productivity and quality through increased employee involvement and commitment, and by eliminating bureaucratic procedures, thus speeding decision making and employee action. The team members identify strongly with their values, and this communally based authority becomes a legitimate force for controlling their actions. (Barker, 1996, p. 116)[7]

Given the negotiative quality of concertive control, the team members naturally saw their community of powerful values, norms, and rules as being legitimate. They could readily make the tacit exchange relationship with their team. They could accept the team's generative discipline as legitimately controlling their behavior. As discussed in Chapter 3, they could readily expect that every person would obey the rules, the ethic, of the team. The teams enforced this expectation very intensely.[8]

THE SACRED QUALITY OF A
CONCERTIVE COMMUNITY

But why, then, are the team members so intense about their values and power relationships? How does their sense of community become so powerful? The answer lies in the work of classical sociologist Emile Durkheim. For Durkheim, the basis for all morality was what he called a "ritual community" (Collins, 1985, p. 145). As members of society, we need to have some anchor point from which we can discern what are good and bad ways of acting together. We have to have some force to steer us toward what we should accept as a moral authority. The catch is that we create morality for ourselves from our shared values, norms, and rules. Ray (1986), in a provocative analysis of today's managerial practices, summarized Durkheim's philosophy on this point:

> For [Durkheim], moral behavior implies conformity to norms, a sense of "ought." It also implies structures or limits within which individuals know what they can legitimately expect to achieve. Finally, morality begins with disinterest in self and attachment to something larger than self; it is a solitary attachment to a group and suggests sacrifice to it. (p. 290)

Certainly, we see this sense of "ought" among the power relationships of ISE's teams. In many ways, the purpose of demarcating power relationships is so that the members of the team will know what they ought and ought not to do as a member of their collectivity.[9]

But the point here is more complex. We develop moral attachments to the groups, to the communities, with which we share values. Our attachment is so strong that we come to see these shared values as sacred, as having the highest value of anything in our lives. The sacred character of our shared values both creates a powerful cohesion and maintains that cohesion over time. In today's world, the work organization has become a puissant source of sacred meaning in our lives, rivaling if not surpassing traditional religion. Again, I want to turn to Ray's (1986) analysis:

> Rather than society as the sacred realm, the enterprise becomes sacred. Employees at all levels in the firm become quasi-parishioners. Indeed, the corporation is spoken of as a potential source of non-deified, non-religious spirituality (Athos & Pascale, 1981). (p. 290)

Within a concertive discipline, the team members, as creators of their own values and power relationships, have also created something sacred for themselves. They have created their own apparent "truth," the *way* to do teamwork. This truth is an essential and powerful source of meaning for the team. It is their definition of themselves and how they *ought* to participate together as a collectivity, a team.

Another way to view the importance of the teams' "truth" is to jump for a moment from an emphasis on Durkheim's ideas to the ideas of Aristotle. From the perspective of Aristotle's work, the teams had developed their own "Nicomachean Ethic" for how to do teamwork.[10] Very briefly, Aristotle's *Nicomachean Ethics* (1998) presents a framework for humans to use in sorting out how we should behave together collectively and morally. We achieve this collective morality by striving (both in action and in democratic debate) for what we perceive to be our highest good. Reaching that good will give us members of the collectivity happiness and enable us to flourish. We determine our virtue, our ethic for working together as a collectivity, through our own day-to-day interactions.

For ISE's teams, their abstract "highest good" was the success of their team, and, naturally, almost all of their meaningful activities, their demarcation of power relationships, were directed toward that end. They felt they were creating a virtuous community in which they could be "good" and could flourish.

Regardless of the terminology, Weber's substantive rationality, Durkheim's sacred truth, or Aristotle's Nicomachean Ethic, the workers had created an "apparent moral truth" for working together as a team, and they believed they "ought" to behave according to that truth.

The team members regarded the "oughtness" of their sacred values with no small amount of fervor. Some of the most powerful examples of this point that I saw at ISE were the nicely framed "Team Codes of Conduct" that began to appear in the team areas during the third phase of their development (see Chapter 3). These framed codes reminded me quite distinctly of framed copies of the Ten Commandments one would see in a church. Earlier in the teams' development, they had framed copies of the ISE vision in their work areas. Some teams even had framed copies of TQM or JIT principles. However, the most visible indicator of the sacred character was the way that the team members talked about their values and the ritualized ways they interacted.

All the aspects of their ritual community, as exemplified by the silver team's near-ritualistic training of Greg to check his work, kept the team focused on their key values, their ethic for doing teamwork. This created and sustained a community of believers and gave the team a sense of secular spirituality, a galvanizing force that held them together as a team. Their power relationships were both meaningful and meaning generative. From Durkheim's perspective, this is a natural and historically expected occurrence. Again, to use Ray's (1986) words, "The rites, rituals, ceremonies and symbolism [of the organization] contribute to the elicitation of sentiment and emotion and, in Durkheim's terms, keep the eyes of all participants fixed on the same goal and concurring in the same faith" (p. 291).

Much of the awareness of sentiment and emotion at ISE was from the meaning-intensive community the team members had created. In their community, the team members naturally saw their shared values and power relationships as sacred and worthy of protection. The "sacredness" of their values often revealed itself when they used the "family" metaphor to describe their work community, as Liz did above when she talked about her team as a developing family. The family metaphor was useful for them as it enabled them to articulate the strength of their feelings for their team. Family is a very meaningful metaphor in our culture, and it instills a sense of Durkheimian secular sacredness into work collectivities. The team members naturally used the family metaphor to express the high value of their team's community.

The team members also used the word *team*, like family, as a metaphor for the sacredness of their work community. These days, the word *team* is more valuable for its metaphorical and rhetorical use than it is as a name for a way of structuring work. "Team" is a powerful metaphor in our culture (see Larson & LaFasto, 1989) that conjures up images of intensity, shared work, sacrifice, commitment, and success. We instill the value of teamwork early in our young children and often as they grow. For ISE's workers, the team metaphor both described their felt experience of working together intensely and gave them a mind-set for organizing their power relationships. The team metaphor reinforced their expectations that each and every team member would uphold the team's sacred values.

Especially when the teams were under stress, I would hear team members make comments such as, "We're a team here. We can't let each other down," and "We've got to pull together as a team and get these boards out the door." Lee Ann, one of the long-term ISE workers, framed the teams' belief in the metaphor, "We may not fit the textbook description of team, but that doesn't matter. We believe that we are a team, and that's what counts."

A concertive discipline is more than just rules for doing good work. Team members place a high value on their discipline because it constitutes both their meaning and their understanding of themselves. They are a community of believers. Their power relationships and values are an integral part of the team members' lives, a point Durkheim (1984) clearly supported:

> It is undoubtedly true that wherever a group is formed, a moral discipline is also formed. But the institution of that discipline is only one of the numerous ways in which any collective activity manifests itself. A group is not only a moral authority regulating the life of its members, but also a source of life sui generis. From it there arises a warmth that quickens or gives fresh life to each individual, which makes him disposed to empathize, causing selfishness to melt away. (p. iii)

A concertive discipline is not just a way of life for the team members. It *is* their way of life.

THE CONSEQUENCES OF DEMARCATION

The first element of how a concertive discipline "works" methodically as a natural part of team interaction is the demarcation of power relationships by the participants in the collectivity, in this case, among ISE's teams. The team members have to demarcate power relationships among their values so that the values will be meaningful and useful for them. When the team members know which values pertain to which situations, they enable themselves to act effectively and usefully together.

As we saw in Chapter 3, ISE's teams demarcated many power relationships early in their team experience, a necessary precondition for forming norms and rules. As the teams' discipline matured, they naturally spent less time creating power relationships and more time using them, especially in their decision making, problem solving, and training of new members. Team members kept focused on their power relationships through their day-to-day negotiation of how to do work. Demarcating power relationships created intense, near-sacred sources of meaning for the teams. Demarcating power relationships, with authority nested in the team members' shared values, also created a strong and legitimate system of control on the teams.

The result of demarcation was the molding of a particular sense of community among ISE's teams. It was a formed, shaped, and patterned community of common policy, common meaning, and intense investment. As Greg told me after his above encounter with Martha and the silver team, "Man, if one person messes up, we all mess up. We're all in this together." And, as noted in Chapter 2, a generative discipline is not neutral. Membership and participation in their concertive community hold strong consequences for the social lives of the team members and ISE.

The Truth, the Way

The first key consequence of demarcation is that the team members create for themselves a perception of apparent truth, which then takes on certain aspects of Durkheim's concept of secular sacredness, Weber's concept of substantive rationality, and Aristotle's concept of a Nicomachean Ethic. The teams have created an apparent truth for what works, a *way* to do teamwork, which they jealously guard and to which they legitimately demand obedience. As we saw in the preceding sections of this chapter, two key activities of demarcation are the teams' development of value configurations and their granting authority to the power relationships that extend from these value configurations.

Once the teams had those two parts in place, the essence of the concertive discipline and its methodology for doing work became real, became meaningful for them. In terms of methodology, the teams now had a way of getting to the truth. They were believers that their power relationships would, if followed correctly, naturally lead them to success, to the true way of working. The team members believed in their values. The longer-tenured members had invested a part of themselves into the values, and they expected new members, like Greg, to demonstrate their own adherence to the values as a condition of membership.

The team members were very comfortable with their discipline and the concertive control it brought to their lives. Their discipline was truthful, tested, legitimate, and easily acceptable. It was their way of working. They created it. They made it real. It *was* their truth. But this powerful sense of "truth" that arises from the demarcation of power relationships brings with it several questions, questions that reveal the other key consequences of demarcation.

Whose Values?

If team members demarcate power relationships to shared values, then just whose values do they draw on? That is a good question. As discussed briefly above, I found that the teams drew their values from a variety of different sources. Some were values from JIT and TQM. Some were business values such as being effective and helping the company make a profit. Others were very democratic and utilitarian values such as equity and fairness. Some, but not all, of the values came from Jack Tackett and ISE's vision statement, although the vision statement was a key catalyst for the teams' forming power relationships.

Certainly, the team members had many values on which to orient, and they naturally gravitated toward those values that looked most useful for them. But were these values representative of all the workers? Or were these the values that the longer-tenured team members chose and enforced among themselves and then forced on their new teammates? For all their use of key democratic values, was there really any choice in the teams' demarcation?

ISE's teams approached demarcation from the perspective of usefulness rather than representation. They tended toward value configurations that worked for them, that helped them to be successful and effective. Though "saying your piece" looked representative and made the team members feel included, the value's central purpose was to help the team make good, well-reasoned decisions. To work together effectively, they had to merge business, moral, democratic, and individual values into a coherent team truth.

Ultimately, then, the answer to the "whose values" question is that the teams used ISE's values. Or better said, ISE's "business" values blurred with the team members' own abstract, culturally influenced understandings of "being" successful and effective both at work and in a group were the foundation of the power relationships the teams demarcated. These were the most important values for the teams, and they configured these values (e.g., the team's effectiveness and success, ISE's profitability, meeting customer needs, etc.) with other, more social values (e.g., fairness, equity) as they needed to make their discipline work. They necessarily demarcated power to the values that helped them to be effective in the eyes of Jack and the other senior managers, as well as their own eyes. They really could not have been expected to do anything else. They had to be effective so that ISE made money, or there would be no teams.

This line of argument could seem to move my analysis here toward a strictly economic model of understanding how ISE's teams worked. But that is too superficial a conclusion. The answer is rhetorical rather than economic. Effectiveness and success became the teams' core values because of their powerful, pervasive, and necessarily abstract cultural meanings. To make their discipline work, ISE's teams had to find a value they all could accept as an anchor for their beliefs. Guided by the broader societal culture, the team members rather naturally turned toward a fuzzy combination of ISE's business values and abstract understandings of effectiveness and success as the core values of their work community.

ISE's business values also played another key rhetorical function in the teams' discipline. These values (e.g., shipping a customer's order on time) were materially "real" for the teams. The teams had to socially construct a discipline for "how to do good teamwork," and, to do this, they had to have some empirical frame of reference on which to do their social constructing. ISE's business values gave them such an empirical, material anchor point. In practice, then, the teams used more social values (e.g., the democratic values of fairness and equity, the teamwork metaphor, the family metaphor) to add a sense of "moral quality" to ISE's business values: "If we are going to be a successful team, we will all have to make sacrifices," "We will all have to do our fair share for the team," "We will all have to work together as a team," "We will have to share the load equally," and so forth.

Left unanswered though are questions such as, in a very diverse workforce, are the "melting pot" values to which ISE's teams gave power (e.g., being effective, working well together, saying your piece, etc.) the right values? Is there any space for individuals with differing values and differing perspectives on how to work together as a team? Yes, the team members created a value-based truth, but that truth necessarily favored the organization.

Resistance Is Futile, or Is It?

What happens to a team member who wants to resist the discipline of concertive control? For the most part, the issue was never one the workers really considered. With rituals such as the training of Greg, most new team members did not really see any other options than to do what the longer-tenured workers wanted them to do. They saw the ritual of investing themselves into the power relationships of the team as a natural occurrence, as a condition of membership. The discipline worked for the teams, so "why rock the boat?"

The teams had what amounted to a "take it or leave it" mentality regarding team membership. I saw this perspective clearly in the harsh treatment longer-tenured team members were willing to mete out on new workers and in the teams' hiring practices. As the teams began to mature, they were given more and more control over who they hired. Eventually, they were allowed to interview potential new hires and make the hiring decisions themselves.

When they started interviewing, the team members, generally longer-tenured members, looked for people who exhibited a clear inclination for and willingness to do "team work." They also were keen on applicants who appeared readily willing to buy into values conducive to teamwork. Larry, who did employment interviews for his team, explained,

> Sure, having previous experience in self-management is important [when considering someone for employment], but I really look for the attitude. I say to myself, "Does this person have the attitude to work on a team? Is this person capable of working the way we want people to work? Can this person learn how to work the way we want them to?"

Randy, who did interviews for a different team, had a similar view:

> When I interview someone, I ask myself, "Do they share some of the same principles that we already have on the team?" Because if they don't share those values, then they won't work out here. We must see some commonality. If we can see two or three of the principles that we believe in showing up in them, then certainly we can build on that. But, if they don't have some of our values already, if they need to be told what to do, if they wait to speak up and refuse to make decisions, if they don't have the principles of honesty and the work ethic of industry and so forth, we can pick that up at the interview. They might be the best technician or the best assembler in town, but if they won't work within our environment, we don't want to put that kind of stress on our teams.

Bonnie, who interviewed for the white team, was even more succinct: "When I interview, I look for someone like me—someone who can work in teams and someone who will thrive in this environment." On the surface, ISE's teams "looked" quite diverse. But beneath that diversity was a collectivity of people with a necessarily common way of viewing their world of work. To use Foucault's (1976) words, the team members had become "docile bodies" prepared to accept their concertive discipline.

The teams would tolerate some resistance to their values as long as that resistance did not threaten their core power relationships. One important example of just such a situation was the representation of ISE's Asian Americans within the teams' community. While observing the team meetings, I quickly noticed that most of the Asian Americans did not actively participate in the team meetings. They were very reluctant to "say their piece." When I tried to explore this issue with some of the Asian Americans on the team, I was met with polite refusals. They did not want to talk with me.[11]

I next approached Liz, one of my most trusted key informants, about the participation of the Asian Americans. She replied that the teams were "OK" with what was happening:

> It's a culture thing, you know. They [the Asian Americans] just aren't used to the give and take of teamwork. They don't like to mix it up like the blacks, whites, and Hispanics do. We like to argue sometimes. But it's OK. We know they prefer to sit back at the meetings, but they work just as hard as everyone else does. They are just as committed as the rest of us. If a problem occurs, they let us know. We've all learned to work with it.

Lu Lee, one of the few Asian Americans to consent to an interview and one of the few Asian Americans who was an active participant in team meetings, echoed Liz's version:

> Most of the Asians here came from a different kind of workplace. You had to do what the boss told you to do and that was it. They don't understand this thing about standing up in a team meeting and saying what you think about something. They don't want to discuss what's going on, they just want someone to tell them what to do. But it's OK here because they all are hard workers. They do what the team needs them to do, like working overtime. They are still a part of the team. It's easier for me because I was born here. I'm an American. If I don't like something, I tell everyone about it. Talking in the meetings is no big deal for me, but it is for the other Asians.

Indeed, ISE's teams were willing to accept the Asian Americans' desire not to participate fully in discussions as long as they were strongly committed to the teams' other key values such as support for the team and the success of the team. Their "resistance" was not rocking the boat. Furthermore, this mutual accommodation also preserved several general stereotypes the team members held of each other (e.g., the Asian Americans' being quiet and not having much input; the Americans' willingness to "mix it up").

Another example of resistance that did not threaten the teams' power relationships was a desire to "do things differently." A team member could voice an idea for working in a different manner or for doing a procedure in a new way. The key was that the team had to perceive the "difference" as being connected to the success of the team. For example, Randy, the aqua team's technician responsible for the testing of the circuit boards, often suggested minor changes to assembly procedures that would cut down on his team's error rate. The aqua team (and the rest of the teams) was quick to accept his changes.

As we have already seen, the teams did not tolerate any resistance that threatened their essential power relationship of effectiveness. If someone came to work late or stayed too long on break or refused to learn a work rule (e.g., check your work), the team would deal with that person harshly, as seen in Sharon's story from Chapter 3. Greg knew that if he did not check his work, the team would not treat him kindly the next time. He would certainly suffer trial by a jury of his *peers*. Under concertive discipline, the members will not let substantive resistance to their powerful values, to their sacred truth of teamwork, go unchallenged. The ultimate penalty for "bad" resistance was banishment from the team community.

A Powerful Enabling and Constraining Moral Discipline

When teams demarcate power relationships, they create a generative discipline that enables them to reason and act in apparently useful and productive ways. This discipline is a powerful force of moral reasoning on the teams. It is the essential ethic that enables them to work together effectively. Demarcating power relationships enables the team to be productive and effective, but it also constrains the team in many ways. Although the teams might encourage "apparently useful" new ideas, they certainly discourage many familiar work behaviors. If a team member was late for work, that person now had to make a justification to a group of peers, not the former line supervisor. Instead of coordinating time off with a single boss, the team member had to work through everyone else. A team member who had a different idea for how best to do work might feel very uncomfortable in rocking the team's boat.

Demarcating power relationships is how the team generates meaning. They create a set of possibilities for themselves, but they necessarily become exclusionary. No ISE member much wanted to risk challenging the legitimate authority of his or her team's moral order. It was a big risk to take. All the structures and strictures that arise in a concertive system help preserve, protect, and defend the team's system of meaning. And the members of a participative environment will go to great lengths to protect what is meaningful for them.

A generative discipline is more than a simple convergence of values. It is also the internalization of those values so that the team members see them as the essential knowledge of a methodical and ethical way of life. The discipline must enable the teams to both demarcate what does and does not have power and bond the individual team members to those power relationships. The day-to-day workings of a concertive discipline represent an ongoing system of concurrent processes rather than a set of sequential processes. Demarcating power relationships is what the participative organization does.

NOTES

1. Webster's Ninth New Collegiate Dictionary.

2. Without knowing Tompkins and Cheney's term for the use of values in decision making, scholars are beginning to employ the concept of enthymeme2, albeit unnamed, in management literature (see Anderson, 1997; Knight, 1997).

3. For a useful example of how such value-based decision making occurs, see Tompkins's (1993, pp. 121-122) discussion of *topoi* and managerial decision making.

4. For an interesting analysis of conversation in organizational change, see Ford and Ford (1995).

5. Along with Weber (1978), please see the classic discussions of authority in Barnard (1938/1968) and Simon (1976).

6. For an interesting discussion of the exchange relationship between the individual and the organization that pertains directly to my ideas here, see Watson (1994, pp. 25-28).

7. For a thorough discussion of authority in concertive environments, see Barker (1996).

8. For an in-depth discussion of negotiating values in participative organizations, see Cheney (1995, 1997).

9. I urge the reader to also consider Kenneth Burke's (1966, pp. 9-13) discussion of human beings as the inventors of the negative.

10. Phil Tompkins (personal communication, May 1998) helped me to make this connection.

11. The Asian Americans were the only ethnic group at ISE with which I had difficulty gaining consent for interviews. Ultimately, I interviewed, formally and informally, only a handful of that population at ISE.

chapter 5

Bonding the Individual

Identification

If you are in it [teamwork] for you only, it's not for you. If you are in it for your own personal gain, it's not for you. Because, believe me, it's not something that anybody would inflict on themselves. People in traditional workplaces, like my husband, for instance, can't understand why we do things the way we do. They can't understand why we get into it so far. It's foreign to them. They just don't understand our level of commitment. My husband even told me I needed professional help. He said, "I don't understand you, Liz. You are supposed to work from 7:00 to 3:30. I understand that you usually stay over, but you never get out of there before 5 or 5:30. How can you do that? Aren't you ready to come home? Aren't you ready to punch the time clock?" I said, "Number one, we don't punch a time clock, and number two, until I feel comfortable with what I've done for the day, I won't leave." He said, "Now that sounds like how you sound when you're home."

Well think about it, I'm married to this place just as much as I am to him. I spend more of my waking hours here than I do at home. People just don't understand. They don't understand that you just don't walk out of this type of environment when the clock says quitting time. I'll go back in there [the shop floor] right now [4:30 p.m.], and I'm willing to bet there are a couple of team members hanging out because they have something that they need to do. They don't care that it's after 3:30. They are committed to doing what needs to be done.

Liz, an original ISE team member

DISCIPLINE, KNOWLEDGE, AND IDENTIFICATION

In the preceding chapter, I wrote that the change to teams at ISE had created something of a hierarchy vacuum. Simultaneously, the change created a turbulence in the organizational identity of ISE and its workers. The new team members were no longer "traditional" (their term) manufacturing workers. They had to take on new identities as self-managed teammates. As Liz described above, this new identity required them to take on a new commitment to their team and to each other, to invest as much or more of themselves into their team's fate as they did into their own families. They had to invent their own personal relationship with their new teams.

The team members accomplished part of this need by demarcating power relationships. With power relationships, the teams had an anchor point from which to make their teamwork meaningful, understandable, and rational. But that is not all they had to do. An organizational discipline is more than just power relationships. A *generative discipline* also requires collective knowledge of those power relationships. A discipline requires its adherents to *accept* their self-created power relationships as the "truth." And a discipline requires its adherents to act in accordance with that truth, *to be committed to it as the truth.* Such a commitment to the truth of power relationships is disciplinary knowledge. Or, stated a different way, the discipline's power relationships do not become "knowledge" until its participants identify with those relationships.

To invent their necessary knowledge, ISE's team members had to identify with their value-based power relationships and reconstruct their own personal identities in terms of these relationships. Then they would have knowledge, knowledge of how to "do" teamwork, and a personal commitment to doing teamwork "right." In her above comment, Liz is revealing her identification with teamwork the ISE way. This shared knowledge, their shared identification with their power relationships, bonded ISE's workers together as a community of believers in teamwork. Bonding the individuals through identification is the next element of what a concertive discipline *does.*

But the process of bonding individuals through identification is even more subtle and unobtrusive than Liz and her coworkers' commitment to staying late to ensure the success of their teams. It is a process rooted in the mundane, almost unnoticeable day-to-day activities of the team members as they act out their values. Identification is what makes power relationships powerful because it enables the team to "know" how to act together *usefully.* As the following example from the white team will show, identification is a key element of the team's ability to reason solutions to everyday problems.

WHAT TO DO?

It was early afternoon on a late summer Thursday, and Rita, the white team's coordinator, was off at a meeting with the salespeople. The rest of the white team was hard at work on an order of T-21 boards for TGE, their best customer. The TGE order had to be finished and shipped by the close of business on Friday so that it would arrive at TGE first thing on Monday. Such a tight schedule, a fact of life in Just-in-Time (JIT) manufacturing environments, was a normal occurrence for the white team. They were used to it and understood enough of JIT inventory philosophy to know why their boards had to ship and arrive on time.

Suddenly, a noticeable buzz crossed the workshop floor. The coordinators' meeting was breaking up. Kurt, who was doing board repair, looked up and saw Rita coming toward the team's area. He saw the look on her face and said loud enough for the rest of the team to hear, "Looks like trouble."

Rita walked into the team's area. "We need to have a quick team meeting." The team members set their work aside and assembled in the middle of the team's work location, which was a small open area framed by assembly, testing, repair, and packing workstations. Some pulled up chairs, others stood. These kinds of meetings usually did not take long.

"Here's the deal," she began. "Sales has just landed an order from a new customer, Northern Telecom. They want 250 G-170 boards shipped by next Tuesday. Sales wants to know if we can do it."

The team could do the figuring quickly. Kevin spoke what they knew, "No way. We'd have to break off the TGE order and reset."

Rita responded, "Right, but sales wants us to think it over. They've been trying to get Northern Telecom for a long time. I told them we would talk it over."

"We can't miss the TGE order," said Christy.

"Could the red team do it?" asked Alex, and she looked around the team. The white team was the only team who regularly built both R-21 and G-170 boards. The red team would have some difficulty in resetting to do the G-170 order.

The white team members shook their heads no. Randy said, "They'd need a day, day and a half, to reset."

"And we need that new customer, too," said Steve.

Again, Kevin voiced what they were all thinking: "What should we do?"

The team had quickly found themselves stuck. They were a hardworking team. They clearly understood and agreed on a shared value of high customer service. They were very proud of their on-time shipping rate. They could easily plan how to get orders out the door and make it happen. But now they had a different sort of problem on their hands. Should they continue work on their best customer's order or should they drop it and start work for the new customer? What to do?

Steve had an idea. "Well, let's go ask Jack about it," he said, which started a mild commotion on the team.

"He's not going to like that," said Kurt. "He'll want us to figure it out for ourselves."

Christy responded, "But what happens if he doesn't like what we do? Will he support us?"

Rita countered, "He has in the past." Some team members nodded in agreement.

"But, this is a big deal," Christy replied. Other team members nodded in agreement with her.

The team members looked at each other and murmured. After a minute or so, Rita said, "OK, I'll go talk to Jack." And she left the area. The rest of the team waited. She was back within 5 minutes.

"Jack says for us to figure it out for ourselves."

"I told you," said Kurt.

Rita got the team back on track. "OK, how are we going to handle this?"

Sandi had the first idea. "We need some kind of priority system. We need some way of figuring this out."

Kevin shot back, "But they're *both* priorities."

JT responded, "But we can't *do* both. We've got to do one or the other." The team debated this point again for a few minutes as they continued to search for some workable alternative with the other teams. They found none.

Finally, Rita said, "OK, our most important goal here is for our team to be successful, right?" The team members nodded.

Steve followed, "We get most of our work from TGE. We can't piss them off."

"Yeah," Christy said. "One TGE order is worth 10 orders from a new customer." More nods as the team was going with the idea now.

Steve continued, "We have to build our best customer's order first. It's the right thing for us to do if we are going to be successful."

Alex added, "You're right, that's got to be our rule of thumb." More team members voiced their consent. Others nodded as each member came on line.

Seeing the agreement, Rita said, "OK, let's keep going with TGE. I'll tell Jack what we are going to do."

Rita left the team's area. The white team returned to the TGE order. Rita told Jack, and he defended their decision to the sales manager. The TGE order shipped on time. Northern Telecom's order shipped the following Thursday.

The white team's "invention" of the "build the best customer's order first" value was a very mundane, commonplace, and seemingly insignificant incident that still shows the intimate, unobtrusive power of identification in a participative organization. The white team, and the other teams, formed many power relationships like "build the best customer's order first." But, for that value configuration to be powerful, the team members had to identify with it. They had to see building the best customer's order first as a decision premise that would lead them to accomplish their essential value of productive success. Their identification with this premise unfolded rhetorically. They argued over the best course of action (the competing values and premises) until they established a line of reasoning that seemed truthful to them. Their identification with "building the best customer's order first" was now practically a natural and seamless occurrence. They had bonded themselves to the value, to their team's power relationships.

The white team's success above helped them to convince themselves that building the best customer's order first was a "true" and meaningful value, a value that would be very useful for them. They bonded with the collective power relationship because they saw it as a useful way of working. This identification enabled them to overcome their natural separations brought on by their initially different ideas for how to solve this problem. It enabled them to commit to a collective course of action. When faced with such decisions in the future, the team could now make a quick and effective decision. They could act as one.

BECOMING ONE WITH THE TEAM

Today, our work organizations are almost consumed by an era of "identity politics." We are all very familiar with popular managerial literature that exhorts leaders to become champions of their organization's values and to inspire workers both to identify strongly with these values and, subsequently, shape their behavior in accordance with these corporate values. For example, a leader in an organization that values customer service could use this value to motivate team members to work overtime or on a weekend to finish an important customer's order. If the team members strongly identify with the value of providing excellent customer service, the leader could readily expect the members to sacrifice their personal time to meet the needs of the company. Our values, our sense of self, our identities have become part of what the organizational theorist Richard Edwards (1979) called the "contested terrain."

Today, we seem to operate on the assumption that we individuals must reshape our own identities to fit the value-based identities of the organization. Certainly, this is not a new phenomenon, as Whyte (1956) instructed years ago in *The Organization Man*. But now the politics of organizational identity are ever more real, confrontational, and, paradoxically (as seen with the white team's experience), unobtrusive.

Much of the scholarly work on organizational identity extends from Albert and Whetten's (1985) highly influential framing of identity as the organization's "central and enduring" characteristics, just as we would think of an individual's identity as consisting of that person's central and enduring characteristics. In this vein, contemporary identity researchers tend to draw heavily from socio-psychologically oriented perspectives of identity construction (e.g., Ashforth & Mael, 1989).[1]

As with the other aspects of my analysis, however, the study of identification in terms of organizational discipline requires a more rhetorical approach, which brings us back to the work of Kenneth Burke. Burke depicted identification as a profound, collective process people use to overcome their natural divisions as individuals. To form any sort of collectivity, we humans have to use language to persuade ourselves that we share "common sensations, concepts, images, and attitudes" (Burke, 1950, p. 21).[2] To be social, to act as a collectivity, we have to discover and bond in some way with our shared interests. As Burke (1950) wrote,

> A is not identical with his colleague B. But insofar as their interests are joined, A is *identified* with B. Or he may *identify* himself with B even when their interests are not joined, if he assumes they are, or is persuaded to believe so. (p. 20)

For Burke, we humans use identification to transcend our divisions so that we can be social. Thus, identification is the essence of organization. Burke (1937) even wrote that identification was the process through which our individual "I's" became *functional* corporate "we's" (p. 140). As Bullis and Tompkins (1989) explained, the implication for the participative organization is that "as members identify more strongly with the organization and its values, the organization becomes as much a part of the member as the member is a part of the organization" (p. 289). In Liz's declaration that she is "married to this place" and in the white team's commitment to building the best customer's order first, we see the outer voices of the team members speaking through an inner voice of identification with their team's power relationships.[3] The more ISE's team members identified with their strong power relationships, the more they became "one with the team."[4]

Identification in this context does *not* refer to the "rah, rah, let's go team!" sense of identification that the team metaphor often mistakenly leads us toward. Indeed, ISE had a good bit of the "rah, rah" spirit early in the change to teams, but it did not last. Immediately after the change, Jack and the other key leaders tried to imbue a sense of team spirit into the workers by giving the teams catchy nicknames (instead of the color codes that prevailed), and they even hung banners with the nicknames in the team areas. But the effect, in terms of identification, was not as strong as the effect of the team's values. Lee Ann, one of the original ISE workers, reflected,

> Yeah, we did go whole hog into the team spirit thing for a while, maybe a year or so. But we just forgot about it after a while. We were too much focused on what we had to do. We were too much focused on doing a good job day to day to worry about silly-ass nicknames, you know. They just went away after a while, and we just called the teams by their color code. That was easiest.

Once more borrowing from Burke (1937), when we speak of identification, we are addressing how we as individuals become *functional* "we's," how we form useful, collective organizational "knowledge." The key is identification with the team's power relationships. Again, Lee Ann makes the point:

> The quickest way to get your butt in the slam around here is to forget that we are a team. We are all responsible for the success or failure of our team. We all have to own up to that. We all have to do what has to be done for our team to meet its goals. If the team needs me to work late, I'll do it. If it needs me to do [board] testing today and assembly tomorrow, I'll do it. We all have to do what it takes to get the job done. We all have to be thinking that way all of the time.

Out of that identification, that sense of becoming a functional "one with the team," comes the individual feeling of being bonded to the team and its power relations, a point revealed in the words of another long-term team member, Mark:

We're bonded all right. We have to bond with each other on the team. When you throw in a new person, it changes everything. The maturity and work level of the team will drop initially until the team accepts that new person. We have to see if that new person is willing to pay the price to be accepted on the team. And there is a price they pay. It is something they feel personally. They feel inside themselves that they have to pay. It could be a requirement that the team puts on them to be accepted. But more than that, it's that we have to trust you as a new person on the team. We have to trust you. You have to have good integrity. We have to be able to know that you will do what we need you to do, that you will add value to our team.

Identification is much more than the team members simply sharing values. Identification invests the team's collective values into the separate identities of its individual members. Through identification, team members become "bonded" to their team community, personally invested in its concertive discipline. In the Durkheimian sense, identification is the individual attachment to the collective solidarity of the team. The power of the team's values becomes the knowledge of the individual, and a strong bond of meaning ensues. As I explored in the preceding chapter, the team members have to demonstrate their identification, prove that they are bonded to the team's values. As Mark said, they have to demonstrate their willingness to pay the price.

PERSUASION, DECISION MAKING, AND IDENTIFICATION

But how does identification unfold as a disciplinary process? How does that "inner voice of identification" come to speak in our actions as team members? The answer lies in a further exploration of the interplay among individual identification, team decision making, and persuasion.

As we saw in Chapter 4, the team's power relationships are useful for its members as a decision-making heuristic. They use their power relationships to reason useful courses of action, solutions to problems, and day-to-day behaviors. Power relationships are the team's apparent "truth" for how to work together effectively. Naturally, the team needs its members to identify with these power relationships. Furthermore, the team needs its members to identify *willingly,* to see the power relationships as good, useful knowledge, just as the white team did above when it figured out what to do. The members of the white team were persuaded that they were doing the right thing for the team, for each other, and for ISE. They had made a "good" decision.

The white team's experience with "what to do" was a natural and seamless part of their workday. They made such decisions all the time. Their key values of team success and effectiveness were very persuasive. They wanted to be successful, to be a good team. Their key values pulled them to create other value relationships that supported team success such as building the best customer's order first. Once they had identified with the team's values, everything else seemed to fall persuasively into place.

In a concertive discipline, the team's day-to-day interaction, so steeped in the team's powerful values, forms a persuasive force for reinforcing and reinventing those power relationships, for re-creating the team's meaningful truth. Ben, who had been with ISE's silver team for about 1 year, reflected on the power of persuasion on the teams:

> When I came here, I could see that the teams all knew what to do to get by each day. In fact, it was pretty overwhelming. I mean, I felt I really had a lot to learn about the way that they did things. But I had a good attitude. I wanted to learn. And, you know, it just seemed to happen naturally. As long as I stayed focused on doing what the team needed me to do, I could do right. All I needed was a couple of months, and I was right in there. They [the longer-tenured members] laid everything out for me. I knew what I needed to do. I just had the right attitude. I wanted to learn and do a good job for them. Learning what I needed to know was pretty easy then.

A concertive discipline requires individuals to be more than just believers in the team's community of values. All the team members have to act in the way that the team needs them to act. They have to make good decisions for the team by using the team's enthymeme$_2$s. As with the white team above, they have to solve problems in a way that supports the team's values. Again recalling Kenneth Burke's words on identification, the more the individual team members identify with those power relationships, the less separated they are as a team, and the more likely they are to do what the team, and by extension ISE, needs them to do. Identification, bonding the workers with their power relationships, moves them to act as functional "we's" for the organization. Kevin, a white team veteran, illustrated this point:

> When we all believe in what we are doing, we can do the right thing. We all have to believe in the team and [in] our own ability to work together. That's when we're truly a team, when we all believe and we all know what to do. You have to be willing, though, you have to be willing to accept the team's way of doing things. That's the key.

Persuasion is ultimately a more powerful tool for a concertive discipline than is coercion. If team members, as seen with Ben above and with the white team's action, willingly accept the team's power relationships as knowledge, then they are ever more strongly bonded to the disciplinary community. The team members want to be a part of their team. They want the meaningful feeling of solidarity that teamwork brings. They want to do a good job by their teammates. Thus, they "allow" the premises, the truth, of the team's discipline to be inculcated into them (see Bullis & Tompkins, 1989, p. 289) through the course of their everyday interactions on the team.[5]

ISE's team members, especially new team members, were ideal targets for persuasion, for the concertive discipline. The team, when its values are threatened, can be powerfully coercive, as we saw in the latter part of Chapter 3 and will see again in the following chapter. But at its root, the process of identification is a process of persuasion. And the team's power relationships are powerfully persuasive.

THE CONSEQUENCES OF IDENTIFICATION

A concertive discipline "works" via its members' demarcation of power relationships coupled with the bonding of the individual team members to these power relationships through identification. As the white team's experience illustrated, once the team identifies with their power relationships as premises, they then "know" how to act as useful, functional team members. They have constructed a collective "team" identity that continually persuades them to act in accordance with their power relationships.

Identification represents the intensely personal character of a concertive discipline. Here is the point at which the individual and the collective merge. Here is the point of transcendence for the natural differences between individual identity and collective identity. Here is the point of strong social consequences for every team member.

I Want to Believe

We all have a need to identify with something beyond ourselves. We all have the need to shape our individual "I's" into a collective "we." We are strongly inculturated to want to believe in values that we perceive to be true, good, useful, and beneficial. In terms of identification, then, the team's power relationships confront the individual members with an irresistible force. Because of the team's persuasive mixture of strong business values (effectiveness, productivity, etc.) and compelling social values (fairness, equity, etc.), the individual team member cannot help but identify. Carol, a temporary worker at the time of this interview, was right in the middle of the identification process:

> Yeah, I feel a lot of pressure to learn the team's rules, but I put a lot of that pressure on me. They want me to be a good team member, but I want to be a good team member even worse. I put a lot of pressure on myself to perform, to learn all the jobs I have to learn. I want to do it right. Sure, it's important to the team, but it's important to me, too.

Kurt, from the white team, got to the point quickly: "Hell, I'm a believer. We all are believers. Who wouldn't want to believe in teamwork? You would be too if you worked here."

Indeed, who in this culture would not want to believe in teamwork? Culturally, teamwork is a prized value, which is taught to children at an early age. In that sense, a new ISE worker comes "wired" to identify with the team values. Who would not want to believe in success, profitability, fairness, and equity? Who would not want to be a team player?

The concertive discipline essentially exploits the team member's need to identify. The team's power relationships seem good. They seem right. They are the truth. A new team member at ISE would find it practically impossible not to identify with the team's power relationships, not to be bonded to the team's discipline. Also, as we saw in Chapter 4, the team members tend to hire people predisposed to believing in teamwork.

So far, my discussion of identification has concerned the role of meaning: the intense meaningfulness of the team's power relationships, the need to make our collective lives meaningful by forming functional "we's," and so forth. Certainly, the team members' very real need to have a job plays a role in their willingness to identify. But, in practical terms, that need melds with the member's need to identify for meaning. Jody, another temporary worker, provided the illustration:

Let's face it, man, I need this job. We all need a job here. If they [the longer-tenured team members] want me to do something, I'll do it. I'll do what it takes to keep my job. But, too, you know, I like working with the team. I'm not all that worried about my job because I like doing my part for the team. They know that, so I'm OK. They know I'll support everyone else here. They know that I'm a team player.

ISE's workers had a need to identify, and they had a need for a job. They wanted to believe in teamwork the ISE way. They were willing to pay the price for identifying with the concertive discipline. Several of the team members I quoted above have mentioned "paying the price" of teamwork. What exactly is that price? The answer takes us to the remaining consequences.

Identification Conscripts

In a separate study of teamwork, Phil Tompkins and I (Barker & Tompkins, 1994) argued that, in a participative environment, the team would actually conscript the identification of the team members. That is, the team can and will demand that its members identify with its power relationships, that the members become good team players. Rita, from the white team, spoke of this expectation:

One of the things we try to do here is to separate our teamwork from our family life. When someone has problems at home or they have something personal that is really bugging them, it's really hard to deal with here. The whole team is affected when something like that affects somebody's work. If someone doesn't think that we can see when they are bothered by something, they are fooling themselves. We can tell when you are not giving 100%. And we expect 100% commitment to the team.

As far as the team is concerned, when someone is not giving 100%, that person is not identifying with the team's values. And that lack of identification cannot go unchallenged, as seen in a comment from Christy, also on the white team:

John [a relatively new team member] was really ticking us off. He was supposed to go to training on testing and repair. But he didn't like doing that, you see. He thought that if he didn't learn it, he wouldn't have to do it. But we have to learn everybody's job here. So, John kept missing the training classes that the company put on [every 2 months or so]. So after he missed like the third class or something like that, I went up to him and said, "Why are you doing this? Do you think that everybody on the team can act this way?" And he said, "Well, what do you want me to do about it?" I said, "I want you to wake up and smell the coffee." I said, "You had better get it together and see what is going on here. You had better get to that training." And he did. Sometimes you have to say that to people, whether they've been around here a long time or what. "Wake up, smell the coffee. You are living in a dream world, come back down."

To be a part of the team, ISE's members had to identify with their team's power relationships. They had to minimize their resistance, and they had to demonstrate their identification for everyone else as a condition of membership. The team members looked to activities such as participating in the meetings and showing up for work on time as tangible evidence of the degree of a member's identification. Members who were not willing to identify did not last, as Rita again explained,

You have to have the right kind of people for a team. Just because you are living and breathing and you're working here doesn't mean that you're exactly right for this environment. And it's OK if you go by the wayside. I'm a firm believer in that. There are people that have been here for years that have left, and I think that was the best thing that could have happened. They just weren't team players.

The necessity of the teams to conscript identification means that a concertive discipline treads a very fine line between persuasion and coercion, and the line gets blurred a lot. But the team's power relationships are so seductive, the values so compelling, the conscription of identification so unobtrusive, so much a natural part of the team's interactions, that the apparency of coercion among the team members submerges and a new, unobtrusive, concertive form of control emerges. Even in an intense atmosphere of conscription, identification in the concertive discipline still appeared to be something the team members did willingly. Even temporary workers who were feeling a lot of pressure to identify with their team's values (see Chapter 3) expressed opinions similar to Jody's in the previous section. They wanted to become good team players. Although some team members could get away with identifying "just enough" to enable them to work together, the team was still the final judge of how much identification was enough. And the team reserved the right to conscript the identification it needed.

Paying the Price of Identification

My choice of the words *bonding the individual* for the title of this chapter refers to the price that the team members had to pay as a consequence of their team membership. When I was collecting data at ISE, I was continually impressed by the team members' use of the words *paying the price* when they talked about their team membership. As seen in some of the excerpts earlier in this chapter, team members often made comments along the lines of "you have to pay a price to work here" and "you have to be willing to pay the price of teamwork." I have argued above that the price involves persuasion, a willingness to identify, and the conscription of identification. But I have not yet explained the depth or degree to which the team members pay that price.

The meaning of paying the price lies in the necessity of the team members to bond themselves to the concertive discipline of their team. We have to pay a price whenever we identify with something new. We have to give up a part of our own individual identity and then reconstruct it to include that something new. When we join a team or engage in participative work, we have to reconstruct our own identity so that it meshes with the team's values. We must take on the team's values, its power relationships. And we must willingly let those power relationships control our behavior.

Paying the price means that the team members had to invest their own identities into the concertive discipline. They had to put a big part of their sense of human dignity on the line to be a team member (see Mumby & Stohl, 1991). A team member who was willing to pay the price, willing to be a good team player, was someone who was willing to identify. That person would be willing to work overtime when necessary, willing to learn all the jobs on the team, willing to deal with the stresses of collaborative work, willing to be harsh to other team members when the situation warranted it. Paying the price meant constructing and investing your identity so that you were willing to do what the team needed you to do. As Liz said to open this chapter, you had to become "married to this place."

I do not want to imply with this line of argument that ISE's team members had become unfeeling robots. That was certainly not the case. But they had become completely bonded to the concertive discipline that they had created for themselves. They certainly were feeling human beings, and what they felt was a burning passion for their team, for their power relationships.

On one level, the team members seemed to find their control by identification to be less objectionable than the hierarchical control of the old ISE. Whereas before they might have rankled at being told what to do, now they "told themselves," and that felt better to them. They knew that they made more choices that supported ISE as opposed to their nonwork interests. But that was OK. They were bonded to their values.

One example that impressed me was the willingness of the team members to work overtime. When ISE's financial fortunes began to recover in 1991, the team members found themselves shorthanded with a lot of customer demand. Overtime work became rampant, as Mike, in his second hour of overtime, told me at the time:

> We have to work a lot of overtime hours because the team needs that now. Sure, I'd like to be home. I've got a hundred things I could be doing. But I'd rather be here. My team needs me, and I have to support that. We have to be successful, and I have to do my part. Look around. People aren't revolting. They're not quitting. They are just taking on the overtime work that is needed. Yeah, we want ISE to make it. I want my team to do well. I made that choice when I signed on here.

I saw a second vivid example of the price of identification in the workers who had left ISE. Late in my data collection, I talked with several former workers who had left ISE to work for a competitor across town. The competitor also was a team-based firm. As these conversations unfolded, I was quite impressed by the workers' stories of how they were "disidentifying" with ISE and reidentifying with their new company.

One of my former-worker conversations was with Sophie, who had participated in the original team planning with Jack. I asked Sophie why she left ISE. Her answer illustrated the price she had paid:

> Basically, I was just burned out, disenchanted. I thought that with ISE, we could have a true team situation. But we could never seem to get that far. We were good, but we never could seem to turn a corner. A lot of the senior management people there still have not accepted teamwork. They still see us [note Sophie's use of "us" even though she was no longer an ISE worker] as regular production workers.
>
> I guess I was just naive, you know. And it took me a long time to open my eyes. I had kind of put ISE and Jack up on a pedestal. I thought teamwork was this great big wonderful thing. But they're really just another company out to make money. There were people there like Jack who had vision and wanted to make a difference, but it was, bottom line, out to make money.
>
> I got into it, too, sure. I spent a lot, I mean a lot, of time there, overtime and all. I thought ISE was special, elite. And I learned a lot. But they were not all

that different. And I just became tired, tired of all the demands on me. Tired of being so committed. I felt emotionally exhausted by the place. I just lost the edge.

I then asked Sophie about her new job with ISE's competitor:

> Now I really like Q-Tech. We've really got it right. We know how to do teamwork here. It's exciting to come in every day and work with a group of committed people who know what to do. We have some space to talk and work things out. We really do a great job of making decisions and getting right to the point of problems. It's much better than ISE. We have a better idea here.

Sophie was following a natural process of disengaging from one company and reidentifying with another. She was reinvesting herself in the apparent "truth" of teamwork at Q-Tech. But she had already paid a price. She had invested much of her own identity in ISE's teams. Here is Sophie's response from *2 years earlier* when I had asked her to describe her feelings about teamwork at ISE:

> ISE is a good place to work. I mean, it's really exciting for me. I really like my team. We're committed to working together, and most of us are good team players. We still have to work on a few people. We're committed. We know how to work together. And I really like that. I'm superinvolved. But I like it that way. I want to do it.

Sophie had willingly paid the price for identifying with ISE's teams, and she was willing to pay the price again with her new company. I could not resist asking Sophie why, if she was so burned out with teamwork at ISE, would she go back to work at another team-based company?

> Well [laughs], I guess I'm just hooked. It's what I know how to do. I mean, I like working in teams. Once you do it, it's hard to go back to traditional work. In my mind, in my heart, I just couldn't go back to any other type of work. So, yeah, some things bug me. But I can work on them here. I believe that Q-Tech is doing teams the right way.

Sophie's words show the powerful effect of identification both before she left ISE and later with Q-Tech. Her inner voice is speaking loudly, especially when she is disengaging and reengaging. The inner voice of identification is a powerful voice. It pulls us, persuades us, and bonds us to the values and power relationships of participative work environments. And we are ready and willing to pay the price.

The price of identification in a concertive environment is its requirement that we invest more of our identity in its discipline than we have to invest to join other organizations. A concertive discipline forms its own community and expects our active immersion into its power relationships. It expects us, as individual members, to bond with its truth. We have to identify, but, paradoxically, we do so with an apparent willingness. Such is the power of the concertive bond.

Through Chapters 4 and 5, I have argued that a concertive discipline, the generative discipline of concertive control, creates a community of believers bonded to each other through identification. Once created, however, the discipline also has to maintain itself over time. The community has to go on. Identification has to continue. The discipline has to withstand turnover and still be robust. The discipline has to work as an *ongoing* methodology for doing good work on the team. The disciplinary system has to maintain itself.

NOTES

1. Whetten and Godfrey (1998) provide a recent, comprehensive, and provocative discussion of our current thinking about organizational identity and identification.

2. Burke (1950) called this necessary sense of rhetorical commonality "consubstantiality" and wrote that it was "necessary to any way of life" (p. 21).

3. Tompkins and Cheney (1983, p. 139) first articulated how identification shapes our outer and inner organizational voices.

4. For five good, quick overviews of the rhetorical perspective on identification, see Cheney (1991, Chapter 1 in particular), Cheney and Christensen (in press), Pratt (1998), Tompkins and Cheney (1985), and Whetten and Godfrey (1998, Part 3). For a structurational perspective on identification, see Scott, Corman, and Cheney (1998).

5. For other empirical studies of the persuasive power of identification, see Barker and Tompkins (1994), Bullis and Tompkins (1989), and Papa, Auwal, and Singhal (1997). For a similar perspective, see Fishbein and Ajyen's (1975) theory of reasoned action. Certo (1997, pp. 433-434) offers a concise overview of the theory.

chapter 6

Maintaining the System

Methodological Control

> Before the change to teams, nobody really gave a hoot about things like coming in late or staying out a bit late for lunch or stuff like that. You only had to worry about your boss. You only had to worry about one person. If the boss wasn't around, you got away with it. Now that we have teams, I don't have to sit there and look for the boss to be around, and if the boss isn't around, I can sit there and talk to my neighbor or do what I want. Now the whole team is around me, and the whole team is observing what I'm doing. It's different, but it works. I don't want to tick off any of my teammates. I want to do what they need me to do.
>
> *Ronald, a team member who joined ISE in 1985*

RULES OF RIGHT, CONTROL, AND SYSTEM MAINTENANCE

Above, Ronald expressed a feeling common among ISE's workers after the concertive discipline matured. They all felt watched. And they felt like watchers. They knew that they were working differently now, that their work life was not as it used to be prior to the change to teams. As Ronald said, it was different, but it worked. For the most part, ISE's teams were doing well. The company was productive. The team members had in place powerful sets of power relationships with which they had strongly identified. They were now maintaining their concertive system. They were controlled, but in control.

The team's demarcation of power relationships molds the members into a disciplinary community. Their identification with the values embedded in these relationships bonds the team members to the community by presenting the

137

power relationships as the necessary knowledge expected of a good team player. They act out their values by acting in ways that are useful and effective for their teams and, subsequently, ISE. The final element of what a concertive discipline *does* concerns the ways and means of maintaining a team's methodology for doing good work, of ensuring that their behaviors stay controlled according to their community's power relationships.

As I discussed in Chapter 3, I knew that ISE's concertive discipline had matured when I saw the widespread use of rational rules among the teams. The teams now had in place "rules of right," rules that specified the right or truthful ways of working at ISE. As we saw in Chapter 2, rules of right along with power relationships and knowledge represent the three elements of *generative discipline.* The teams could now effectively control their work because they had the power, the knowledge, and the rules. By following their rules, they knew that their methodology for teamwork would lead them to apparent "truth," to effectiveness, to success, as we see in the following example from the blue team.

THE 7:00 A.M. MEETING

Tommy wished he could leave the cold chill of the February Monday morning behind him as he punched in the cipher code on the back door of ISE's production shop and went inside. He said "hi" to a few friends also arriving for the day and walked over to the production workers' lunchroom. Tommy was the blue team's facilitator. It was 6:40 in the morning. He now had only 20 minutes to get ready for the team meeting, and his team had some important decisions to make. He poured himself a few sips of coffee to warm up. A minute later, he tossed the cup away and hung up his overcoat, but he left his jacket on for now. He walked over to the blue team's work area and sat down in a cold chair to make his plans.

Before ISE's change to teams, the shift supervisors and line leads made all the work-related decisions. The workers focused on separate tasks (assembly, testing, repair, etc.) while the supervisors did all the necessary coordination. Supervisors communicated information down to the workers (e.g., how many boards to build by when, who would work overtime, etc.), and workers communicated information up to the supervisors (production problems, machinery breakdowns, etc.). Although some workers had input into what work was done, this input was the exception rather than the rule.

But in ISE's self-managing system, there were no supervisors to make decisions for the team; they had learned how to do it for themselves. The teams had already completed this learning phase of their development as team workers. Now Tommy's blue team and all the other teams had to teach the new employees how to be effective team workers. The longer-tenured workers on the blue team could make good decisions, and they could react to problems that arose during the workday. But now their team had added eight new members over the last few months. The blue team had to get these new people working effectively as soon as possible.

That was one of the reasons why Tommy was the blue team's facilitator. Tommy, an original team member, knew how to run a team meeting so that his team could make good decisions on work issues. He also knew how to help new workers distinguish between the right ways of doing teamwork and the wrong.

That morning, Tommy studied his production schedule. This was a weekly schedule the teams received that told them how many boards of a particular type they had to build and when they had to ship them. Tommy had used this schedule as the basis for structuring the blue team's meetings. He knew that the team needed to answer four basic questions:

1. What needs to be done today? (e.g., How many boards need to be built?)

2. What parts, supplies, or help do we need to do this?

3. Who is going to do what tasks? (e.g., Who will put boards together, test for malfunctions, package finished boards?)

4. Can we get this done today? (Do we need to work overtime? Should we borrow help from another team?)

Tommy's role, as the facilitator, was to ensure that the team talked through these questions, set goals for how many boards they had to finish, and determined the sequencing necessary to meet their schedule.

By following this pattern, the blue team could organize its work activity and coordinate for necessary supplies, parts, and extra help. Also, each of the teams normally took time at either the beginning or end of the meeting for two other important functions: disseminating general company information (announcements, safety inspections, etc.) and dealing with problems that the team was experiencing (personality clashes, unacceptable team behavior, etc.). Following this pattern allowed the teams to effectively manage the necessary ancillary issues to their production functions. When he became the facilitator, Tommy had gotten himself a white butcher-paper flip chart, and he used the key questions above to write out today's outline for the team to follow during the meeting:

Today's Meeting
1. What we're doing.
2. What we need.
3. Work assignments.
4. Coordination.
5. Announcements.
6. Other stuff.

Tommy wrote these items out in bold black letters and set the flip chart out in the middle of the blue team's area. He looked at his watch. "Almost 6:50, I'd better get a move on if I'm gonna run this show."

Tommy's role as the facilitator had undergone several changes since ISE had converted to self-managing teams. At first, the teams had "coordinators." These were team members who took on the role of coordinating team information for 1-month periods. After about a year, the teams started to elect coordinators for 3-month terms instead of for 1 month as they had done originally. The teams had learned that continuity in the coordinator role made for good teamwork. Coordinators then got an extra 10% in pay as recognition of the increased responsibilities they had assumed. After a few years, the teams and ISE's management formally acknowledged that the coordinator role had grown into something of a "first among peers" leadership position, so they formalized the role (see Chapter 3). Jack, Juli, and a few team members solicited applicants for the leadership position in each of the now six teams. To recognize the formalization of the role, they renamed it from coordinator to "facilitator." Tommy applied, interviewed, and was chosen to be the blue team's facilitator.

As before the influx of new workers, the facilitator role involved coordinating the team meetings and ensuring that information flowed into, within, and out of the team. The facilitators were still, seemingly, not supervisors. Their sole job was to facilitate the flow of information. But the reality was that the teams now placed some supervisory expectations on the facilitators, and the extra pay was a tacit recognition of that fact. The blue team expected Tommy to take complete responsibility for running the morning meetings, to facilitate all communication with other teams and ISE's managerial staff, and to take the lead in solving any problems that came up during the day. As we saw with other facilitators in Chapter 3, Tommy knew he was a de facto supervisor.

Tommy looked over the day's schedule and made some notes. The other team members continued to arrive for work. By 6:55, several workers had begun to arrange some chairs in a semicircle around Tommy's flip chart. Within a few minutes past 7:00, the 15 members of the blue team were gathered, some sitting, some standing, around Tommy's chart. Seven of the team members were original team workers. The remaining eight were new workers who had been hired since the past November. Tommy finished with his notes and walked to the front by the chart. "All right, let's get started."

Tommy wrote under the "What we're doing" heading "TGE, Dynatrax, Howard Mill" and then turned to the team. "OK, TGE has 100 F-101 boards that have to ship by Thursday. Dynatrax has 100 F-105s, and Howard Mill has 150 F-101s to ship by Friday." He looked at the team members expectantly.

Tonya, one of the longer-tenured workers, got the ball rolling. "Well, we've gotta have those TGE boards assembled and sent to wave solder today because we'll need Tuesday and Wednesday to get them tested and packed." Several other older team workers nodded, and many of the new workers saw this and followed suit.

Randy, another original team worker, countered, "But those 105s take a lot longer to build. We can't let them slide. We'll have to start them today or tomorrow."

A couple of the other longer-tenured workers voiced their ideas about which to start first. Tommy tried to keep the group focused. "OK, we know we have to get going on both of these, which should we do first?"

Lucy, a longer-tenured worker, had the answer: "TGE is our best customer, and it's gotta ship first. Let's get going on it."

Tonya followed, "Yeah, if we push assembly today and tomorrow, we can get both orders tested on Wednesday."

"We're gonna need some help on test then," Randy said. "Do you think that the silver team could spare a person to help us test on Wednesday?" He looked at Tommy.

"I'll check it out. So, we're agreed then?" Tommy looked around to see nods of consent.

Marla, hired just the past month, had something to say, though. "Since we're talking about borrowing a couple of people from the other teams, I wanted to tell you that I have to take my baby to a doctor's appointment Friday afternoon."

Tommy nodded, but replied firmly, "OK, but we don't want to get into that right now. We'll deal with that later on. Now, I'll see if the silver team can spare a couple of people to test later this week."

The team spent the next few minutes agreeing on the sequencing of the work. Almost all of the team would work on assembly today and tomorrow. After noon on Tuesday, they would start breaking people off the assembly line to start testing and troubleshooting the F-101 boards as they came back from wave solder.

Although all of the longer-tenured workers had contributed to the group discussion here, only two of the new workers, Lisa and Miguel, who each had been with ISE since November, had said anything regarding the decision. The older workers were not really trying to dominate the discussion; they just knew what needed saying, and they modeled this behavior for the new workers. Miguel's and Lisa's limited participation still showed the longer-tenured workers that the new people were learning their roles in the meeting.

The next new worker spoke when Tommy moved into the second topic by saying, "I need somebody to come with me to get the parts from supply." Steve, hired 2 weeks ago, quickly volunteered. Tommy said that he and Steve would go get the parts for the TGE order from supply and request that the parts for the Dynatrax order be ready to pick up by 10:00. The other workers would begin setting up the line to build the TGE boards.

Randy and Lucy volunteered to start testing as soon as the boards arrived back from the soldering room. Lucy added, "Hey, Tony [who had been hired in January], you've been wanting to learn testing, why don't you work with us when we start."

Tony replied, "Sure."

Tommy looked back at his chart to review. "OK, we've taken care of one, two, and three," he said as he checked them off. "Everybody knows what to do?" Nods of agreement. "I'll take care of coordinating with the stockroom, shipping, and the silver team," and he checked off point four on the chart. "I've got a couple of announcements," he said and read a notice from human resources about compensation claims. Then he announced, "Here's one for you new people," and read a notice from safety about proper storage of repair tools. He looked at Marla. "OK, we know that you have to go to the doctor on Friday. Why don't we work that out later in the week?" He looked around to see the other older workers nodding along with Marla.

"As long as we're on the subject, don't forget that we have to start tracking vacation time for the year," Lucy said.

"OK, we'll try to get to that tomorrow, too." Then Tommy checked off point five on the chart. "One last thing, a couple of people have told me that some people are staying out too long on break." The team looked at each other; some people shifted in their seats.

Randy spoke up, "It's important for us that everybody is back and ready to work when the break's over."

Tonya added, "Yeah, that's right."

Tommy followed, "OK, let's all work on that. I know it's hard to come back from the break room sometimes, but we have to get our work done." He looked around to see the new workers nodding in agreement. "Let's get going." It was now 7:20.

A METHODOLOGY FOR DOING GOOD WORK

While drawing on the ideas of Kenneth Burke in Chapter 2, I wrote that organizational disciplines create a "methodology for living" at work. A methodology represents a means of control that relies on a rational rules system, a set of rules of right. As its scholarly connotation implies, a methodology will, when followed correctly, lead us to an apparent truth. In the blue team's example, we see the subtle but powerful working of a methodology for doing good, truthful teamwork, a methodology that certainly was leading the team in their perceived direction of "goodness."

Tommy and the members of the blue team were doing good work. They had identified with their power relationships, and they had material mechanisms in place to keep them acting in accordance with their values. In short, they were *disciplined.* Their work was regular and recurring. When deviant behavior occurred, such as people being late from break, they fixed the problem by reminding themselves to stay disciplined.

Within their methodology, Tommy and his teammates had a method for "doing" team meetings. They had a method for making decisions. They had a method for deciding issues, such as the common "build the best customer's order first" power relationship described in Chapter 5. They had a method for solving personnel issues. They had a method for instructing and checking new members. They had a method for keeping themselves in line. They all knew the apparent truth of teamwork, and their methodology helped them to both make their truth an everyday reality and keep acting out their truth day in and day out as members and problems came and went on the team.

In Chapter 3, I discussed Weber's assertion that our substantive rationalities, our value-based power relationships, would naturally take on a methodical character. According to Weber, we would, out of the necessity for regular and recurring ethical rational action, ultimately turn our substantive rationality into formal systems of rational rules, in other words, a methodology for action (Kalberg, 1980). What we see among ISE's teams now that their discipline had matured is what Weber would call a formal rationality. They readily used a formal, disciplinary methodology for doing good work. And as we saw in the blue team's vignette, their methodology worked well for them.

The teams' methodologies were very useful and very subtle. To move to Durkheim's perspective for a moment, the methodologies elicited emotion and sentiment from the teams. It was the material application of their solidarity. It kept "the eyes of all participants fixed on the same goal and concurring in the same faith" (Ray, 1986, p. 291; see also Durkheim, 1973, pp. 48, 92, 161). Through identification, the team members had now become bonded to their concertive discipline. As we saw with the blue team above, the team members felt perfectly natural and comfortable with their concertive discipline. They felt they had become a real team.

Liz, now a team facilitator too, revealed the "naturalness" of the methodological bond when she described her team's ability to solve a serious problem:

> Last week, we had 200 boards ready to ship, and they were all boxed and everything and ready to go out the door. But a problem came up, and engineering put a hold on them. They told us we had to change a diode and they had a change on them. And, when I told this to the team, I didn't hear one person, and I keep a pretty good tune in, one person complain that they had to unbox, change out, suck out four parts on the board, and add four parts to the board. But we still had a problem. We all got together and we said, "We're going to miss the shipment but we have to give the customer a day when we can ship. When is the soonest we can get them back out?" So, instead of management coming out and saying, "You've got to get these done," we did it ourselves.
>
> My team cared enough to get together as a real team and say, "We're not going to build anything else for a couple of days. We are going to get this problem fixed and get the boards out the door in the right way." And we turned those changes around so fast that Jack came out to commend the team. In the time of a crisis, you see the maturity of our team. It's part knowing what to do, doing what's right, and all of us being committed to the same goal.

Certainly, all meaning construction on the teams was not completely fixed. For the blue team, and all the other teams, their concertive discipline still represented something of a formative "rough draft" (see Chapter 2). They had some room to maneuver (as we saw in Chapter 4) but not a lot. Their methodology was a formative rough draft for how to act as a good team. It was not the final project, but it almost was. Their methodology guided and directed what became the team's material reality.

When the concertive discipline of ISE's new teams matured, they had in place a methodology for the effective self-control of their behaviors. All of ISE's teams, as we saw with the blue team above, had their own methodologies. Some teams did things a bit differently, but they all had regular and recurring formalized ways of working together. But if the teams now controlled their work through disciplinary, concertively developed methodologies, what had happened to the more familiar mechanisms of organizational control such as supervision or punishments and rewards? The answer is that these functions had been merged and blurred into the new system.

WHAT HAPPENED TO SUPERVISION?

Traditionally, we think of the word *supervision* as describing the methodology for control in an organization. Managers supervise, or apply a methodology, so that the work gets done. But, as we know, ISE's teams, and participative workers in general, do things differently. The traditional methodology of supervision does not transfer completely into the participative work culture. What happens, instead, is a different manifestation of traditional notions of control and supervision that better fits the teams' concertive environment. The control methodology unfolds through a different process, a process that emanates from the teams' concertive discipline.

Phil Tompkins (1990) has argued that traditional control consists of three interrelated processes. The first process is *directing,* essentially "telling" people what to do by "informing, advising, suggesting, even outright ordering, or issuing a statement of purpose, objectives, or core value premises" (p. 228). Before the change to teams, Jack Tackett and his shop foremen and line leads "gave" directions to the workers, mostly by issuing orders. They told people what to do.

The second process is *monitoring.* Traditionally, the supervisor monitored work for compliance with the directions. In the old ISE, Jack could monitor work by examining production goals. His supervisors monitored line work by walking the assembly line and spot inspecting an assembler's work on the boards. If an assembler had to get 20 B-150 boards assembled by 10:00, the line lead could check at 10:00 to see if the work had indeed been accomplished. Essentially, monitoring represents the deviation-counteracting loop in any control process (Tompkins, 1990, pp. 228-229).

The third process is *deviation elimination,* the familiar dispensing of rewards and punishments (Tompkins, 1990, p. 229). Before the change to teams, line leads and the shop foreman held the power to reward workers who accomplished their orders and to punish those workers who did not. Bonuses, raises, time off, dockings, "ass chewings," and firings were the order of the day.

But with the concertive discipline of self-managing teams came a new methodology for accomplishing these processes. Actually, the traditional methodology of directing, monitoring, and deviation elimination would not have worked in ISE's concertive system anyway. It was no longer legitimate.

In Chapter 4, I discussed how authority represents what the members of an organization legitimately allow to control their behavior. In ISE's concertive system, the locus of authority had moved from the former hierarchical system to the value-based power relationships of the teams. Authority was now nested in the teams' community to which they had all bonded themselves. Directing, monitoring, and deviation elimination still occurred, but they now occurred in ways that better fit what the teams accepted as the legitimate authority of the concertive system. Essentially, the teams' disciplinary methodology worked because the teams now supervised themselves.

Concertive Discipline and Directing

In their new participative environment, what the teams needed most from ISE's management was direction, a particular kind of direction. They needed to know what they had to do to work together as a team and what was expected of them. But they did not need highly specific orders. Rather, they needed general guidance, as we saw in Chapter 4; they could readily fill in the blanks themselves. Once the teams had some direction, some general sense of what to do as a team, everything else started to fall into place. For example, once the teams had an initial understanding of their core values, they could easily form power relationships. For Jack Tackett, this meant shifting his manufacturing vice president's role from being mostly a supervisor to being mostly the orchestrator or director of ISE's team environment.

Jack always believed that teamwork was a fundamentally better way of working on both quantitative (productivity) and qualitative (a more humane environment) grounds. He believed that teamwork helped unleash the human potential of ISE's employees. He believed that the team members were smart workers who needed to be set free of bureaucratic constraints and supervisory dehumanization. Jack also knew that he would have to change his way of managing if his radical change to teams would be fulfilled. As discussed in Chapter 3, when ISE changed to teams, Jack reinvented himself as a manager. Now Jack referred to himself less as a vice president and more as a leader and a coach:

> Before the change to teams, my principal focus was on planning and directing. I determined what needed to be done and sent my instructions out to all my elements. I was the focus. I gave the directions, the orders, and everything flowed

back to me. I had systems in place to determine how things were going, and if something went wrong, I got it fixed. Decision making was focused on my level. My staff carried out my orders. It wasn't as autocratic as it sounds. I tried to be more participative, but I was still the focus.

Today, I spend very little time concerned with what's going out the door. I let the teams handle all those details. We will have a staff meeting to go over general issues, but the teams will meet on their own to decide what they have to do today and how they're gonna do it. Rarely do I get involved in their business. They have called on me to mediate a dispute between or within teams or to do conflict-resolution sessions with people who can't get along.

But now I mostly coach the teams by helping them get oriented and focused, by helping them figure out for themselves what they need to do. I do more actual hands-on training than I ever did before. I spend a lot of time on new product developments. I do a lot of reflective and analytical work, projecting trends, figuring out what we need to do to stay on the path of continuous improvement, strategic planning, that sort of thing. I don't have to be looking over everyone's shoulder out there. They can do that for themselves.

A big part of Jack's transformation, then, was shifting his attention from the day-to-day details of work at ISE to a personal model that better fit the teams' new need for general direction and guidance. In the participative environment, the teams needed general direction and focusing from Jack so that they could construct and maintain their power relationships. For his part in control at ISE, Jack had to shift from being a detailed order giver to being a more general direction giver. He had to shift from closely monitoring day-to-day operations to more of a coaching role in which he got involved only in things the teams could not handle for themselves.

When the conversion to teams first occurred, Jack's primary "direction" was his vision statement for the manufacturing area. As discussed in Chapter 3, ISE's vision laid out the general values for the teams, values that the team members formed power relationships around. After the teams began to form useful power relationships, Jack could afford himself the luxury of coaching and keeping the teams focused on the broader strategies of ISE. The teams no longer needed specific orders from Jack, just his general guidance. One of the few specific pieces of direction that came from outside the teams was the weekly production schedule. This schedule showed when customers had been promised delivery of their orders. The teams, who did have some input into the schedule, quickly formed a power relationship around the schedule. They saw it as their material goal for good customer service. As we saw with the blue team, the teams could figure out for themselves the specifics of meeting the schedule. In the end, Jack's ability to successfully shift his directing role was a key piece in ISE's puzzle coming together.

As we saw in Jack's comments above, he also shifted his tactics for monitoring and eliminating deviation. Again, in a participative culture, Jack's role did not require him to monitor or otherwise supervise in the same manner as he did before. In fact, if Jack had tried to monitor or punitively discipline the teams as he had with the assembly workers before the change, the whole experiment would have crashed down around him, as Tommy, the blue team's facilitator, told me:

> When it gets down to it, the success of the teams depends on Tackett. If he doesn't walk his talk, there'd be chaos here. If he micromanages or doesn't let us do our work, then nothing has changed. If he rides us all the time, then nothing has changed. We would be right back to ground zero. He's the one who has to step up and be the model for how things are supposed to work. He has to let us do our thing.

Jack adapted to his new role quite well. He focused on general directions and, for the most part, got involved in specifics only when he was needed. In fact, if a team came to him with an issue, Jack tried to have the team work it out for themselves first. He could now afford to look at general trends within ISE and not worry about monitoring every little thing. As Jack indicated at the end of his comment above, he did not have to supervise his teams closely. They could do that for themselves.

Jack's reformation created the conditions for the teams to create their own methodologies of control. They could create power relationships. They could identify with those relationships, and they could create mechanisms for acting out those relationships over and over again only if they were operating under the right conditions. That was perhaps Jack's most significant contribution to teamwork at ISE. Even during the initial change to teams, Jack was careful to ensure that the teams had the latitude they needed. Juli Patterson, who had served a stint as the red team coach immediately following the change to teams, described her role in creating the conditions that the teams needed:

> Well, Jack had worked with us [the new team coaches] a lot on how to help the teams get along. We weren't there to supervise. While I was there, I tried to help them as much as I could and let them learn how to be a team their own way. A lot of the times they would be struggling trying to make a decision or figure out

what they should be doing. They would come to me and say, "You tell us what you want us to do to solve these problems." But I wouldn't do it for them.

Sometimes they complained that they weren't trained well enough on how to be team members, or they said, "You don't give us the proper tools to solve problems." When that happened, we tried to arrange the training they wanted, mostly on interpersonal issues. A lot of times, they just needed someone as a coach to say, "Yes, you are doing the right thing," someone they felt was accessible and who could be a sounding board. I didn't do anything spectacular. A lot of times I just listened.

With Jack's ability to create good conditions for the teams to reach value consensus and to demarcate power relationships, the teams had an environment from which naturally evolved the methodology for teamwork that we saw displayed in the blue team's vignette at the start of this chapter.

The teams' methodology also helped them to give themselves specific directions and orders. Because they had power relationships in place that fit Jack's general guidance, they could readily deduce good and effective ways of solving problems and making decisions, as we saw with the blue team above. Furthermore, as we have seen in Chapters 3 and 4 and in the blue team example, the longer-tenured team members were the keepers of the power relationships. As Tommy and his contemporaries demonstrated, the longer-tenured team members naturally took on the role of keeping their team focused and directed on their shared values. Because the longer-tenured workers also became the coordinators, later called facilitators, the team members naturally looked to the facilitator as the key person to keep the team focused. Tommy's actions in both organizing and conducting the team meeting illustrate how he, as well as the other facilitators, had warmed to that role. The facilitators certainly functioned as team leaders, and they led primarily by helping the team identify and realize their necessary specific directions.

Concertive Discipline and Monitoring

In ISE's team environment, Jack and his staff spent more time monitoring general trends within and outside the shop floor, such as sales forecasts for particular types of boards. They did monitor the weekly production schedule and offer their assistance to any teams that were having difficulty. But with the legitimacy of the concertive system now resting mainly with the teams' community of power relationships, Jack and his staff really could not dig much deeper than that level without being seen as violating the values of teamwork. Besides, the teams could monitor themselves.

As ISE's concertive discipline matured, the teams created a number of methods for monitoring their own behavior. Initially, they just watched each other, rather openly, as Ronald reported at the beginning of this chapter. But as time went on, they developed more sophisticated ways for monitoring their own adherence to their community values. In Chapter 3, I described the highly detailed attendance policies that the teams devised for themselves, including charts on which they could monitor each other's attendance. At the beginning of Chapter 4, I described the "check your work" power relationship, which is essentially a form of monitoring.

The teams very much enjoyed adding levels of complexity to their monitoring. One day, I came into the green team's area and sat by Lee Ann, who was the facilitator at that time. I saw that she was drawing some type of model, and I asked what she was doing. Lee Ann said that she was drafting a reporting system for the team. Five other team members were going to take on the responsibility of, as she put it, "watching over" specific functions of the team and reporting these statuses at team meetings. One person was going to oversee safety issues, one was going to monitor human resource issues, and one was going to monitor the team's work with the supply room. Another person was going to be a liaison with the scheduling people on Jack's staff, and a final person would monitor tool security. As Lee Ann finished explaining her system, she said, "It really just formalizes what we are already doing. We have a lot of responsibilities, and this should help us keep control of them."

The teams got good at monitoring themselves. Tommy described another example from the blue team:

In April of this year, a couple of us went over the team's SPC [statistical process control] charts. We saw that the number one cause of defective boards on our team was raised parts [a board component that is not accurately seated on its board]. You know, I then looked at the history of the blue team, and raised parts have been an issue for over a year. So we went back to the team and said, "Has anybody ever done anything about it?" And they said, "Well, no." Someone said, "We let wave [the soldering process personnel] do it." I said, "Are we finger-pointing another area? What can we do to prevent it because it's still our fault? We eat the defect." So a couple of us got together with the ME [mechanical engineer, a member of the support staff], and he said to me, "Why don't you try some crimping?" Well, that entails a lot of labor, crimping parts. So I said to the team, "We need to do some experimenting and do some crimping." They grumbled about it a while, but we did it. And lo and behold our raised parts dropped from 15,070 parts per million to under 1,000 in a month's time. So we had it in black and white what that bit of extra work did for us.

But guess what? Not everybody bought into it, or they just got tired doing the extra crimping. And we had added some new people on the line, too. But the next month, our defect numbers started to go back up. So I went into the team meeting, and I held up the defect sheets. They stretched out as tall as me. I said that, when we were crimping, the defect sheets were only two pages. I said, "What do you think the major number one defect is? I'll give you a hint," and I made a squeezing motion with my hand. And everybody said crimping. And I said, "OK, why is that?" I said, "Let's bring some ideas why it's back." Jane goes, "I don't think it's all that important." And I said, "Data doesn't lie, but liars can make data." And I said, "This data shouldn't be lying to you. It's telling you something is not happening on this team and it's crimping. You guys need to get it together." That's all I said. So we talked about it for a few minutes. Then we decided to put an extra person on assembly to help crimp. You know, we do all right most times, but sometimes somebody has to snap the team back to reality.

In a concertive discipline, the teams claim the legitimacy to monitor their own behavior carefully and closely. The team members welcomed inventions such as their attendance charts, their team meeting confrontations, and their self-created monitoring systems because these items represented tangible manifestations of their status as self-managing teams. The tangible evidence of their monitoring along with the known observation of everyone else on the team showed that the team was both controlled and in control.

Concertive Discipline and Eliminating Deviation

In the team environment, Jack's main concern for deviation elimination was to keep to the weekly production schedule. But even when production lagged, he looked to the teams to identify and fix the problem. He would work as a liaison with ISE's other departments, such as engineering and sales, to head off potential crises or to work on big problems that were beyond his teams' purview. Jack and his staff got involved in fixing team problems only when something happened that the teams could not handle.

One such instance occurred during the period when ISE was hiring a large number of temporary workers. After a temporary worker had been with ISE for 6 months, that person became eligible for full-time employment. At first, the teams were given the power to hire whomever from the temporary pool they wanted. After a few months, some temporary workers began to feel that some longer-tenured workers on two of the teams were not being fair and had been playing favorites. Two temporary workers who had been passed over for selection to full-time status complained to Jonie Ross, ISE's human resources vice president:

> The problem was that the teams were just not as mature as they needed to be. We probably gave them more credit for knowing things than we should have. When this problem came up [temporary hiring practices], we discovered that we had not given the teams enough training in hiring skills. We fixed it by training the people on how to do interviews and on federal hiring regulations. We monitored their interviews and hiring decisions for a while to ensure that everything was OK. They're back to doing their own hiring now, and everything is going smoothly. But we always keep our ears open for problems on the team. We are here to help them when we can.

Jonie's example depicts how ISE's more senior managers dealt with the teams. They helped the teams solve problems that the teams could not handle themselves. But the senior managers did not take away the teams' ability to control their own behavior.

Again, and as seen in Jonie's example above, ISE's senior managers had to acknowledge the legitimacy of ISE's power relationships. They had to let the teams handle everything that they could. They could help the teams solve a problem, but they had to let the teams return to running the show. Too much control by Jack, Jonie, or anyone else would have endangered the whole system.

For the teams, two words characterize their legitimate form of deviation elimination: peer pressure. Peer pressure made their world go around. It made their concertive-control methodology work. In the concertive disciplinary system, the team members had the legitimate right to control each other's behavior. As Ronald said at the beginning of the chapter, the old supervisor was not around anymore. Now the team watched everything everybody did, and the team took corrective action. The team supervised itself.

Most of the examples and vignettes I have used in this and preceding chapters have shown longer-tenured team members directing peer pressure toward the newer team members, such as Sharon's team disciplining her for bad attendance in Chapter 3 and Greg's learning to check his work in Chapter 4. Certainly, most applications of peer pressure occurred to eliminate the deviations newer team members were prone to make until they "learned" how to work as a good team member, as happened with Greg.

But other applications of peer pressure occurred to help keep people in line, that is, acting in accordance with the team's power relationships. The longer-tenured team members were not exempt from this form of deviation elimination. One morning, Christy, who had been with ISE for several years, came in to work to find Jennifer, another longtime worker, eating at her workstation:

> One thing we don't tolerate is eating and drinking on the line. It's really detrimental to electronic parts if something gets spilt. So, I come in one morning, and there is Jennifer eating her breakfast out on the assembly table. And I went right up to her and I said, "Jennifer, you know you can't eat on the floor. You know the rules. You cannot eat on the floor, and you cannot have paper cups on the floor. Come on, you've been here a long time. You know better." And she said to me, "Hey, it's before 7:00, and nobody's here. Christy, it's just you and me." And I said, "I don't care. We all have to follow the rules around here." So, she was a little angry at me, but she got up and went to the break room. She did come up to me later and say that I was right.

As I discussed in Chapter 3, Weber has argued that once we began to turn our substantive rationalities into formal rationalities, our control system would take on a heightened intensity (Kalberg, 1980). We would guard our rationalities, our system for working together, very tenaciously. Certainly, ISE's teams became intense about their hard-won knowledge for doing good teamwork. They did not hesitate to enforce their rules on each other. And, sometimes, the intensity got rough indeed.

In mid-1991, I walked into the silver team's area one morning and found the temporary workers very agitated and the full-time workers nowhere around. I asked Katie what was happening. She said that the full-time workers had gone off to fire Joey. Joey was a temporary who worked hard but had a tendency to wander off across the shop and socialize. Although he did not do this often, he had a knack of doing it when Martha, the coordinator, or another full-time worker happened to notice his absence. The previous day, Joey had been caught again. That morning, after the team meeting, the full-time workers said that they were going to go to the conference room to talk about Joey's problem. Right before I came to the team's area, they had called him back to the conference room. Katie looked back over her shoulder toward the conference room and sighed. "He's a good worker, but they [the full-time workers] don't see that. They don't know him. Now they're back there, judge, jury, and executioners."

The heightened intensity of the teams' methodology of control meant that the team members could be their own judge, jury, and executioners. The nesting of authority in the teams' value-based communities gave such actions legitimacy. The team members themselves thought it necessary. They had to maintain their concertive disciplinary system. They had to withstand turnover. They had to keep the power relationships in place over time. They had to eliminate any deviance from their methodology. The heretics got burned.

Legitimate Self-Supervision

In ISE's concertive system, the team members had become their own supervisors. They had taken over responsibility for directing their own work, for monitoring their own conformance with their rules, and for eliminating any deviation from their methodology. The key point to remember here is that, from the perspective of the team members and from the perspective of ISE's management, the teams' exercise of power is perfectly legitimate. As discussed in Chapter 4, the team members had the authority, the legitimacy, to control their own behaviors. They exercised peer pressure because that was a legitimate tool for maintaining order in their work community. Jack, Jonie, Juli, and the other managers and staff arranged their behaviors to fit with the legitimacy of the concertive discipline. In short, the generative discipline of concertive control disciplined everyone in the manufacturing area.

Not even Jack could get away with violating the values of teamwork. During the transition to a team-based structure, Jack had explained to the teams the differences between Theory X and Theory Y management (see McGregor, 1960). "You all know I can be a pretty Theory X manager, " he had said. "But I'm trying to change. I want you all to let me know when I get out of line."

Lee Ann took him at his word. One day, Jack came out to her team's area angry because her team was behind on a customer's order. Lee Ann interrupted him, saying, "Theory X, Theory X, Theory X." Jack raised his hands in a surrender gesture and backed off. Jack and the team then had a civil discussion of how to solve the problem.

The facilitators, however, found themselves in a difficult position. The power relationships of the teams called for the facilitator to help direct her or his team and do some monitoring, but the facilitator was not to cross the line into being a supervisor. This was difficult ground to tread, as all the facilitators expressed to me. Rita described how she dealt with the problem:

> Before the change to teams, supervisors used to go to line leads and say, "We need 500 of these boards today. We don't care how you get it done, just get it done." They would go to the line with a baseball bat and say, "You have to do

500 of these boards. I don't care how you get it built, get it built." They would go over to the touch-up people, and they would say, "You have 500 boards to get touched up today. I don't care how you get it done, get it done." Every day the supervisor would come out to the line lead, "How many boards do you have done? Do you have enough done?" It was like browbeat, browbeat, browbeat. It was put on the line lead's back. If they missed the shipment, it was their fault. They could go home at 3:30, but 9 chances out of 10 you would see that line lead here until midnight packing or whatever it took. The line lead had power. If the line lead didn't like somebody on the line, they could just go to the supervisor and say, "She doesn't do good work, and we really need to get rid of her."

But now, it's like you really have to take personalities into account. Is my problem a personal thing with me and that person? Usually, the team peer pressure will pick up on somebody not performing and correct them. I'm not going to do that for them, and they don't want me to. The team has to correct people.

Before, the line lead would have your future lying in her hands. It was your destiny what she thought of you. And what price were you willing to pay to be her friend? I can't do that sort of thing now as the facilitator. With facilitator, it is more or less coaching. It's not, "You got to get it done." It's more, "How are we going to do it?" When we get the readout for what sold for the week [the production schedule], our team's scheduler goes through and puts in what sold, and then they do a manpower count for me. And usually on Monday mornings, I'll say to the team, "We have this, this, and this to ship." It's listed on a board. As it's shipped, we cross it off so we know exactly where we stand.

And this week, ironically, we only have 15 people. There are three on vacation. And the manpower counts for 17. So on Monday, we sat down and we decided we would all come in early every day this week to make up for the two people that weren't with us this week. That way they know what it is going to take to reach the goal we want to reach. I mean if I couldn't get them to work overtime, it wasn't going to be held out on me. If they said, "No, we're not working overtime, and we'll probably miss that shipment," that is their decision. They, we really, have to be willing to pay the price of a missed shipment. And the price of a missed shipment can be real high. We could have Jack coming out there. We could have it reflected on our team reviews. We could note that some people are not committed enough on their individual reviews. Ultimately, if we miss a customer shipment, it could mean our jobs down the road. Say it's TGE and we miss their shipment, and they withdraw and don't buy from us anymore. So sometimes I have to remind them of things like that. "Come on, guys, this is a TGE shipment. It's critical to get there on time, let's go for it. I know we can do it." So the facilitator also has to be a motivator when it comes to getting things done. You have to keep the team focused on its goals. You have to keep things going. But you can't go overboard. And, boy, people will tell you if you do.

Liz was a bit more blunt in her account:

I won't allow the monkey [of supervision] to sit on my shoulder. If it's the end of Friday at 3 o'clock and we don't have everything done and everybody leaves, do I look like a fool? Am I going to stand here and pack 50 boards? No. If the team doesn't take the initiative to stay and resolve it and get it done, that's not my monkey. I make the goals clear to them. They know exactly what ships. They know what their responsibilities are. They didn't let me down; they let the team down. We are all in this together.

Yes, management does try to put the monkey on your back when you're the facilitator. But you have to not let them. Because, granted, yes, Jack and Juli and all of them are into this team building, but, when the pressure's on, they can revert right back to seeing the lead guy as the whipping boy. They won't whip me; it's not on my shoulders. And they will accept that when I remind them of it. I told Jack one day, "Do you see a monkey on my back?" That's what I told him.

I was gone last Thursday and Friday. I come in on Thursday morning to do the team meeting. We were focused on the goal we had to meet by Friday. But on Friday morning, they let a real aggressive member of the team convince them it wasn't necessary to get it all done. So they went home on Friday early and didn't get done. So this morning [Monday] Jack said to me, "How many boards did you get into burn-in?" And I knew exactly to the board: "There are 102 in burn-in, and 156 on the assembly floor." He got all huffy and said, "Liz, you promised me they would be into burn-in." I said, "No, Jack, you are using the wrong word. The word is *we*. We means not just Liz Adams. We entails the whole team. Now, Liz Adams wasn't here Friday and the team got weak and tired and didn't do what we decided we were going to do. So this monkey is not here [points to her back]. You know what I mean?" You have to let them have it sometimes, even Jack, because they are all human beings. We're all human beings.

That's all part of my job as facilitator. I help everybody. I try to keep us focused on our goals. Sometimes, I wake people up. But I don't take all the heat. And I'm not easily intimidated. Maybe that's why they wanted me to be the facilitator. It is very important to me that my team's a success, yes. I love to see people grow, I want my team to grow. And I'd love to see the team be able to say, "We don't need you anymore, Liz." I would love that. It would be great because then I would say, "Look, I helped them." Yes, that's the personal satisfaction I get out of it. "You guys really grew, and I'm so proud of you guys."

ISE's team workers had grown, and they were proud. When their concertive discipline matured, they had a very workable methodology that controlled their work toughly but effectively. They had become their own supervisors.

THE CONSEQUENCES OF CONTROL

The team members took both pride and comfort in their methodology of concertive control. Their generative discipline enabled them to feel comfortable with disciplining each other. More important, out of this comfort grew a naturalness. Their formal methodology seemed natural for them, a natural part of their work life on ISE's teams. It was intense, but it appeared right and true. The social consequences of the teams' disciplinary methodology of concertive control, their way of maintaining their system, also reflect this seeming naturalness. Nevertheless, the consequences are important and demand our critical consideration.

Tendency Toward Formalization

The first social consequence of the teams' disciplinary methodology is that it can become overformalized and rigid, much like the bureaucracy teamwork purports to replace. The danger, as Weber warned, is that such a system can become oppressive. We would focus too much on following the formal rules and forget or lose focus on the usefulness of the substantive values that formed the rules in the first place. We would follow the rules simply for the sake of following the rules.

Three tendencies push concertive disciplines in this direction. The first is that the formation of rational rules in a concertive system is a necessary process. The teams must be able to maintain their community of power relationships and identification over time. They must be able to withstand turbulence from turnover and other environmental changes. The longer-tenured team members cannot re-create the formative conditions from ISE's past during which they developed and identified with the core values of teamwork. The teams must create a set of rational rules out of their power relationships. They must create a methodology for maintaining their concertive community; such is the way that language works for us. They had no choice.

The second tendency is Weber's assertion that our formalization processes take on a heightened intensity, which I have mentioned several times above. On a team, our values are very important to us. We have created them, and we have strongly identified with them. They elicit emotion and sentiment in us. We viciously protect them. The team members always acted, especially when it came to peer pressure, to protect their community of values and their methodology for living out those values.

The third tendency is the preeminence of utilitarian ethics in a team environment. On the one hand, it is quite natural for the teams to take a very utilitarian approach toward their concertive discipline. They have a community of power relationships founded on tightly held, shared values. What better way to support a shared community than to act with the "greatest good" for that community in mind? But the tendency of such a highly utilitarian system is to always see the *ends* of the team's concertive discipline (the team's true way of doing teamwork, their community of shared values) as justifying the *means* for maintaining the concertive discipline (peer pressure), which reflects Weber's concern that we would come to privilege our formal rationality over our substantive rationality. The team can seemingly justify any type of peer pressure, no matter how harsh and severe, as long as it appears to help maintain the team's methodology.

When we put these three tendencies together, we get a strong pressure to *over*formalize the team's discipline, to re-create Weber's iron cage in a new and powerful form. We saw several examples of such a process in Chapter 3 with the teams' desires to "get things written down," to create team codes of conduct, and to create complex attendance policies. Formalization seemed the cure for anything that ailed the teams. Tommy told me how his team had formed its code of conduct:

> How it [the code of conduct] came about was that we were spending all this time fighting over who was and was not doing what. Accusations were flying. So I said, "Look, let's all get together and get this dirty laundry aired." I told Jack that we needed an hour off, and we went over to a conference room. I said, "We need to decide what we want to see in each other as teammates and coworkers." I started writing things down on the board. We finally came up with a list of all the important things that made a good team member. We had about 10 things. That was how we did it. It came out of people's anger over everyone not having a clear understanding of the true ideals of teamwork. So we got it out and got it written down. There are no excuses now.

Formalizing the team's methodology is alluring, seductive, and, to a certain extent, necessary, but it is ultimately problematic. The team has to formalize, but once formal rationalities are in place, the team is then bound by those rationalities. For example, about 3 months after the teams began creating the complex attendance policies I described in Chapter 3, the teams found themselves spending a lot of time in meetings arguing over exceptions to their new rules. The attendance policies had become a cumbersome trap, as Kurt from the white team explained:

At first, we used more peer pressure. If someone had been late, we'd talk to them as a team type of thing. But that didn't work to everyone's satisfaction. I mean, we still had to talk to people about being late. So we got together as a team and put together this humongously cumbersome attendance policy. It was really tight because we were saying stuff like, if you're late four times and late means more than 5 minutes, and on and on. I had been here for 2 years without any attendance policy, and now all of a sudden, it was just as bad as a time clock—except that we didn't have the actual time clock itself. I felt like we were saying, "We don't trust you anymore. We don't think you are old enough to keep track of your own time." It's really causing us a lot of trouble.

Lee Ann often used the term *rule overload* to describe her team's knack for making a rule for every kind of behavior on the team. She once told me,

Whenever something comes up, we make a rule for it. I'm not sure that it's all that good either. I think everybody gets too rushed, too stressed out. They just don't want to talk about things anymore. All they want to do is to make a rule, and they believe that everything will take care of itself if they do that.

The overformalization certainly caused stress on the teams. Sophie, who, as mentioned in Chapter 5, had left ISE for a competitor, cited the overformalization as one of her reasons for leaving:

Things had gotten really bad. We had rules for every little thing you could think of. I mean, I'm all for team codes of conduct, but we overdid it. We tried to pack everything into a code of conduct. And we spent a lot of time on little behavior things when we should have been working. I was always stressed out from worrying about what I was doing and what everyone thought of me and that everyone was constantly looking at me.

The teams had not exactly re-created a bureaucracy with the maturation of their concertive discipline, although their substantive and formal rationalities had, as seen in Chapter 3, certainly become blurred. While they definitely had a methodology of rational rules, the authority for their methodology lay with the teams' concertive values, their own power relationships. The teams had their own legitimacy. Peer pressure was OK because the teams agreed to it. A concertive-control system is a bit more open and, in certain ways, allows for more creativity than a bureaucracy, but it is still a powerfully controlling system. The team workers in a concertive discipline can be more open to the discussion of possible courses of action, and they can be more open to generating new ways of doing things. But they have such openness *only* as long as their actions fit with the team's values.

Just as Weber warned, in participative environments, we have a tendency to overformalize our methodologies for doing good work. And we can place intense pressure on each other to follow the formal rules. What the teams tended to do with their formal rules, their attendance policies, their codes of conduct, and the like, was to create a system of control that was more powerful and more complete than the bureaucratic system that marked the old ISE.

Under Peer Pressure

All of us have been subjected to peer pressure at many points in our lives. All of us have felt its power. All of us know how difficult peer pressure is to resist. When we create a disciplinary system that revolves around peer pressure, we have created something very powerful indeed. We have created something that has the potential for doing both much good and much harm. We have created something that we must handle carefully.

All through this chapter and the three preceding chapters (Chapters 3, 4, and 5), I have detailed many examples of how the teams used peer pressure and why they found it necessary to use it: the public punishment of Sharon in Chapter 3, the training of Greg in Chapter 4, the pressure to identify with team values in Chapter 5, and the tracking of attendance in this chapter. Sometimes peer pressure worked for the good of the team, other times it did not. Peer pressure could quickly turn ugly, as we saw in Joey's sad circumstance earlier. As with the need to identify, peer pressure has a price.

Consider this moving comment from Harvey, who had been a temporary worker for about 6 weeks when we spoke:

> I'll tell you, man, I'm worried. I feel like they [the longer-tenured team members] are watching me all the time. I'm afraid that I will mess something up and they'll let me have it. I need this job, so I really watch every little thing I do.

And compare Harvey's comment with the many examples of peer pressure's pervasiveness among the teams found in Chapter 3 and with the comments from Ronald at the beginning of this chapter and from Sophie just above. The team members felt the heat from the system. They felt the pressure. But they also thought it was necessary. Kevin from the white team voiced a common feeling:

Yeah, I do feel under a lot of pressure to perform here. But we have to do that. We all get tired. We all have a bad day sometimes. So we all have to look out for each other. We all have to help each other remember that we're a team, and we all have to work together as a team. Someday I jump on someone's back, the next day someone jumps on mine. That's how it works. We have to use peer pressure. That's our tool.

As we have seen throughout the last four chapters, the teams readily wielded the big stick of peer pressure. Tonya, from the blue team, felt the imperative to use peer pressure:

What do you do if somebody doesn't do their job? Who is ultimately accountable? Well, gee, we all are. Of course, the team should get together and say to this person, "You're not doing your job." But the team is not going to do that unless one person steps up first and says, "You're not doing your job. We all have to talk about it." There's gotta be that, that somebody to be the bad guy. Literally, to be the bad guy and say, "You're not attending to your work. I really enjoy you. I think you're a good worker when you're here, but you're never here." There are people who've worked here a couple 3 or 4 months who've quit because they couldn't take it. They couldn't take being held accountable by the rest of us. They couldn't take the fact that we all have to watch what we're doing. It was too much for them.

What Kevin and Tonya have described is the "panopticon" effect of concertive control. The concept of a panopticon is generally traced to the work of Jeremy Bentham (see Zuboff, 1988, Chapter 9), and the term refers to an architectonic principle for controlling behavior, as normally seen in a prison. Essentially, in a panoptic system, "prisoners" never know when their behavior is being scrutinized. The guards can see them, but they cannot see their guards. Their only option is to "behave" in a controlled manner or risk punishment. The public display of attendance and the feeling of being "watched" on ISE's teams have a panoptic effect. The workers know that they are under surveillance, so their only option is to act in the way the team wants them to act. I can still vividly recall the sense of pride in Liz's voice when she described her team's attendance chart: "So now, we can all see who's on time and who is not. And we have the peer pressure of knowing that to back it up."

Peer pressure had become a naturally accepted part of the teams' concertive discipline, of their lived experience at ISE. Peer pressure was as much a "truth" in their community as was their power relationship of building the best customer's order first. Peer pressure helped them to be effective, but they paid for it in terms of stress, trust, and that ugly feeling of someone always looking over their shoulder.

In the Eye of the Norm

When we mix formalization and peer pressure, we get a very powerful and very complete system of control. That is the consequence of a concertive discipline. Writers on concertive control have warned that this new discipline could become a stronger social force than traditional bureaucratic control. Tompkins and Cheney (1985) asserted that concertive control would increase the strength of control in its system, and Tannenbaum (1968) proposed that if management would give up some of its authority to the workers, it would, in turn, increase the effectiveness of control in the firm. Tannenbaum wrote that participative organizations could not be productive

> unless they have an effective system of control through which the potentially diverse interests and actions of members are integrated in concerted, that is organized, behavior. The relative success of participative approaches, therefore, hinges not on reducing control but on achieving a system of control that is more effective than that of other systems. (p. 23)

The disciplinary methodology of concertive control is such a system.

Peer discipline increases the total amount of control because the concertive workers have created this methodology from their own community of shared values with which they have strongly identified and subsequently enforced on each other. They have put themselves under their own eye of the norm, resulting in a powerful system of control.

At the end of Chapter 3, I discussed the strong and prevalent sense of stress that ISE's workers felt from being in the eye of the norm. As with the other consequences I have described, the team members certainly felt the cost of living in their discipline. Liz, who in Chapter 3 complained of getting superinvolved and burned out, told me more about how the conflicted facilitator role, having to be something of a leader but not being a supervisor, was taking a toll:

> You've got to learn to be thick-skinned as the facilitator because of the fine line everybody expects you to walk. If you had a lot of friends before, you'll lose them fast when you become a facilitator. You have to be a hard ass sometimes. You have to keep reminding people of what's important and what we have to do. Sometimes they think you're a part of management, but they want you to be

part of the team. You know, I even eat lunch alone now. Sometimes they push me like I was a line lead. But I try to push back, too. I'm kinda getting tired of it, I'll tell you that.

Another key aspect of this consequence is that the increased power of concertive control becomes manifest in a manner much less apparent than bureaucratic control. Team members are relatively unaware of how the system they created actually controls their actions (Tompkins & Cheney, 1985).[1] The team workers have, essentially, socially constructed themselves to fit their concertive discipline. They readily accept that they are controlling their own actions. It seems natural to them, and they willingly submit to their own control system. Creating team codes of conduct, deducing ways of acting from power relationships, demanding identification with team values, and even publicly punishing team members were all natural and, in a way, easy for them to do.

However, as mentioned above, all analyses eventually come back to the ultimate paradox of a concertive discipline. The workers are more controlled, but they do not want to go back to the old system. Teamwork is more stressful, more demanding on their time and on their individual identities, but they do not want to give it up. After all, this is a discipline of their own creation. Their dignity, their sense of self, is invested in its success. Toward the end of my data collection, as I was assimilating and making sense of all I had seen and heard at ISE, I found myself drawn to Lee Ann, who had been my closest confidant during my years of study. I asked Lee Ann what she thought about teamwork now after all the years and experiences she had invested in it:

Teams make it more cost-effective for management, because they can put responsibilities that were theirs onto the team, and it can make employees more flexible. It can make you have a lot of frustrations because you are expected to know everything and be able to do everything at the same high level as every other person. Most of what the team does that is good is that it is yours; you are the one who did this, you know. It's not spread out so much; the responsibility is not spread out so much. We own it in a way.

But it is frustrating when things don't go well. It's both good and bad. You see a lot more people willing to put in a lot more time for their teams than they would for their manager. If the team and the product are working right, you really have a sense of accomplishment. This is what we're doing, and we're damn proud of it. If the team is not working right, you have that same sense of responsibility and the stress to succeed that a manager does. You take it home with you. You do take teamwork home with you.

When I was working straight [traditional assembly-line work], you worked your 8 hours and you went home, that was it. If you didn't make the shipment on time, that's tough. Let the line lead worry about it. You didn't see people working 24 hours a day to make shipments, and it wasn't your fault if something, if the parts didn't come in. You didn't have to think that, "Well, if I just do this, if I just stay late 1 more day, then we can still make it." That was somebody else's job to think of. That part was really nice about the old way. It was really nice. If your time card didn't get turned in, you didn't get chewed out, the manager did. In some ways, it was easier to work in a traditional environment because you are not responsible, and you are not at fault. It's not your job. You don't have to be involved if you don't want to. In teamwork, you are there. You've gotta be there, and you've gotta be doing it 100% of the time.

I asked her, "So, what keeps you coming in each morning?"

Damned if I know [big laugh]. You feel successful when your team is successful. And when things are tough and you miss a shipment and have to work overtime or something, you look around to each other and you commiserate with your fellow sufferers. When it comes down to it, we are responsible for what we do, and I like that.

And we are like a family in a twisted sort of way. It happens like that with the people that you are working with here. You get to where you know what they're gonna do, and they know what you're gonna do. You don't let them do something like miss a part because they can't. They don't let you do that because they know you can't. That part is really nice. There may be a few bad apples, but, on the whole, we're pretty close to each other. I mean, even with the old job, you had some days when you didn't want to come to work 'cause you didn't want to face your boss. Well, in this way, you don't want to come to work because you don't want to face your team. But I still come in, I still face them. No matter what, I still don't want to go back to the old system. Would you?

Thus, ISE's team workers are both under the eye of the norm and *in* the eye of the norm. From their perspective, *in the eye,* all seems natural and as it should be. Yet their community of power relationships winds tighter and tighter about them, continually fed by their strong identification and intense methodology, which compel their willful obedience. Their methodology descends on them as a "lacy, steel-filigree cage" (Barker & Tompkins, 1994, p. 237) of concertive discipline that replaces Weber's famous iron cage. Paradoxically, the team members feel somewhat less alienated, more committed, and happier in their work. They feel more in control, but, certainly, they are more controlled. They are *disciplined.*

NOTE

1. The perspective that the reader often receives from an analytical account of concertive control can be deceiving. Because many of the excerpts and accounts I have used illustrate analytical points, they can seem jarring and very apparent forms of control. But, in the pace of day-to-day work, much of this effect is lost. For the team members, concertive control is a natural, seamless, and exceedingly subtle part of their lives.

7

Responding to the Generative Discipline of Concertive Control

Yeah, I've read what all those high-priced consultant types say about teamwork. They say that they've got this five-step program or this four-step program to be an effective team. Do this and you'll be a "Super Team." It sounds like something from AA.

I don't really believe all that. I don't believe that you can get to be a perfectly functioning team. I believe that being on the team is like living on the edge, that no matter how good you get, you are still going to be living on the edge, just because that is the nature of human beings. Nothing is permanent. Things change too fast. Personal conflicts, if not handled right, will wreck the team. It is easy in a crisis to try and find some person to dump the responsibility on. Given that, how can a team still function? Why do we do what we do?

My team gets products out the door. All the teams get products out the door. How? We do it because we're a team. We do it for each other. We've made this ourselves. We all know what we have to do to make it work. We know the right way to work together. And we went through a lot of hell figuring out the right way to do it. We know what it's like to be a real team.

I wish all those big money consultants would come out here and live with us for a while and find out what it's like. Then they could find out what it's really like to work out here where the team makes the rules.

Lee Ann, a long-term ISE worker

HOW CONCERTIVE CONTROL WORKS
AS A GENERATIVE DISCIPLINE

Back in Chapter 1, I wrote that I wanted to analyze the "great social experiment" of participation in today's world of work. My desire was to describe how we control our behavior in such participative, team-based organizations, to identify the most salient social consequences of this new form of control, and to provoke us toward considering ways of making such work better for all concerned. Responding to Lee Ann's charge, I had gone out to "where the team makes the rules" and into the discipline of teamwork.

In Chapter 1, I described the general trend toward participative, team-based work and demonstrated how ISE's teams offered a highly useful exemplar. The teammates at ISE constituted an "everyteam" whose experiences, successes, trials, and tribulations as participative workers would relate to our own. In Chapter 2, I argued that *generative discipline,* as a concept, offered us a rich opportunity for understanding and assessing the highly discursive methods of participation. Because team workers control their own behavior concertively, acting in concert with each other, I argued that the generative discipline arising from their discursive practice of concertive control would reveal the social consequences of their participation.

In Chapters 3, 4, 5, and 6, I sought to answer three questions about concertive discipline in today's teamwork environment: (a) How do concertive disciplines work in team-based organizations? (b) what are the consequences of our concertive disciplines? and (c) how should we respond to these consequences? In Chapter 3, I chronologically described the creation of a generative discipline of concertive control (a concertive discipline for short) among ISE's teams from its point of origin to its maturation as a clear and present mechanism for controlling work. My concern here was to identify the more clearly evident mechanisms of the concertive discipline. I argued that the teams first reached consensus on key values and then, quite naturally, turned these values into behavioral norms, followed by strong formal rules. Their apparent system of value-based rules worked well for the teams. They were effective and successful. However, the team members also felt the disciplinary pressure of being self-supervisors. They readily enforced their discipline, sometimes quite severely. And they all felt constrained by their concertive discipline, even though they also felt that the discipline was a necessary element of their ability to work together effectively.

In Chapters 4, 5, and 6, I focused more on the latent elements of concertive control, seeking a more discursive understanding of how it worked as a generative discipline while revealing the social consequences the discipline brought with it. In Chapter 4, I argued that ISE's workers had molded themselves into a community shaped around their shared values for doing good work on the teams. For a concertive discipline to work, the teams had to demarcate power relationships from these values, indicating what were and were not "good" ways of working. Essentially, they created their apparent "truth": what Lee Ann described above as their own perception of the right way to do teamwork, or, in Weber's terms, their substantive rationality for doing teamwork. They formed themselves into a community of believers. New members gained admittance into this community by "proving" their willingness to be bound by its concertive discipline.

In Chapter 5, I described how the team members bound themselves to their community by requiring each other to identify strongly with their value-laded power relationships. The team members had reconstructed new individual identities that accounted for their concertive community. Or, said another way, they had invested themselves, their sense of human dignity, into their concertive discipline. They expected new members coming on the team to pay the same price.

Finally, in Chapter 6, I detailed how ISE's concertive discipline worked as a methodology for controlling team behaviors over time. The teams knew that if they followed their methodology for doing teamwork, it would lead them to the truth, to being an effective and successful team. The teams could not tolerate deviance from their methodology; it had to be followed. Peer pressure was their main enforcement device. The teams monitored their own obedience to their methodology and punished miscreants readily and often publicly. They had to maintain their methodology and, thus, their disciplinary community at all costs.

ISE's experience with concertive control, then, is consistent with two theoretical predictions about the future of organizational activity. The first, which extends from Weber (1978) to Foucault (1976, 1980), asserts that organizational life will become increasingly rationalized and controlled. The second, which emerges primarily from Tompkins and Cheney (1985), Tannenbaum (1968), and Edwards (1981), posits that organizational control will become less apparent and more powerful.[1] ISE's teams had created for themselves a robust, viable, and intensely meaningful concertive discipline that paradoxically gave them freedom to manage themselves while tightly controlling their own behaviors. This seeming conundrum answers the question of how the generative discipline of concertive control works.

Ultimately, the discipline of concertive control, as I have described it here, is an ideal type, a general conceptualization of how we control participative work organizations (see Chapter 2 as well). Concertive disciplines may not become manifest in all participative organizations in the same manner as it did at ISE, and the exact "ways and means" of concertive control may not hold consistent from organization to organization. That said, we can recognize the general characteristics of concertive control, as described here, in other participative organizations.

Furthermore, and in yet another paradox, concertive environments, despite their tightly constrained methodologies, are still highly volatile. As Lee Ann said above, if team members do not handle their constraints well, irreparable social damage can result. In the midst of this volatility, though, one element of concertive control, as an ideal type, will remain consistent, and that is its consequences.

THE CONSEQUENCES OF CONCERTIVE CONTROL

In Chapter 1, I mentioned that all organizations have their goods, their bads, and their uglies and that ISE's team environment would be no exception. Certainly, the enhanced productivity and social meaningfulness of teamwork can be good, the conscription of identification by the teams can be bad, and their intense peer pressure can get downright ugly. In the preceding three chapters, I detailed the significant social consequences of concertive discipline, the effects teamwork has on us as social beings.

Perhaps in these consequences, too, we find some of the reasons why we often see articles in popular journals such as the *Economist, Business Week,* the *Wall Street Journal,* and *Fortune* that discuss the problems and difficulties of forming and, especially, maintaining team environments. Teamwork worked at ISE but, as we have seen, not without social costs. The team members enjoyed working together, but they also keenly felt the stresses, pain, and burnout of constantly being in the eye of the norm. As a means for focusing our attention on these consequences and for formulating a response to them, I have, below, condensed the consequences I discussed in Chapters 4, 5, and 6 into what I see as the four most significant.

The Powerful, Useful Truth

I have used several different concepts to describe the "truth" of teamwork that molds the participative community: Weber's substantive rationality, Aristotle's Nicomachean Ethic, and Durkheim's solidarity. Regardless of the specific descriptor, the point remains that participative teams must demarcate an intensely meaningful community. That community is their shared power relationships, which grows from their consensus on values for doing good work together and reflects their understanding of the right way of working together as a team. More than merely a part of their social fabric, their apparent truth *is* their social fabric. Belief in their truth molds them into a community and compels their identification. It is who they are.

Of all the terms that apply to this sense of a team-based community, the most interesting fit is with Aristotle's *Nicomachean Ethics* (see Chapter 4), even though this fit is somewhat more tenuous than that of Weber's or Durkheim's concepts.[2] For ISE's workers, their community gave them a shared perspective on what was and was not moral, a perspective they formed through a negotiative politics best illustrated in the "What to do?" vignette from Chapter 5. They had a hierarchy of abstract moral goods, with "transorganizational" conceptualizations of being productive and successful as a team at the top, meaning that their understanding of success and productivity was more than, say, a quantitative indicator of meeting the production schedule.

Fulfilling their abstract truth of productivity, success, and effectiveness as a "team" gave them happiness. They believed that they had created a system in which "good" team members could flourish. And it certainly was not an ethical system of "anything goes." Their ethical community became a meaning-intensive anchor point that kept them feeling safe and comfortable in turbulent and changing conditions. It was a foundation that forged the bonds of identification. It won their hearts and minds. As we have seen, they certainly practiced their ethic.[3]

As with any politics, their truth was not completely fixed. It was a formative rough draft for living in their team community that shaped and guided their actions always toward their apparent truth. Their truth enabled them to be self-managers, to realize a greater sense of contribution, commitment, and success. They felt they were more than what they were in the old ISE because they were a part of an intimate community of their own creation. Their truth enabled them to create and feel creative, to be in control while they were controlled.

The key element of this consequence, we must not forget, is that participative work is an intensely meaningful experience. As I discussed in Chapter 4, "team" is much more important for its metaphorical and rhetorical value than for any other purpose. Who wants to be branded as "not being a team player"? Who among us fears the shame of "not making the team"? The bond we create through our identification with our team community is exceedingly powerful because it is so meaningful for us. If we break that bond, we lose a part of ourselves.

The Ever-Increasing Formalization

Weber warned us that bureaucracy was the ultimate trap for all forms of organization. The concertive discipline does have many elements that seem bureaucratic, such as its reliance on rational rules and its blurring of substantive rationality and formal rationality. But ISE's experience with concertive control still calls forth the question, Does the concertive system offer a form of control that conceptually and *practically* transcends traditional bureaucratic control? My analysis of ISE's experience with teams indicates that, on the one hand, a concertive system creates its own powerful set of rational rules, which resembles the traditional bureaucracy. On the other hand, the locus of authority has transferred from the hierarchical system to the teams' community of values and power relationships, which does not resemble the bureaucracy. Concertive control works by blurring substantive rationality and formal rationality into a "communal-rational" authority system (see Chapter 4). Concertive workers create a community value system that eventually controls their actions through rational rules. This rational, concertive community also gives the team members a feeling of comfort as they navigate the turbulence created by technology, globalization, increasing education, and increasing diversity in our general organizational environment.

More important, as I discussed in Chapter 6, my analysis suggests that concertive control does not free workers from Weber's iron cage of rational rules, as the culturalist and practitioner-oriented writers on contemporary organizations often argue. Instead, an ironic paradox occurs: The iron cage becomes stronger. The powerful combination of peer pressure and rational rules in the concertive system creates a new steel cage whose bars are almost invisible to the workers it incarcerates. ISE's team workers, as Weber (1978, p. 988) warned, apparently have harnessed themselves into a rational apparatus out of which they truly cannot squirm.

Is entrapment in the steel cage of concertive discipline the unavoidable fate of participative systems? Theory suggests a yes answer, but the reality is that we do not know yet. We have not been experimenting with participation on a grand scale long enough for us to understand and appreciate the complete future of concertive systems. Given this uncertainty, what "the ever-increasing formalization" consequence does illustrate for us is that concertive control relies, out of necessity, on a methodology of rational rules. We simply do not have a better way of working together in complex environments over a long period of time. Because of this reliance, concertive systems will incite intense rushes toward formalization. The team must ensure that its methodology maintains its community over time, day in and day out. Formalization comes with the territory of participation, and we must be vigilant lest we fulfill Weber's dire warning.

The Price of Identification

In Chapter 5, I discussed how intrigued I was by the team members' continual mentioning of "paying the price." What they meant was the investment of themselves, their own identities, required by the concertive discipline. They had to bond with and be bonded to their team community. Creating such a bond meant that they had to reconstruct their own identities and become one with the team. This personal investment of individual identity is the price they had to pay. It is the ante for participating in a concertive discipline.

The price of identification brings with it a number of issues that I explored in the preceding chapters: the fear of not making the team, the stress and burnout of continuous self-supervision, the sacrifice of personal family for the team family, and the risks inherent in appearing unwilling to pay the price. Yet most of ISE's team members willingly paid the price. If they did not pay up, they did not last. The team's community of values is an irresistible force that compels our identification with it. We want to believe in the truth of teamwork, so we do. Then we realize that feeling of inclusion into something collective and bigger than ourselves. We add a new element of meaning to our lives. Being on the team meant a lot to ISE's workers in many complex ways.

Following Burke's reasoning again, identification is a necessary part of our social lives. Identification allows us to overcome our natural separations so that we can "be social." Bonding ourselves to the team community is a natural consequence of concertive discipline. When confronted with attractive and appealing participative environments, we willingly pay the price for membership.

The Peer-Pressured Eye of the Norm

For better or for worse, we, like Liz at the start of Chapter 5, find ourselves "married" to participative work. The concertive community's "truth," the meaningfulness of the right way of doing teamwork, exerts a strong appeal. We willingly and readily enter into the "eye of the norm" and close the steel cage behind us.

From my perspective, the effects of being in the eye of the norm represent the most serious consequence of concertive control. Once we are members of the team, enclosed in the eye, all seems natural. We willingly use peer pressure as the necessary enforcement tool of our methodology. The team's work seems right, correct, and, of course, true. Driven by peer pressure and the legitimate authority of the team's community, concertive control represents a form of control more powerful than its bureaucratic predecessor. Authority and the possibility of appeal first and finally reside in the peer pressure of the teams.

Certainly, the powerfully collective character of participation may grate our Western, individualistic selves (see Ezzamel & Willmott, 1998; Nahavandi & Aranda, 1994). But once a concertive disciplinary community forms, such as we saw at ISE, the swirling storm of power relationships, identification, and methodology is practically irresistible. We are not so individualistic that we can easily avoid being pulled into the eye of the norm.

The striking element of being in the eye of the norm is its naturalness, unobtrusiveness, and comfort. When we engage in participative work, we enter the eye of the norm. We are confronted by a powerful system of control, but we cannot readily or easily see our constrained condition, much less analyze it. The eye of the norm represents a near-totalizing experience. We create the concertive community. We identify with it. We live by its methodology. Concertive control is us. It is how we do participative work. We *discipline* ourselves generatively and punitively.

Evidence From Related Research

Other studies of teams and participative work support my arguments about the discipline of concertive control and its consequences. Grenier (1988), in his ethnography of teams, described similar consequences and effects from peer pressure and the disciplinary eye of the norm. Although not writing explicitly about teams, Kunda (1992) and Watson (1994) published ethnographies detailing similar effects of identification, persuasion, and language use in participative organizations. A recent article in the *Wall Street Journal* (King, 1998) presented a graphic and compelling account of the tribulations of peer pressure during a team-based experiment at Levi-Strauss.

Prior to my first publication on ISE in 1993, Tompkins and Bullis (Bullis, 1991; Bullis & Tompkins, 1989) studied concertive control in the U.S. Forest Service. They concentrated on the empirical analysis of how Forest Service workers used language rhetorically to create and identify with key organizational decision premises. Essentially, they studied how the workers concertively persuaded themselves to act in ways functional for the organization. They found that workers persuaded themselves to identify strongly with core decision premises of the Forest Service, which created a very unobtrusive disciplinary process. The workers were so intensely involved in creating a collaborative form of control that they did not really notice that they were indeed controlling their own work.

In 1997, Papa, Auwal, and Singhal took a fascinating approach to the study of concertive control. They investigated the consequences of concertive control, as it became manifest among the members of the Grameen Bank Cooperative in Bangladesh, focusing on the rhetorical accounts of cooperative members as they described their activity in the organization. Though they found the same elements of value consensus, rational rules, identification, and peer pressure I have discussed above, they argued for a different understanding of the role of peer pressure.

Papa, Auwal, and Singhal argued that the forms of peer pressure manifest in a concertive system are more culturally acceptable in Bangladeshi culture than in Western culture. The members of the cooperative readily accepted and acknowledged that peer pressure caused them stress and pain, but they *knew* they had to exert strong peer pressure to maintain their cooperative methodology. Adding another paradox to the workings of concertive control, the authors asserted that the cooperative's members felt enabled and empowered by their concertive system because they knew it would work when they maintained accountability via peer pressure. However, Papa, Auwal, and Singhal did not deny that concertive control still represented a very powerful discipline.

In an interesting contrast with Papa, Auwal, and Singhal's (1997) arguments, Ezzamel and Willmott (1998) found that team workers in a British firm, StitchCo, deeply resented the expectation that they bond their identity to their forced concertive community. The authors described a situation of "competing truths" or value systems that destabilized the formation of concertive control at StitchCo. Prior to the change to teams, the workers had strong identities as "machinists," as opposed to teammates, and they were unwilling to reform these tightly held values and embrace the collectivism and peer pressure of concertive control. They certainly were not convinced, as were ISE's workers, that their job depended on their success as team workers. They did not have the same sort of community, level of identification, or potent methodology.

I asked a consultant friend who specializes in team-based interventions to comment on both Ezzamel and Willmott's findings and the extensive problems Levi-Strauss experienced with teams, as described by King (1998) in the *Wall Street Journal.* Her answer was that the teams at both organizations were not trained well enough in teamwork and that management did not prepare the teams adequately:

> If they had been prepared well enough for teamwork, none of this would have happened. They needed to take ownership of their own team processes. They needed to decide for themselves how to make teams work there, and they needed to commit themselves to making teams work. They just needed to know how to work together and how to be committed to each other.

Essentially, my friend was saying that the teams needed a new and better community, a new truth of teamwork. If the teams had been able to demarcate a more workable set of power relationships that they could identify with more strongly, then they would have created a good methodology and "everything would have worked out." My friend's comments illustrate how much faith we have, whether we are cognizant of it or not, in the team metaphor. We believe that teamwork is that irresistible force that will overcome all resistance and lead us to the truth of productivity and success.

I want to note one additional research report concerning the discipline of concertive control. Graham Sewell (1998) has issued an important caution that we do not forget the effects of traditional hierarchical control in concertive environments. At ISE, the teams did most of their own monitoring, but that situation is not the case in many participative organizations. Sewell asserted that when we mix horizontal, or peer, monitoring (concertive control) with vertical, or hierarchical, monitoring (managerial control), we get an even more powerful and total system. Sewell persuasively argued that, as we add more and better information systems for managerial monitoring and tend more and more toward participative forms of work, the potential for oppressive and tyrannical control methodologies dramatically increases.[4]

My fear, after considering the available research, is that concertive control is the next step on our long march toward totally organized lives. Concertive environments require us to give more of ourselves to the organization, while getting mostly a heightened sense of meaningfulness in return. But when we consider the consequences of participation, we can easily see a more totally organized and constrained world of work looming on the road to our future. I am not willing, just yet, to go quietly down that rough and rocky road. And I do not believe that Jack or Liz or Tommy or anyone else at ISE would want to go down that road either. So where does that leave us?

Well, it is tempting, from a strictly organizational perspective, not to respond at all to these consequences. ISE was ultimately successful and productive with teams. The team members with their generative discipline of concertive control had created a powerful system for shaping their behavior so that they could be successful. The consequences of concertive control might be a reasonable price to pay for the larger organization's success. What is so bad about being in the eye of the norm when the organization's life is at stake?

But Jack Tackett, as the architect of teams at ISE, would not agree with that line of reasoning. Sure, Jack bet ISE's future on making teams work, but he was just as fervent an apostle of teamwork as a *qualitatively better* way of working. Jack saw teamwork and participation as a means for making today's workplace more humane, and the consequences I have outlined above address the humanity, the social character, of participative work. It is Jack himself who gives us the moral imperative for responding to the consequences of concertive control.

HOW SHOULD WE RESPOND?

Participative organizations, like ISE, reflect many goods, bads, and uglies as teams blend abstract and material values while they argue and develop their own meanings for team success and ethical behavior. We must respond to the consequences I outlined above because the consequences facing ISE's teams are our own consequences. We all face these consequences anytime we engage in participative work. Concertive disciplines embody political and dialogic processes (Deetz, 1995). Because of this, the participants in concertive work will need some discursive room to maneuver as they deal with the formation of concertive control and its consequences. Our requirement, then, is to recognize the goods, bads, and uglies and to create, continually, the conditions that enable us to work with them and mediate their effects. That is, we must create that discursive room to maneuver.

How can we do this? How can we mediate the social consequences of concertive control? How can we respond to the imperative for action clearly evident in these consequences? Answering these questions has vexed me in the years since I first studied ISE and has consumed most of my research since. But now I am prepared to deliver a response, which I hope will further provoke us toward mediating the consequences described above. What follows are my assertions for how we should respond to the generative discipline of concertive control.[5]

All of the responses that I discuss below have one assumption in mind: I believe that concertive control is inevitable. When we organize ourselves into participative work groups, we will control those work groups more or less concertively and immerse ourselves into their generative discipline. Given this, we must respond to the consequences of concertive control as a part of creating its discipline. Or said another way, *we must embed a response to these consequences into the discipline itself as we are constructing it.* We must make responses to these consequences a regular and recurring part of our participative work.

Cultivate a Continuing Criticism

Our first response to the discipline of concertive control requires the realization that we apply powerful and potentially highly oppressive controls to our activity in participative organizations. Armed with the knowledge that concertive control represents such a strong and unobtrusive form of control, we must respond by subjecting concertive control to a constant scrutiny: a continuing criticism purposefully designed to determine its good and bad effects. We must ensure that we remain aware of concertive control's power over us and aware of the consequences it entails for our social lives. I use the word *we* here to signify that *we* must be the ones doing the continual criticizing. We have to have the ability to critique our own collective participation in today's organization.

There is another and perhaps more important reason for continually critiquing concertive control. The power relationships we create in a concertive community take on a sense of truth, the right way to do participative work. That truth (or substantive rationality, or solidarity, or Nicomachean Ethic, or whatever term we want to use) answers several meaningful questions for us (e.g., what are we doing? why are we doing it? and how should we go about doing it?) and provides the foundation on which we build a concertive discipline.

Once we create that truth, once we move through the process of reaching a consensus on shared values, demarcating power relationships, and molding communities, we have created a moral compass for our team. We subsequently use the knowledge gained from the demarcation process as a foundation for moral reasoning in team decision making. Team members themselves reason what is and is not moral, what are and are not "truthful" ways of working together. Because we give such a high status to our team community's truth, we must recognize that status, understand the power of our shared truth, and criticize it. We must be able to ensure that our participative community is working for us, not against us.

Doing Well and Doing Good

David Whetten has argued that an essential element of working in today's value-intensive organization is for all of us to understand that we have to "do well and do good."[6] Doing well refers to the need for success and effectiveness common to any organization. To survive, all organizations and the people in them must know how to make their organization a success. They have to do "well" as an organization. Professor Whetten called doing well the organization's "economic logic."

But organizations and the people in them also need a "moral logic." They have to act, individually and collectively, in moral or "good" ways, both toward themselves and toward their external environment and stakeholders. As we saw, ISE's teams certainly created and used their own morality of teamwork, much akin to Aristotle's (1998) concept of *Nicomachean Ethics.* What was "good" extended from the teams' value consensus. The team members had determined for themselves what doing well and doing good meant for their team. Recall how ISE's teams decided to build their best customer's order first and strongly punished those team members who were shirking their team responsibilities.

How does a team sort out what is well and what is good for them? Professor Whetten suggested that organizations must stay focused on utilitarian ethical concepts because of an organization's basic need to have some degree of success doing whatever it does. The greatest good for the greatest number of organizational members is that which helps the organization to be successful. In terms of concertive control, ISE's teams had to concentrate on demarcating what was and was not effective work on the teams. They had to figure out such knowledge as "building the best customer's order first" just to survive.

With these points in mind, the teams naturally placed the more "business" values of team success and effectiveness at the top of their power relationship chain. As we saw in Chapter 4, they used more commonly understood "moral" values, such as fairness and equity, to add an ethical quality to their business values. They had to be successful, but they also tried to share work equally. Their concertive system did allow them to do well and do good as they saw it from within their own concertive discipline.

But the need to do well and do good, with its utilitarian foundation, tends the team toward overformalization and intense peer pressure. How can the teams still do well and do good while resisting the strong pull naturally exerted by the eye of the norm? How can teams maintain their virtue, their integrity, their collective sense of what is and what is not good? The answer brings us back to the need to *cultivate* a continuing ability for the teams to criticize their own actions. The teams, supported by management, must create for themselves the time and space required to pause and reflect on their own moral reasoning.

Know the System, See the Consequences

For the teams to gain the perspective necessary to criticize their own ability to do well and do good, they must know how their concertive system affects them. They must realize that they are working in an intensely meaningful and powerful disciplinary system. Team members need to know that their concertive system works via the molding of a community through demarcated power relationships. Team members must realize that they bond themselves tightly to that community, and they create methodologies that constrain and shape their behavior. They must understand that they exist in an environment of peer pressure, formalization, and constant self-scrutiny that has consequences for their social well-being.

To cultivate a means for critiquing these powerful and unobtrusive processes, the team must deliberately set aside time to review how they are controlling themselves. They must gain the ability to openly discuss their methodologies for controlling their own behavior and to assess the toll that the eye of the norm is taking on them. They must be able to identify the consequences of their concertive work and determine what they want to do about those consequences.

Unfortunately, I am not describing a naturally occurring process. Gaining a critical perspective takes time, and time is a precious resource in the modern organization. ISE's team members were certainly constrained by time in the form of an unrelenting schedule of customer orders. They could sense problems and trouble, and sometimes they would halt work for a bit to talk over a serious issue. But they never developed a regular and systematic mechanism for reflecting on their concertive processes.

What I am arguing for here is just such a regular, recurring, and systematic method for the team to assess its own moral reasoning. We managers, scholars, consultants, and participative workers alike must realize that teams have to take time to criticize these processes if they are to avoid the pitfalls of concertive control. I am not making a completely unusual assertion here; team scholars such as Hackman (e.g., 1986, 1992) have also noted that teams need to review their activity regularly. We also find this sense of the team needing to reflect, converse on values, and improve itself in other current writings on participation, such as those of Senge (e.g., 1994) and Wheatley (e.g., 1994).

I am, however, urging that we extend this review beyond performance measures to an open and active discussion of the team's morality. Periodically and regularly, say once or twice a month, a participative team needs to assess how its moral community is doing. The team has to assess its concertive system, maintain what its members like (such as a shared value for learning all the jobs on the team), and change those elements (such as too-strong peer pressure) that cause them difficulty. A continuing criticism must be as much a part of the discipline of concertive control as demarcation, identification, and methodology.

We are certainly not used to such moral reflection in our organizational lives, which is why I use the word *cultivate*. All of us will have to work diligently toward creating an environment safe enough for the members of a participative team to engage in adequate critical reflection. Management, through training and other means, must create a safe environment for the team to do its own criticism. The team must openly and honestly assess how well its own morality works. As Lee Ann said at the opening of this chapter, in the discipline of teamwork, "*the team makes the rules.*" The team demarcates a moral concertive community from the myriad of possible values in its realm. The team members must criticize their own habit and practice.

Negotiate the Values, Find the Virtue

The collective power relationships of a concertive community may have a sacred quality, but these relationships are not sacrosanct. They can evolve and change. Teams can negotiate and renegotiate the shared values from which they form the power relationships that mold their community. When the teams critically reflect on the consequences of their concertive discipline, they must realize that they are assessing their values. They have to feel that they can change a value if they see the need.

Though ISE's team members did not use the same terminology that I have used here, they did understand that they had to talk about their values. Whether they were trying to solve a problem or teach a new team member, they all knew that they had to talk about what was important to them collectively. They knew they had to talk about what made for a good team member. They knew that the team needed all its members to say their piece. On perhaps some deeper level, they knew that they bonded with their values when they talked about them with each other.

If, as I have argued, the team molds its own moral community and then powerfully controls behaviors in accordance with its morality, then the team must actively and knowingly negotiate the values that form that community and evaluate the usefulness of those values as the team evolves. When ISE's teams became bogged down with their cumbersome attendance policies, they had great difficulty working through the problem. They did not know how to criticize a rule that seemed so naturally connected to their value for supporting the team. They did not understand how to gain perspective and reinvent a new attendance rule that was less problematic but still functional. The teams did not have a cultivated system for reflective critical thinking that could move them toward a candid and open discussion of the problem. If part of their discipline required them to spend an hour once a month reflecting on their problem areas, perhaps they could have easily negotiated a useful solution that still maintained their values and methodology.

ISE's teams were exemplars of the growing diversity among workers in today's participative organizations, a diversity that requires our organizations to place a premium on inclusion. In a concertive-control system, the team has to take collective responsibility for being inclusively moral. Their shared power relationships, their community, must be molded through their own negotiation of competing values. This negotiative, molding process, to hearken back to Aristotle for a moment, enables the team to find its virtue. As the team negotiates its own habit and practice and navigates the difficulties of competing or conflicting values, it will create its own sense of morality, its own utilitarian golden mean, which we saw ISE's workers do many times. Participative teams must learn how to make the delicate balance among necessary utilitarian values, the tendency toward formalization, and the power of peer pressure. But they must negotiate that balance for themselves. No one else can create it for them.

The values from which the teams form power relationships originate in many different realms, as discussed in Chapter 4. The generative discipline of concertive control draws on business values, democratic social values, and individual values of work, among others. Regardless of the origin, participative teams must have a regular and recurring mechanism for assessing their values, for negotiating differences, and for arguing out changes. They must determine and subsequently evaluate their own definitions for success, effectiveness, fairness, equity, and all other pertinent values.

Again, we must not forget that, in participative work, the team makes the rules. They create a concertive discipline and reason morally with it. The team's responsibility is to ensure that they openly decide what is moral for them and that this morality works for them over time. They must learn to be their own critics and cultivate useful mechanisms of reflection and negotiation. Management must support them in this difficult task with time, training, and any other requirements. The organization must not forget its responsibility for cultivating a continuing criticism among the teams.

Create a Positive System of Discipline

If cultivating a continuing criticism facilitates the moral reasoning of the team, creating a positive system of discipline facilitates its ability to maintain the integrity of that system. *Integrity,* like moral reasoning, is another difficult term for our diverse culture in which the meaning of such expressions is abstract and contentious. But we as society members do feel a need for integrity, albeit an abstract feeling. ISE's team members were no exception. An expressed desire for integrity popped up many times during my interviews, such as this comment from Jonie Ross: "What they [the team members] want most is integrity. They want to know that they can depend on each other and that everything will work for them."

Integrity for the team members, then, had a dual meaning. On the one hand, they needed to believe that all the team members would act in accordance with their community's power relationships, and they enforced such behaviors, as we have seen. On the other hand, the teams needed to believe that their system, their concertive discipline, would work for them as well. Both the individual members and the system had to have integrity if the team was to realize its goals and fulfill the truth of its community.

Carter (1997) has defined a useful, three-point definition of integrity as (a) discerning what is right and wrong, (b) acting on what one has discerned even at personal cost, and (c) saying openly what one is doing. Though Carter's definition addresses the more individual side of integrity, creating a positive system of discipline represents a more collective requirement. Through the workings of their generative discipline, the team members could discern what was right and wrong for their team, and they could act on what they had discerned. But, in terms of a positive system of discipline, I want to focus more on creating a system that minimizes the personal cost involved and facilitates the need to openly discuss what the team is doing. If we can maintain such an abstract sense of integrity within a concertive discipline, we can mediate some of its consequences. We can create a system that is positive and that has the potential to stay positive.

What exactly does "positive" mean in this situation? My point here is that we must create disciplinary participative systems in which the team members can pursue the openness, trust, inclusion, and candor required for a "positive" demarcation of values and power relationships as they build their concertive communities. A positive system of discipline, then, is a discipline in which the team members can still be creative, even if that creativity is contentious and difficult. It is a system in which the participants can learn for themselves how to adapt to the conditions, consequences, constraints, and unknowns of concertive discipline. It is a system in which they can do this creating and adapting without so much risk of personal cost.

Share the Values

Team members must ensure that the values on which they mold their community are indeed shared by all participants, at least to the greatest extent possible. All the team's stakeholders must participate in this process, and the process itself must be transparent, open, and clear. As diverse political beings, we need a healthy tension between our values, both *business* and *social*. As we work through those tensions, we create a more inclusive community and a more positive discipline.

Graham Sewell (e.g., Sewell & Wilkinson, 1992) has called for workers and managers in participative organizations to engage in an ongoing political discussion about how they control their own work. This is a novel and provocative idea, as Phil Tompkins and I (Barker & Tompkins, 1994) commented on Sewell's call:

> Although the notion of a political debate within the factory may sound foreign to our ears in the United States, we endorse the idea because it implies upward- and downward-directed involvement in discussion about these new mechanisms of control. (p. 239)

The teams have to sort through many different, conflicting, and competing values as they demarcate power relationships and mold their community. They must have the time for such discussions throughout the course of their work as teams, not just in the beginning.

The myriad of different, conflicting, and competing values must be voiced as well. Jack Tackett did not hide his belief that teamwork was a fundamentally better way of working. He also did not hide his belief that teamwork *had* to work at ISE for the company to survive. The team members heard and sorted through both directives. The team members did spend much time discussing values, naturally but not deliberately, early in their transition to teams. However, they later relied on their rules rather than on reevaluating their values and processes. The team members did take time to talk indirectly about values when they demarcated key power relationships (e.g., build the best customer's order first) and when they worked out team problems, but they did not take steps to ensure that the values were uniformly shared.

My desire here is to remind all of us in participative work of the necessity to discuss our community's values openly, candidly, and often. We have to ensure that we do share the values of our work community and that we actively address the differences, conflicts, and competition among our values. Although not everyone agreed with all the values, ISE's teams did, for the most part, have a consensus on the core values of their communities. That general consensus, openly derived, is the best result that we can hope to achieve, with the caveat that we must continually criticize that consensus to ensure that it remains viable.

The manifest consequence of working through shared values is the high identification and buy-in that the team members so treasured. The latent consequence is the internal perception of the team members that they are participating in a system that is good and in which they and their teammates can flourish. If the teams mold their community through persuasion, rather than coercion, and if they stay focused on demarcating values that are central for all concerned, then they have the best chance possible for creating a positive system of discipline.

Ensure a Voice

For the teams to have this kind of open and honest discussion, the voices of the team members and stakeholders must be heard. As Jack Tackett did, management will weigh in with its values, and the longer-tenured team members will have theirs, but what of everyone else? The teams must ensure that all parties are heard.

ISE's teams did have some mechanisms for getting the voices heard, such as their power relationship of "saying your piece." They had also worked out something of an arrangement with the Asian American workers who felt very uncomfortable saying their piece. My concern here is that a concertive discipline is not naturally a friendly environment for resistance or for even different ideas on how to do work. In participation, we must give resistance a fair hearing.

Team members and managers must recognize this natural tendency and develop mechanisms to ensure that everyone can say their piece. More important, we all must realize that participative work requires inclusion: honest, open, persuasively created, and deliberated inclusion. Not to ensure a voice for the underrepresented means losing the community benefits of persuasive argument and identification, and it necessarily tilts the team in the direction of coercive peer pressure.

Create a Safe Environment

At one point in my interview with Sophie (see Chapter 5), I asked her to describe the most important factor in a team's being successful. She replied,

> We need the right conditions. We need the space to talk with each other and to work out our differences. We may not fully agree all the time, but if we can get that space, if we can relieve some of the stresses to keep busy all the time, then we can work things out for ourselves. When we do that, we will all be happy with what we decide.

Her comment and the pervasiveness of similar comments from other team workers pushed my thinking toward the problem of, How do we create the ideal conditions for teamwork? Not so much ideal in the productivity sense but, rather, ideal in the social sense: How can we create ideal conditions that enable participative workers to flourish as human beings?

A few years ago, I began work with a professional mediator, Kathy Domenici, designed to develop a means for helping teams create environments in which they could continually criticize their actions, solve day-to-day problems, argue over values, and maintain a sense of collective integrity. Our initial work toward this goal has been to craft a team-based system in which the team members learn how to practice some of the techniques common to third-party mediation (Barker & Domenici, in press).

Our model unfolds in five parts. The first is *creating a safe environment.* Here we discuss how team members and managers can create environments in which team members feel safe to voice objections, differences, and concerns, and in which they feel safe to engage in persuasive arguments about these issues. The second part is *learning collaborative communication,* which refers to mechanisms that enhance the team members' ability to talk through issues and problems collectively.

The third part of our model is *learning power management,* in which we help the teams to understand how they form power relationships and to manage for themselves the issues of power both in terms of powerful people and powerful values on their teams. *Learning process management,* the fourth part, refers to the team's need to understand and criticize its own day-to-day work processes. We describe how team members can assess the consequences of their disciplinary processes and gain enough perspective to work through changes in a constructive manner.

The last element of our model is *learning face-saving techniques,* and it directly addresses the need for constructive but inclusive arguments on the teams. Team members must be able to argue and persuade each other as they mold and remold their truth for doing good work. They must be able to solve deviations from their methodology without tending themselves toward oppression. To that end, we describe a set of techniques that allow the team members to engage each other on a personal level while still maintain their cohesion and ability to work together.[7]

Our work on mediation in team environments reflects my own drive to develop ways of mediating the consequences of participative work, which my study of ISE has compelled me toward. I have become a believer in both the inevitableness of concertive control and the imperative to create ideal social environments in which we mediate the consequences of that work.

ISE's workers did understand the need to have an environment in which they could work on their teamwork. They would break their normal work routine for emergency meetings when problems arose. They encouraged saying your piece at regular team meetings. They did show compassion and consideration for each other. Sometimes they would leave the team area to discuss difficult problems. Jack Tackett tried to support their efforts.

But, again, they did not have a systematic method for dealing with serious conflicts. The teams worked on them as best they could. When they felt the heat of scheduled production, the team members quickly called on strong peer pressure to solve their problems and maintain their team's methodology. When the work environments became unsafe, the bads and uglies of participative work ruled the day.

We, all of us involved in participative work, must create safe environments for team members to flourish, in all the many meanings of that term. The team members must be able to look openly for problems, identify them, and fix them creatively. Only within a safe environment can team members create a positive system of discipline. Our thinking about and construction of team-based organizations must be focused on that end. The social consequences of concertive control demand just that orientation.

Hold an Enduring Faith in Our Use of Language

George Cheney (1995) has written that participative organizations have "an acute need for a dynamic, self-reflective and comprehensive communication system" (p. 195), which is a point I have been supporting in these last two sections. Cultivating a continuing criticism and creating a positive system of discipline both depend on a participative organization having such a dynamic, self-reflective, and comprehensive communication system. Mediating the consequences of concertive control requires us to have faith in our ability to use language, persuasively and creatively, to work through the problems inherent in our organizational participation. Positive concertive control requires a politics, and that politics requires rhetoric.

Team members have to control their own behavior in a concertive system, but they also have to stay creative so that they can mediate the consequences of that system, which is a terrible tension to endure. The teams will have to find a way to stay creative despite these consequences and in light of their shared values.

ISE's team members knew that they needed time to talk, to work through problems rhetorically, and they knew that time was their wolfsbane. But, if they could only get the time, if they could find a way to talk, they could solve their problems in positive ways. They could make substantive changes to their concertive system.

For Randy, an ISE team member, the more the team members talked, the more they came to trust and depend on each other, and they became more creative:

> The most difficult thing to develop here is trust among the team members. We can't really resolve any problems and get any behavioral change without it. We have to have that trust because confronting people when there is no trust won't accomplish anything. The key, to me, is developing the trust, and that comes from how we talk to each other. We can't give each other negative strokes all the time. When we trust each other to talk, we treat each other fairly and openly and honestly. We are able to take constructive criticism. We can confront each other on quality or quantity or behavioral issues. When that happens, we can believe that we are being confronted for the best interests of the team and ourselves. We can create win-win situations that way. It's a struggle. We have to keep working it. We always have to look for ways to talk with each other.
>
> You know, we will never reach a utopia here. This will never be the ideal place to work. That doesn't exist anywhere. Sure, we're successful, but, certainly, we have our problems. It's always going to be that way. But the key thing is that we can be happy. If we're having fun in our work, if we feel good about ourselves and the work that we do, then we will be happy. If we know that the people around us are focused on task, quality, and cooperation for the 8 to 10 hours we're at work, then we will be happy. The only way we can get there is to talk with each other. We always have to find the time to do that.

Randy's perspective was a common one on the teams. The team members did not really expect that they would reach an ultimate form of teamwork or become a perfect team. They just wanted to strive for their abstract values of success and productivity, and they wanted to flourish in all its abstract meanings. They knew that talking with each other, their use of language, was their key to reaching that goal. They knew that the path toward changing their work lives, toward mediating the consequences they felt, lay in language. Lee Ann, as she usually did, put the common feeling succinctly: "Hell, if we can just talk with each other, everything will be OK."

Liz loved to call her experience with teams "a never-ending journey," which is a very apt analogy. The participative world of concertive control is a journey because the generative discipline of teamwork is language bound. We are continually inventing and reinventing the discipline. Concertive control is how it is because of the way people use language in collective environments. The goods, bads, and uglies of participation all arise from our uses of language. All of us, all of us who think about, manage, or work in participative environments, must realize the dual necessity for critiquing how we use language in these environments and subsequently using language to change the way we do teamwork. If we are to realize the goods of participation and mediate the bads and uglies, we have to change the way that we talk about concertive discipline. And only the team itself can do that. Only the team can change its generative discipline.[8]

Just as Lee Ann said in the quotation opening this chapter, the character of concertive control, with its sensitivity to market changes, personality fissures, contradictory power relationships, and asymmetrical power relationships, is very fragile indeed. Team members respond to this fragility by using language to create a powerful, generative discipline of concertive control. They mold a value-intensive community that becomes sacred for them. They find meaning in their lives by identifying strongly with their team community. Their subsequent methodology gives them direction and motivation to live in alignment with their community. We should not be surprised when the team resorts to strong pressures for maintaining their collective way of life.

We can only navigate the consequences that naturally arise in participative work through the rhetorical use of language, through the deliberate consideration by each team of its underlying power relationships, its demand for identification, and its controlling methodology. Likewise, we can only navigate the paradoxes of concertive control through the same critical reflection and creative use of language. We must cultivate conditions that enable team members to criticize their own work and to develop positive disciplinary systems. We cannot tell the teams what values to demarcate. They must find their own way through their own language use. The final lesson we can draw from ISE's experience is that, in participative environments, we must have faith in our ability to create positive collective environments and to solve collective problems through reasoned talk.

I began my analysis by describing the importance of the team's rhetorical language use, and I end my analysis back at that point. Ultimately, then, I am left with a rather simple answer for the complex world of participation: It all comes down to rhetoric. I ask you, the reader, to consider that the team needs this requisite simplicity. The team needs to have faith in its use of language. Language is truly the team's tool. They create their environment with it, and they live their lives through it.

The participative age we have entered requires us to have an enduring faith in our own ability to use language to find creative ways of working together. Such language use can either be good or bad because rhetoric cuts both ways. We will have to deal with that last paradox, for we are in the age when the team makes the rules. We are a part of the discipline of teamwork. Recalling what Jack Tackett has charged us to do, we must work to ensure that our ways of doing participative labors are both productive and humane. Without a continuing criticism to help us reason morally, without a positive system of discipline to maintain our collective integrity, and without our faith in using language, we will indeed be trapped and doomed to the concertive steel cage of our own creation.

A FINAL WORD

Throughout this book, my task has been to provoke our thinking about the social consequences of participation in general and the generative discipline of teamwork in particular. I have gone out to where the team makes the rules, engaged the disciplinary practice of concertive control, and uncovered a compelling set of consequences to consider. I believe that we must discover, analyze, and resolve the consequences of concertive control rhetorically. I have sought to foster such a rhetorical argument.

As I reach the end, I am reminded again that, if nothing else, concertive control and participative work represent intensely meaningful experiences. We are inextricably pulled to concertive systems, into the eye of the norm, just because they are so richly meaningful. Viktor Frankl (1988) wrote in *Man's Search for Meaning* that we can tolerate the "hows" of life if we know the "whys." Lee Ann, Liz, Kurt, Sharon, Diego, Christy, Jack, and all the rest of ISE's team workers were willing to put up with the hows—the consequences— of concertive control. They were willing to live in the eye of the norm because they knew the why. Their work at ISE, their self-created community of concertive control, gave their lives a special meaning. And the rest of us, myself especially, have no right to charge that they were wrong in their belief.

The renowned social critic Gibson Burrell once cautioned me not to go beyond discussing how we create meaning in organizations.[9] He warned that going beyond that point, to venture into prescriptions regarding our creation of meaning, tilted our organizational thinking toward fascism, both intellectually and practically. In this last chapter, I have delicately danced around Burrell's warning.

But I firmly believe that we must actively pursue the "right" ways of doing participative work, whatever we decide those ways to be. For participation is like nitroglycerin, a highly volatile rhetorical concoction: good and productive in some contexts but devastatingly destructive in others. We must look for ways of stabilizing participation, keeping it useful for all of us, both individually and organizationally. The team makes the rules by working its way through a haze of business values, social values, family values, leisure values, and everything else. Those of us involved in participative work have a moral obligation to support these participants in their difficult journey. Such is our task, our imperative, as scholars, as consultants, as managers, and, especially, as participants. In this new era of participation, we must do well, *and* we must do good.

NOTES

1. The development of concertive control at ISE also complements the traditional literature on work-group norms and team development (e.g., Hackman, 1992; Sundstrom, De Meuse, and Futrell, 1990). ISE's experience with concertive control illuminates the linkages between the emergence of group norms and the broader organizational issues of discipline, authority, rationality, power, and control.

2. The apparent connection between the team members' activities and Aristotle's concepts is not altogether surprising when we consider the powerful influence Aristotle's work and other Western philosophies would have had on the educational upbringing of most of ISE's team members.

3. Bill Rhodes helped me formulate this connection to Aristotle.

4. For another related research report, see McKinlay and Taylor (1996).

5. I first began formulating these responses during my initial study. As these responses took shape, I cross-checked their usefulness with workers in team-based organizations in Milwaukee, Wisconsin, and Albuquerque, New Mexico, while I was teaching and researching in those locations.

6. Professor Whetten shared most of the information that follows in a personal communication (September 1996). I subsequently drew on two of his unpublished manuscripts (Whetten, 1996a, 1996b).

7. Subsequent to our developmental work described here, Kathy and her colleagues in mediation have developed and implemented a successful training program that teaches these five skills to team members and managers.

8. Billig and his colleagues (Billig et al., 1988) present a fascinating discussion of the necessity for using language for social change.

9. Personal communication, August 1996.

References

Adler, P. A., & Adler, P. (1987). *Membership roles in field research.* Newbury Park, CA: Sage.

Adler, P. A., & Adler, P. (1991). *Backboards & blackboards: College athletics and role engulfment.* New York: Columbia University Press.

Albert, S., & Whetten, D. A. (1985). Organizational identity. In B. M. Staw & L. L. Cummings (Eds.), *Research in organizational behavior 7* (pp. 263-295). Greenwich, CT: JAI Press.

Allaire, Y., & Firsirotu, M. E. (1984). Theories of organizational culture. *Organization Studies, 5,* 193-226.

Anderson, C. (1997). Values-based management. *Academy of Management Executive, 11,* 25-46.

Aristotle. (1998). *The Nicomachean ethics* (Oxford World's classics ed., D. Ross, Trans.). London: Oxford University Press.

Ashforth, B., & Mael, F. (1989). Social identity and the organization. *Academy of Management Review, 14,* 20-39.

Athos, A. G., & Pascale, R. (1981). *The art of Japanese management.* New York: Warner Books.

Barker, J. R. (1993a). *Concertive control in the self-managing organization: Changes in communication and control practices during a period of organizational transformation.* Unpublished doctoral dissertation, University of Colorado, Boulder.

Barker, J. R. (1993b). Tightening the iron cage: Concertive control in self-managing teams. *Administrative Science Quarterly, 38,* 408-437.

Barker, J. R. (1996). Communal-rational authority as the basis for leadership on self-managing teams. In M. Beyerlein, D. A. Johnson, & S. T. Beyerlein (Eds.), *Advances in the interdisciplinary study of work teams III: Team leadership* (pp. 105-126). New York: JAI Press.

Barker, J. R., & Cheney, G. (1994). The concept and the practices of discipline in contemporary organizational life. *Communication Monographs, 61,* 19-43.

Barker, J. R., & Domenici, K. (in press). Mediation practices for knowledge-based teams. In M. Beyerlein, D. A. Johnson, & S. T. Beyerlein (Eds.), *Advances in interdisciplinary studies of work teams V.* New York: JAI Press.

Barker, J. R., Melville, C. W., & Pacanowsky, M. E. (1993). Self-directed work teams at XEL: Changes in communication during a program of cultural transformation. *Journal of Applied Communication Research, 21,* 297-312.

Barker, J. R., & Tompkins, P. K. (1994). Identification in the self-managing organization: Characteristics of target and tenure. *Human Communication Research, 21,* 223-240.

Barley, S. R. (1996). Technicians in the workplace: Ethnographic evidence for bringing work into organizations studies. *Administrative Science Quarterly, 41,* 404-441.

Barley, S. R., & Kunda, G. (1992). Design and devotion: Surges of rational and normative ideologies of control in managerial discourse. *Administrative Science Quarterly, 37,* 363-399.

Barnard, C. (1968). *The functions of the executive.* Cambridge, MA: Harvard University Press. (Original work published 1938)

Barnett, G. A. (1988). Communication and organizational culture. In G. M. Goldhaber & G. A. Barnett (Eds.), *Handbook of organizational communication* (pp. 101-130). Norwood, NJ: Ablex.

Billig, M., Condor, S., Edwards, D., Gane, M., Middleton, D., & Radley, A. (1988). *Ideological dilemmas: A social psychology of everyday thinking.* Newbury Park, CA: Sage.

Bolweg, J. F. (1976). *Job design and industrial democracy.* Leiden, Netherlands: Martinus Nijhoff.

Brown, M. H., & McMillan, J. J. (1991). Culture as text: The development of an organizational narrative. *Southern Communication Journal, 57,* 49-60.

Brown, R. H. (1978). Bureaucracy as praxis: Toward a political phenomenology of formal organizations. *Administrative Science Quarterly, 23,* 365-382.

Bullis, C. (1991). Communication practices as unobtrusive control: An observational study. *Communication Studies, 42,* 254-271.

Bullis, C., & Tompkins, P. K. (1989). The forest ranger revisited: A study of control practices and identification. *Communication Monographs, 56,* 287-306.

Burke, K. (1937). *Attitudes toward history.* New York: New Republic.

Burke, K. (1950). *A rhetoric of motives.* Berkeley: University of California Press.

Burke, K. (1964). Art . . . and the first rough draft of living. *Modern Age, 12,* 155-165.

Burke, K. (1966). *Language as symbolic action: Essays on life, literature, and method.* Berkeley: University of California Press.

Burke, K. (1984). *Permanence and change: An anatomy of purpose* (3rd ed.). Berkeley: University of California Press.

Carrier, J. G. (1982). Knowledge, meaning, and social inequality in Kenneth Burke. *American Journal of Sociology, 88,* 43-61.

Carter, S. L. (1997). *Integrity.* New York: HarperCollins.

Certo, S. C. (1997). *Modern management* (7th ed.). Upper Saddle River, NJ: Prentice Hall.

Cheney, G. (1991). *Rhetoric in an organizational society: Managing multiple identities.* Columbia: University of South Carolina Press.

Cheney, G. (1995). Democracy in the workplace: Theory and practice from the perspective of communication. *Journal of Applied Communication Research, 23,* 167-200.

Cheney, G. (1997). The many meanings of "solidarity": The negotiation of values in the Mondragon Worker-Cooperative Complex under pressure. In B. D. Sypher (Ed.), *Case studies in organizational communication 2: Perspectives on contemporary work life* (pp. 68-83). New York: Guilford.

Cheney, G., & Christensen, L. T. (in press). Identity at issue: Linkages between "internal" and "external" organizational communication. In F. Jablin & L. Putnam (Eds.), *The new handbook of organizational communication.* Thousand Oaks, CA: Sage.

Cheney, G., & McMillan, J. J. (1990). Organizational rhetoric and the practice of criticism. *Journal of Applied Communication Research, 18,* 93-114.

Cheney, G., & Tompkins, P. K. (1988). On the facts of the text as the basis of human communication research. In J. Anderson (Ed.), *Communication yearbook 11* (pp. 455-481). Newbury Park, CA: Sage.

Christensen, L. T. (1991, June). *The marketing culture: The communication of organizational identity in a culture without foundation.* Paper presented at the International Conference on "Organizational Culture," Copenhagen, Denmark.

Christensen, L. T., & Cheney, G. (1994). Articulating identity in an organizational age. In S. Deetz (Ed.), *Communication yearbook 17* (pp. 222-235). Thousand Oaks, CA: Sage.

Clegg, S. R. (1989). Radical revisions: Power, discipline, and organizations. *Organization Studies, 10,* 97-115.

Collins, R. (1985). *Three sociological traditions.* New York: Oxford University Press.

Coombs, R., Knights, D., & Willmott, H. C. (1992). Culture, control, and competition: Towards a conceptual framework for the study of information technology in organizations. *Organization Studies, 13,* 51-72.

Cooper, R., & Burrell, G. (1988). Modernism, postmodernism, and organizational analysis: An introduction. *Organization Studies, 9,* 91-112.

Crosby, P. B. (1979). *Quality is free: The art of making quality certain.* New York: McGraw-Hill.

Dahler-Larsen, P. (1991). *Corporate culture and morality: Durkheim-inspired reflections on the limits of corporate culture.* Unpublished manuscript, University of Odense, Denmark, Department of Economics.

Daudi, P. (1986). *Power in the organisation.* Oxford, UK: Basil Blackwell.

Deetz, S. (1992). *Democracy in the age of corporate colonization.* Albany: State University of New York Press.

Deetz, S. (1995). *Transforming communication, transforming business.* New York: Hampton Press.

Drucker, P. F. (1988, January/February). The coming of the new organization. *Harvard Business Review,* 45-53.

Drucker, P. F. (1992). *Managing for the future.* New York: Truman Talley/Plume.

Drucker, P. F. (1994). The age of social transformation. *Atlantic Monthly, 247*(5), 53-80.

Durkheim, E. (1973). *On morality and society: Selected writings* (R. Bellah, Ed.). Chicago: University of Chicago Press.

Durkheim, E. (1984). *The division of labor in society* (W. D. Halls, Trans.). New York: Free Press.

Eccles, R. G., & Nohria, N. (1992). *Beyond the hype: Rediscovering the essence of management.* Cambridge, MA: Harvard Business School Press.

Edwards, R. (1979). *Contested terrain: The transformation of the workplace in the twentieth century.* New York: Basic Books.

Edwards, R. (1981). The social relations of production at the point of production. In M. Zey-Ferrell & M. Aiken (Eds.), *Complex organizations: Critical perspectives* (pp. 156-182). Glenview, IL: Scott Foresman.

Ezzamel, M., & Willmott, H. (1998). Accounting for teamwork: A critical study of group-based systems of organizational control. *Administrative Science Quarterly, 43,* 358-396.

Fay, B. (1987). *Critical social science.* Ithaca, NY: Cornell University Press.

Fishbein, M., & Ajyen, I. (1975). *Belief, attitude, intention, and behavior: An introduction to theory and research.* Reading, MA: Addison-Wesley.

Follett, M. P. (1941). *Dynamic administration: The collected papers of Mary Parker Follett* (H. C. Metcalf & L. Urwick, Eds.). London: Pitman.

Ford, J. D., & Ford, L. W. (1995). The role of conversations in producing intentional change in organizations. *Academy of Management Review, 20,* 541-570.

Foss, S. K., Foss, K. A., & Trapp, R. (1991). *Contemporary perspectives on rhetoric.* Prospect Heights, IL: Waveland.

Foucault, M. (1972). *The archaeology of knowledge* (A. M. Sheridan, Trans.). New York: Pantheon.

Foucault, M. (1976). *Discipline and punish: The birth of the prison* (A. Sheridan, Trans.). New York: Vintage.

Foucault, M. (1980). *Power/knowledge* (C. Gordon, Ed.; C. Gordon, L. Marshall, J. Mepham, & K. Soper, Trans.). New York: Pantheon.

Frankl, V. E. (1988). *Man's search for meaning.* New York: Pocket Books.

Frost, P. J., Moore, L. F., Louis, M. R., Lundberg, C. C., & Martin, J. (Eds.). (1985). *Organizational culture.* Beverly Hills, CA: Sage.

Frost, P. J., Moore, L. F., Louis, M. R., Lundberg, C. C., & Martin, J. (Eds.). (1991). *Reframing organizational culture.* Newbury Park, CA: Sage.

Giddens, A. (1984). *The constitution of society: Outline of the theory of structuration.* Berkeley: University of California Press.

Gray, B., Bougon, M. G., & Donnellon, A. (1985). Organizations as constructions and destructions of meaning. *Journal of Management, 11,* 83-98.

Grenier, G. J. (1988). *Inhuman relations.* Philadelphia: Temple University Press.

Guest, R. H. (1989). Team management under stress. *Across the Board, 26,* 30-35.

Hackman, J. R. (1986). The psychology of self-management in organizations. In M. S. Pallak & R. O. Perloff (Eds.), *Psychology and work: Productivity, change, and employment* (pp. 89-136). Washington, DC: American Psychological Association.

Hackman, J. R. (1992). Group influences on individuals in organizations. In M. D. Dunnette & L. M. Hough (Eds.), *Handbook of industrial and organizational psychology* (Vol. 3, 2nd ed., pp. 199-267). Palo Alto, CA: Consulting Psychologists Press.

Hackman, J. R., & Walton, R. E. (1986). Leading groups in organizations. In P. S. Goodman & Associates (Eds.), *Designing effective work groups* (pp. 72-119). San Francisco: Jossey-Bass.

Hammer, M., & Champy, J. (1993). *Reengineering the corporation: A manifesto for business revolution.* New York: Harper Business.

Helms, M. M. (1990). Communication: The key to JIT success. *Production and Inventory Management Journal, 31,* 18-21.

Homans, G. C. (1950). *The human group.* New York: Harcourt, Brace & World.

Jermier, J. M., Slocum, J. W., Jr., Fry, L. W., & Gaines, J. (1991). Organizational subcultures in a soft bureaucracy: Resistance behind the myth and facade of an official culture. *Organization Science, 2,* 170-194.

Jorgensen, D. L. (1989). *Participant observation: A methodology for human studies.* Newbury Park, CA: Sage.

Kalberg, S. (1980). Max Weber's types of rationality: Cornerstones for the analysis of rationalization processes in history. *American Journal of Sociology, 85,* 1145-1179.

Kanter, R. M. (1989). *When giants learn to dance.* New York: Simon & Schuster.

Katz, D., & Kahn, R. (1978). *The social psychology of organizations.* New York: John Wiley.

Ketchum, L. D. (1984). How redesigned plants really work. *National Productivity Review, 3,* 246-254.

King, R. T., Jr. (1998, May 20). Jeans therapy: Levi's factory workers are assigned to teams, and morale takes a hit. *Wall Street Journal,* pp. A1, A6.

Knight, J. A. (1997). *Value based management: Developing a systematic approach to creating shareholder value.* New York: McGraw-Hill.

Knights, D., & Morgan, G. (1991). Corporate strategy, organizations, and subjectivity: A critique. *Organization Studies, 12,* 251-273.

Kunda, G. (1992). *Engineering culture: Control and commitment in a high-tech corporation.* Philadelphia: Temple University Press.

Larson, C. E., & LaFasto, F. M. J. (1989). *Teamwork: What must go right/what can go wrong.* Newbury Park, CA: Sage.

Lentricchia, F. (1985). *Criticism and social change.* Chicago: University of Chicago Press.

Lewin, K. (1948). *Resolving social conflicts: Selected papers on group dynamics.* New York: Harper & Row.

March, J. G., & Olson, J. (1989). *Rediscovering institutions: The organizational basis of politics.* New York: Free Press.

McGregor, D. (1960). *The human side of enterprise.* New York: McGraw-Hill.

McKinlay, A., & Taylor, P. (1996). Power, surveillance, and resistance: Inside the "factory of the future." In P. Ackeres, C. Smith, & P. Smith (Eds.), *The new workplace and trade unionism* (pp. 279-300). London: Routledge.

McLagan, P., & Nel, C. (1995). *The age of participation.* San Francisco: Berrett-Koehler.

Miller, P., & O'Leary, T. (1987). Accounting and the construction of the governable person. *Accounting Organizations and Society, 12,* 235-265.

Morin, E. (1984). La societe: Un systeme auto-organizateur. *Sociologie.* Paris: Fayard.

Mumby, D. K., & Stohl, C. (1991). Power and discourse in organizational studies: Absence and the dialectic of control. *Discourse & Society, 2,* 313-332.

Nahavandi, A., & Aranda, E. (1994). Restructuring teams for the re-engineered organization. *Academy of Management Executive, 8,* 58-68.

O'Donnell-Trujillo, N., & Pacanowsky, M. E. (1983). The interpretation of organizational cultures. In M. S. Mander (Ed.), *Communications in transition: Issues and debates in current research* (pp. 225-241). New York: Praeger.

Ogilvy, J. (1990, February). This postmodern business. *Marketing and Research Today,* 4-20.

Orsburn, J. D., Moran, L., Musselwhite, E., & Zenger, J. H. (1990). *Self-directed work teams: The new American challenge.* Homewood, IL: Business One Irwin.

Ouchi, W. G., & Wilkins, A. L. (1985). Organizational culture. *Annual Review of Sociology, 11,* 457-483.

Oxford English dictionary. (1989). Oxford, UK: Oxford University Press.

Pacanowsky, M. E., & O'Donnell-Trujillo, N. (1982). Communication and organizational cultures. *Western Journal of Speech Communication, 46,* 115-130.

Papa, M. J., Auwal, M. A., & Singhal, A. (1995). Dialectic of control and emancipation in organizing for social change: A multitheoretic study of the Grameen Bank in Bangladesh. *Communication Theory, 5,* 189-223.

Papa, M. J., Auwal, M. A., & Singhal, A. (1997). Organizing for social change within concertive control systems: Member identification, empowerment, and the masking of discipline. *Communication Monographs, 64,* 219-249.

Parker, M. (1992). Post-modern organizations or postmodern organization theory? *Organization Studies, 13,* 1-17.

Parker, M., & Slaughter, J. (1988). *Choosing sides: Unions and the team concept.* Boston: South End Press.

Perinbanayagam, R. S. (1985). *Signifying acts: Structure and meaning in everyday life.* Carbondale: Southern Illinois University Press.

Perrow, C. (1986). *Complex organizations: A critical essay.* New York: Random House.

Peters, T. J. (1988). *Thriving on chaos: Handbook for a management revolution.* New York: Harper & Row.

Peters, T. J., & Waterman, R. H., Jr. (1982). *In search of excellence.* New York: Warner Books.

Pratt, M. G. (1998). To be or not to be: Central questions in organizational identification. In D. A. Whetten & P. C. Godfrey (Eds.), *Identity in organizations: Building theory through conversations* (pp. 171-207). Thousand Oaks, CA: Sage.

Putnam, L. L. (1982). Paradigms for organizational communication research: An overview and synthesis. *Western Journal of Speech Communication, 46,* 192-206.

Quinn, J. B. (1992). *Intelligent enterprise.* New York: Free Press.

Ray, C. A. (1986). Corporate culture: The last frontier of control. *Journal of Management Studies, 23,* 287-297.

Riggs, F. (1979). Introduction: Shifting meanings of the term "bureaucracy." *International Science Journal, 31,* 563-584.

Rothschild, J., & Whitt, J. A. (1986). *The cooperative workplace.* Cambridge, UK: Cambridge University Press.

Sackmann, S. A. (1990). Managing organizational culture: Dreams and possibilities. In J. A. Anderson (Ed.), *Communication yearbook 13* (pp. 114-148). Newbury Park, CA: Sage.

Schein, E. H. (1990). Organizational culture. *American Psychologist, 45,* 109-119.

Scott, C. R., Corman, S. R., & Cheney, G. (1998). Development of a structurational model of identification in the organization. *Communication Theory, 8,* 298-336.

Senge, P. N. (1994). *The fifth discipline: The art and practice of the learning organization.* New York: Doubleday.

Sewell, G. (1998). The discipline of teams: The control of team-based industrial work through electronic and peer surveillance. *Administrative Science Quarterly, 43,* 397-428.

Sewell, G., & Wilkinson, B. (1992). "Someone to watch over me": Surveillance, discipline and the just-in-time labour process. *Sociology, 26,* 271-289.

Simon, H. A. (1976). *Administrative behavior: A study of decision-making processes in administrative organizations* (3rd ed.). New York: Free Press.

Smircich, L., & Calas, M. B. (1987). Organizational culture: A critical assessment. In F. M. Jablin, L. L. Putnam, K. H. Roberts, & L. W. Porter (Eds.), *Handbook of organizational communication: An interdisciplinary perspective* (pp. 228-263). Newbury Park, CA: Sage.

Smith, R. C., & Eisenberg, E. M. (1987). Conflict at Disneyland: A root-metaphor analysis. *Communication Monographs, 54,* 367-380.

Soeters, J. L. (1986). Excellent companies as social movements. *Journal of Management Studies, 23,* 299-312.

Stewart, A. (1990). The bigman metaphor for entrepreneurship: A "library tale" with morals on alternatives for further research. *Organization Science, 1,* 143-159.

Stohl, C. (1995). *Organizational communication: Connectedness in action.* Thousand Oaks, CA: Sage.

Sundstrom, E., De Meuse, K. P., & Futrell, D. (1990). Work teams: Applications and effectiveness. *American Psychologist, 45,* 120-133.

Tannenbaum, A. S. (1968). *Control in organizations.* New York: McGraw-Hill.

Thomas, R. J. (1989). Participation and control: A shopfloor perspective on employee participation. *Research in the Sociology of Organizations, 7,* 117-144.

Tompkins, P. K. (1985). On hegemony—"he gave it no name"—and the critical structuralism in the work of Kenneth Burke. *Quarterly Journal of Speech, 71,* 119-131.

Tompkins, P. K. (1987). Translating organizational theory: Symbolism over substance. In F. M. Jablin, L. L. Putnam, K. H. Roberts, & L. W. Porter (Eds.), *Handbook of organizational communication* (pp. 70-122). Newbury Park, CA: Sage.

Tompkins, P. K. (1990). On risk communication as interorganizational control: The case of the Aviation Safety Reporting System. In A. Kirby (Ed.), *Nothing to fear: Risks and hazards in American society* (pp. 203-239). Tucson: University of Arizona Press.

Tompkins, P. K. (1993). *Organizational communication imperatives: Lessons from the space program.* Los Angeles: Roxbury.

Tompkins, P. K., & Cheney, G. (1983). Account analysis of organizations: Decision making and identification. In L. L. Putnam & M. E. Pacanowsky (Eds.), *Communication and organizations: An interpretive approach* (pp. 123-146). Beverly Hills, CA: Sage.

Tompkins, P. K., & Cheney, G. (1985). Communication and unobtrusive control. In R. D. McPhee & P. K. Tompkins (Eds.), *Organizational communication: Traditional themes and new directions* (pp. 179-210). Beverly Hills, CA: Sage.

Tompkins, P. K., & McPhee, R. D. (1985). Introduction and afterword. In R. D. McPhee & P. K. Tompkins (Eds.), *Organizational communication: Traditional themes and new directions* (pp. 7-14). Beverly Hills, CA: Sage.

Trist, E. L. (1981). The evolution of socio-technical systems. *Occasional paper no. 2.* Toronto: Quality of Working Life Centre.

Trist, E. L., Higgin, G., Murray, H., & Pollock, A. B. (1963). *Organizational choice.* London: Tavistock.

Tuckman, B. W. (1965). Development sequences in small groups. *Psychological Bulletin, 63,* 384-399.

Van Maanen, J. (1988). *Tales of the field: On writing ethnography.* Chicago: University of Chicago Press.

Walton, R. E. (1982). The Topeka work system: Optimistic visions, pessimistic hypothesis, and reality. In R. Zager & M. P. Roscow (Eds.), *The innovative organization* (pp. 260-287). New York: Pergamon.

Walton, R. E., & Hackman, J. R. (1986). Groups under contrasting management strategies. In P. S. Goodman & Associates (Eds.), *Designing effective work groups* (pp. 168-201). San Francisco: Jossey-Bass.

Watson, T. (1994). *In search of management: Chaos and control in managerial work.* New York: Routledge.

Weber, M. (1958). *The Protestant ethic and the spirit of capitalism.* New York: Charles Scribner's Sons.

Weber, M. (1978). *Economy and society* (G. Roth & K. Wittich, Eds.). Berkeley: University of California Press.

Webster's Ninth New Collegiate Dictionary. (1985). Springfield, MA: Merriam-Webster.

Wellins, R. S., Byham, W. C., & Wilson, J. M. (1991). *Empowered teams: Creating self-directed work groups that improve quality, productivity, and participation.* San Francisco: Jossey-Bass.

Wheatley, M. J. (1994). *Leadership and the new science: Learning about organization from an orderly universe.* San Francisco: Berrett-Koehler.

Whetten, D. A. (1996a). *If beauty is only skin deep, what about virtue? Applying the concept of identity congruence to socially responsible businesses.* Unpublished manuscript, Brigham Young University, Center for the Study of Values in Organizations, Provo, UT.

Whetten, D. A. (1996b). *The costs and benefits of business' commitment to "doing good and doing well."* Unpublished manuscript, Brigham Young University, Center for the Study of Values in Organizations, Provo, UT.

Whetten, D. A., & Godfrey, P. C. (Eds.). (1998). *Identity in organizations: Building theory through conversations.* Thousand Oaks, CA: Sage.

Whitley, R. (1977). Organizational control and the problem of order. *Social Science Information, 16,* 169-189.

Whyte, W. H. (1956). *The organization man.* New York: Doubleday.

Willmott, H. (1991, July). *Strength is ignorance; slavery is freedom: Managing culture in modern organizations.* Paper presented at the International Conference on "Organizational Culture," Copenhagen, Denmark.

Womack, J. P., Jones, D. T., & Roos, D. (1990). *The machine that changed the world: The story of lean production.* Cambridge, MA: MIT Press.

Zuboff, S. (1988). *In the age of the smart machine: The future of work and power.* New York: Basic Books.

Index

201

About the Author

James R. Barker is Director of Research and Associate Professor of Organizational Theory and Strategy in the Department of Management at the U.S. Air Force Academy. He received his PhD from the University of Colorado and his MA from Purdue University. His recent projects include collaborative research with scientists at the Los Alamos and Sandia National Laboratories. He has previously held faculty positions at Marquette University in Milwaukee and at the University of New Mexico in Albuquerque, and has also consulted with a variety of public, private, and service organizations. His research interests focus on the development and analysis of participative control practices in technological and knowledge-based organizations. His teaching interests focus on the application of theoretical principles to solve day-to-day organizational problems, and he has taught a number of courses that emphasize the development of critical thinking and decision making skills.

His work has appeared in a number of professional journals, including *Administrative Science Quarterly, Communication Monographs,* and *Advances in the Interdisciplinary Study of Teamwork.* He serves as an associate editor of the *Western Journal of Communication,* and on the editorial board of *Administrative Science Quarterly.* In 1993, he won the Outstanding Publication in Organizational Behavior Award from the Academy of Management for his research on self-managing teams, and he recently lectured on teamwork in organizations at the Sloan School of Management at the Massachusetts Institute of Technology.